The Pam Show

*My Adventures with
the Andrews Sisters
and Beyond*

For information, contact: henrygraypub2022@gmail.com

Publisher's Cataloging-in-Publication Data

Names: DuBois, Pam, 1957—.
Title: The pam show: my adventures with the andrews sisters and beyond / Pam Dubois.
Description: Granada Hills, CA : Henry Gray Publishing, 2026.
Identifiers: LCCN 2026900107 | ISBN 9781960415677 (pbk.) | ISBN 9781960415684 (hbk) | ISBN 9781960415691 (ebook.)
Subjects: LCSH: Andrews Sisters (Musical group) — Biography. | World War, 1939 – 1945 — Social aspects — United States — 20th century — Biography. | Show business — United States — History — 20th century. | DuBois, Pam — Autobiography.
BISAC: BIOGRAPHY & AUTOBIOGRAPHY / Entertainment & Performing Arts
Classification: LCC ML420.A575 D73 2926 | DDC 781.65092 — dc23

LC record available at https://lccn.loc.gov/2026900107

Library of Congress Control Number: 2026900107

Made in the United States of America.

Published by Henry Gray Publishing, 17020 Chatsworth Blvd. #1125, Granada Hills, California 91394.

For more information, or to join our mailing list,
visit HenryGrayPublishing.com

My Adventures with the Andrews Sisters and Beyond

Pam DuBois

HENRY GRAY
HG
PUBLISHING

Granada Hills, CA
"Select books for selective readers"

DEDICATION

I dedicate this book to my grandmother,
Alice Oppenheimer—
My angel in heaven, my angel on earth.

ACKNOWLEDGEMENTS

First and foremost I have to thank David Altieri.
Without him this book would never have been possible.
He worked tirelessly to bring it to fruition
(and besides which, I owe him my life).

I would be remiss in not thanking Kim Spile
for her input and creativity
at the onset of this project.

I also have to acknowledge my ex-husband, Andrew,
for putting up with me and my crazy adventures
for over 50 years.

Thank you, Bruce Scivally, my publisher,
who is absolutely the best!
I could not have been luckier
to have found him.

To my author friends:
Cassandra Danz (*Mrs. Greenthumbs*)
and Christina Crawford (*Mommie Dearest)*
for paving the way and encouraging me to do the same.

And finally —
PATTY, MAXENE, and LAVERNE!

It's been a hell of a ride.

"THE PAM SHOW"

I have always been a controversial person who is not afraid to express my opinions.

A comment I posted regarding the Andrews Sisters generated a negative reply from someone I used to work with. I defended it and suddenly there were hundress of responses (both positive and negative), and the blog went viral.

The next day I went viral and "THE PAM SHOW" was born.

The content of this book is derived from materisl previously presented on "THE PAM SHOW."

INTRODUCTION

My father Bill had a huge crush on the Andrews Sisters. One in particular. He would sit in the balcony of The Paramount Theatre in New York and drool over Patty—the blonde one in the middle of the trio who sang the solos. I wish he had lived long enough to see his daughter become her daughter as well.

Quick background—I was born to Bill and his wife Jane in the 1950s. Jane did not want children. She despised them. But that's what married women did in those days—had kids, dressed them up and proudly paraded them around the neighborhood as if they were a prize or a new mink coat. If Jane got any satisfaction out of having me, that was about it.

She spent most of her time pushing me onto her own mother, Grandma, who was recently widowed and only too happy to take on the responsibility.

Thank God.

If not for her, I doubt I'd be alive today.

Want to know more?

Keep reading....

CAST OF CHARACTERS

Jane — (Bio) burdened biological mother

Bill — biological father; picture Ralph Kramden

Grandma — my savior

Andy — gay ex-husband

Emma / David —the closest thing I've ever had to a sister. Or a brother, depending on how you look at it...

Jill — suicidal roommate

Joanna — a/k/a Joanna Pettet, actress, and current roommate

Patty — an Andrews Sister, adoptive mother

Maxene — aunt; an Andrews sister

LaVerne — aunt; an Andrews Sister

The Andrews Sisters — popular 1940s sister singing trio

Wally — adoptive father, a controlling hypochondriac

Gayle — 500-pound childhood friend

Lynda — Maxine's adoptive daughter

Mrs Airfart — friend of Grandma's; think Kate Smith

Kim — scatterbrained on-again, off-again best friend

Mari's and Carrie — Liza and Lorna's friends' kids that stayed with me for awhile

Hillary and Stewart — my kindergarten teacher's children that I loved like my own

Edith —overbearing Hungarian ex-mother in law

Cassandra —actress/Mrs. Green Thumbs, morning regular

Christina Crawford — author of *Mommie Dearest*, longtime friend

The Birth of the Andrews Sisters

Once upon a time there were three little sisters who had absolutely nothing in common other than the fact that they all liked to sing. Then one day in 1923, the oldest one hit a key on the piano, and said to one of her sisters, "You sing this note," while to her other sister, "You sing this one." And the Andrews Sisters were born.

Fifteen years later, after doing their time in Vaudeville and being on the road, they burst into 1938 with a blockbuster chart-topping number, one hit song called "Bei Mir Bist du Schoen," and they were on their way.

The Andrews Sisters knew Abbott and Costello from the Vaudeville days. They liked the boys alright, but they did go into *Buck Privates* with a bit of trepidation. What if they encountered some more insanity like they had with The Ritz Brothers? Instead, they found invaluable guidance and show business wisdom from a tall skinny straight man and a short, squat, deeply religious Italian funny man.

Patty learned a great deal from Abbott and Costello. From Lou, most importantly he taught her comic timing, and her sense of "ethics." Actually, all three of the girls got their "the show must go on, no matter what" discipline famously from the evening after Lou, Jr. drowned, and his devastated father did his radio show despite his crippling anguish and sorrow, in the hope that the baby, wherever he may have gone after this life, would hear him. That night in particular left a branded impression on Patty, Maxene, and LaVerne, about the dedication and devotion that was both required and embraced in this field called entertainment.

Maxene and her children would frequently go to the Costellos for barbeques and pool parties. She loved the pride he had for his family, in his three daughters Paddy, Carole and Chris. Remember it was not so long before that Maxene had been one of three daughters. In Lou Costello, she saw all the things that she wished her stern Greek father would have been. He took time for his children, and for her son and daughter when they visited. He got down on the floor and played with the children as if he was one of them. A slightly bigger kid, but nevertheless just another child in the pool. But she did notice a vast difference in his demeanor after the death of his only son, and thought him to be more serious than the clumsy clown she had worked with previously. Maxene was adamant that Lou never let his pain or sense of loss infiltrate into his relationship with his girls. She believed his love for his daughters is what sustained him in the last years of his life.

LaVerne was oblivious to anything other than what people were wearing, though she was fascinated by the dynamics of "Who's On First?" Never quite getting it, but nonetheless knowing it was comic genius. I know this from her husband named Lou, or Louie, who at times got into a card game or two (high stakes) with Abbott and Costello.

Patty always told me that "Paddy Costello" was named after her. And she believed it. Unfortunately this was not true. Paddy was born two years before the Andrews Sisters achieved fame, and before it was common practice to name your cats, dogs, and children after the popular stars of the day.

LaVerne died eight years after Lou Costello, and seven years before Bud Abbott. Perhaps propelled by a wave of nostalgia, Patty and Maxene visited Bud and his wife Betty in Woodland Hills sometime between the resurgence of Bette Midler's rendition of

"Boogie Woogie Bugle Boy of Company B in 1972 and the opening of their Broadway show *Over Here* in March, 1974. Both sisters found that time had mellowed the usually gruff Bud Abbott. He told them stories of his youth in Coney Island and in Burlesque. And they left him that day knowing that it would be the last time that the last surviving members of the great quintet of Universal Studios 1941 would ever see each other.

They were correct.

Maxene lived until 1995, and Patty to 2013. And for the rest of their lives, people would inevitably come up to them and say, "Hey, I saw you last night in that Abbott and Costello movie!"

And they would smile.

Angelyn Andrews

One hundred years ago today A baby girl was born.
She was only on this earth For 8 months and 2 days.
A life never lived.
But what a life it would have been. Her name was:
ANGELYN ANDREWS
And she will always be:
One of "The Andrews Sisters."

Batter Up!

She had just moved here from someplace called Leeds in England, and her family, particularly the mother did not know what to make of a rambunctious teenager from New York. Gail's mother, who we shall call "Mum Skibbins" (well, that WAS her name) used to call me "a bloody cow" (whatever that was?), and really downright hated me. She took great pleasure in tormenting me (as I did her).

When Doris Day's autobiography came out that summer, Mum Skibbins was among the first to read it. And boy did she have a time with me. She started by making fun of the part in the book when Doris tells about Patty finding out that her affair with Marty Melcher (Patty's then husband). According to Doris, Patty drove to Doris' house with a baseball bat, screaming and pounding away at the door until Doris' mother finally answered.

The Skibbins' lived on the bottom floor. We were up in the penthouse. After listening to Mum Skibbins call Patty "a mad woman, a lunatic, and a mental case," to the entire first floor, I decided enough was enough and I was going to tell Patty what was being said about her.

So I went back upstairs. Patty was in the kitchen cooking something (no doubt some kind of chicken) and I was almost crying while breathlessly blurting out the terrible things that were being told about her. I don't know if I was more upset with the neighbors, Mum Skibbins, or Doris for saying such ridiculous nonsense about Patty.

So Patty stood there and listened quietly to the whole thing, ending with me saying, "Bubby— you didn't go after Doris Day with a baseball bat, did you?"

Stop for a minute now, and picture Patty. PATTY. The Boogie Woogie Bugle Girl. The girl next door. The cute one in the middle. America and apple pie during the Second World War, singing for the boys as they marched off to fight. How could somebody accuse her of such a brutal act??

Again I repeated, "Bubby, you didn't go after Doris Day with a baseball bat, did you?" almost pleading with her to say, "NO!"

She pulled me into the dining room and we sat down. Very calmly, she said, "Pammy, you know me. You know me better than anyone. Now be sensible...Would I go over to someone like Doris Day's house swinging a baseball bat? Come on now..."

Now, feeling a bit foolish, I remember muttering to her, "No. No, of course not. I'm sorry."

We stayed there a bit longer, and then Patty got up, wiped her hands on her apron, and started heading for the kitchen. As it was about to swing open, she turned, looked at me, and said, "It was an 8 iron golf club, and I would have killed the fucking bitch if she had opened the door!"

Wally's World

Here on "THE PAM SHOW" I am going to share some WW stories. No, not World War II, or even World War I; I'm talking Walter Weschler, or as the passport office knows him: Baby Boy Weschler.

Now many, many times people have asked me how, with the obvious strong hold Wally has on Patty, was I able to spend so much time alone with her?

Well, I'll tell you. Wally had two activities which kept him very busy throughout the early mornings way into the night. He was addicted to 12 Step Meetings. That's right, folks. Bet this is a first for you. He was addicted to going to 12 Step meetings for addictions he didn't have.

First it was just AA, then it moved on to everything from Stutterers Anonymous to Children of Cults Anonymous. He loved these meetings because he loved to talk—and they had to listen to him—and it was the one place where he commanded respect, and actually got it. He would say that he was a "long timer" or "old timer", so all these newbie schmucks would go to him for sponsoring. He used to do up to five meetings per day. From a sunrise meeting at Shop-oholics (they always started early before the stores opened) to a midnight meeting of Parents of Transgender Children, he was there, spewing guidance and information.

And then in between meetings, he indulged in his second favorite pastime—going to car dealerships and haggling and fighting over the price of cars he had no intention of buying. I remember answering the phone one day at the house, and a call from Honda came in for Percy Faith, and another for Frankie Laine from Casa De Cadillac, and finally I turned around to Patty and asked why we were getting all these calls asking for all these people that you know? (At that point, I had no idea that these men were famous, I just thought they were people Wally played golf with back in the day.) And she said, so matter-of-factly that this in itself was hysterical... "OH, Wally's been banned from all the car dealerships in town, so now he's going down the list of the County Club roster and using their names when he goes in to argue about a car he's never gonna get!"

Wally Wechsler and the Andrews Sisters

Patty & Wally

As I read over the comments on yesterday's show, I was both thrilled and fascinated. Thrilled that you guys have found "THE PAM SHOW" to be a safe place to say what you feel. And fascinated that I am not alone in my thinking. This has always (even long before Patty) been a topic that has been near and dear to my heart—women who sell themselves out for their men. And I suppose that there are also men who sell themselves out for a woman. So, how about if we continue this subject on today's show, and I'll make you a deal...if you keep on contributing your thoughts and opinions, as to why women do this, and give me some kind of clue into this way of this thinking, I'll spill a few more secrets that I'll wager you did not know. I especially want to thank you for your candid honesty. Yes, I agree there are some women who enjoy, or rather need to be, "shitted on" by a man. Patty was one of them. She felt like she was nothing without a man. As I try to point out to the Joan Crawford fans, who say terribly disparaging things about my friend Tina because she dared to point out her mother's less than stellar child-raising abilities. The fact that Joan Crawford made terrible mistakes in that department in no way takes away from her ability to be an Academy Award-winning actress (*Mildred Pierce*, 1945). A great actress, if you will. Same here...Patty made the worst possible decisions in the "Man" department, but that in no way takes away from her amazing vocal, dancing, comedic, and acting talents. And that is what, I hope, she will always be remembered and loved for.

But why do they do it? I think Maxene was just being nice when she said that Patty needed a father figure. She was baffled as the rest of us. Although, as little kids, Maxene and LaVerne used to send Patty into their parents' room, very early in the morning, and have her steal a nickel off their father's dresser. He ran a restaurant, and a pool hall, and would empty the day's take up, there until he could get to the bank the following day. With the nickel she took, Patty would run down the street and buy three donuts—one for her and one for each of her sisters. It's ironic though that in married life, that was also her way of obtaining money, even though the tides had turned, and she was the one earning it.

Wally brainwashed her, no doubt about it, Marty Melcher did the same before him. But let's go back to Bob's comment...did she enjoy it? I know she never wanted to have a "MR. Andrews" for a husband. She was "MRS. Weschler" through and through. And in moments of just sheer meanness, I've seen her sign an autograph "Patty Weschler," leaving a disappointed fan speechless. I watched, as did her sisters, and her sisters, as he slowly took away everything and everyone that meant anything to her.

In the late 60's, after LaVerne died—Wally blamed her and a lost lawsuit he filed against her years earlier regarding the Andrews parents' estate) for a financial predicament he and Patty had found themselves in. I never told anybody this before, so here's something new for you Andrews Sisters: he made Patty sell her jewelry. All of it, except her "PATTY" pin, the gold record I wear around my neck, and her wedding rings. All the rest was melted down and sold for its gold, silver, and stone value. Wally was still a young-is man in his 40s and could have gotten a job, could have done anything, like played the piano in a band. But no. Wally Weschler said, "Sell your jewelry." And so she did.

And when the gay male fans became too close, Wally would doubt their homosexuality, and decided that they were in love with Patty. He would say, "Dump your friend so-and-so." And so she did.

Why? Why do they do it? I remember standing on the top of the stairs in New York, a fucking child, screaming at my biological mother, "It's either him or me..." as she took off down the street with her latest boyfriend. I think the need is so much greater than just the desire to please themselves, or their man. I think certain women feel, no matter how famous or successful they are, they are nothing without their man.

In the house, the awards, the Grammy and Emmy certificates, the plaque they award the artist when they are given a star on the Walk of Fame, the letters from the presidents, were all kept hidden under the dining room table. Wally's golf trophies adorned the coveted shelves and walls.

Wally and Patty, 1951

So let's see...I've already told you how Wally made Patty sell ALL of her jewelry. The sickest part of this, Patty was never to know. After they died, and their safe deposit box was opened, it revealed that Wally had stashed away a gold watch, probably worth more than all of Patty's jewelry combined.

I've told you how he slowly rid Patty's life of her fans and friends. I've told you how he tried, unsuccessfully, to make her hate her sisters (the one thing he never could do!).

But I didn't tell you what an awful, horrible, degrading feeling it was when she would have an argument with him, then find me later, seeking me out to console her, as she would cry and say: "He's all I've got in the world...What would I do without him? He's all I've got. I have nothing, I have no one, without him."

All the while I was fighting the urge to scream at her: "Open your eyes! Look right here in front of you!"

There's more, so much more...but we have to have something for next week, next month, etc....

I will be in bed doing my time with my back, hopefully for the last time. That did not go well yesterday!

But I urge the rest of you to go out and do something fun this weekend. It's April, after all!

When Pam Met Patty

45 years ago today I came to California. I slipped in quietly a little before midnight. Nobody knew I was here. Patty and Wally had finally left New York a couple of weeks earlier, and were staying at a hotel in Encino, having sold their house before going East to do the Broadway show. They could not decide after the show closed if they wanted to go back to California or buy an apartment in Manhattan. I'm pretty sure the weather decided for them.

I don't know why I didn't tell anyone where I was going. I guess I was afraid someone would say "Don't" and I knew instinctually that I had to be here. You see, tomorrow is May 8th, and I promised Patty that she would never again spend another "May 8th" alone. Eight years earlier, on May 8th, her beloved sister La-Verne died. And without me, or Maxene, Patty had no outlet for her still-consuming grief. She had tearfully told me the story of LaVerne's death, and the nine months leading up to it, one night after the show, as the two of us drove through a quiet, snowy, yet beautiful Central Park. It was then that I vowed, "Never would she suffer through that sad anniversary by herself again."

I had no idea which room Patty was in, nor was I about to go find her, and potentially deal with the wrath of you-know-who in the middle of the night. By where the car was stationed, I pretty much had an estimation. Suffice to say, I didn't sleep much that night. I'll be honest, I was nervous. Yeah, they had custody papers to be able to take me on the road with *Over Here*. But since that didn't come to fruition, I didn't know what to expect. What would be their reaction? Happy? Pissed? Glad to see me? Or maybe really angry?

I didn't have long to wait. At 6AM, I parked myself at the pool, a pretty good vantage point to the room I assumed they were in. I kept reassuring myself it really didn't matter, I was only going to be here a few days, a week at the most.

At 6:15 the door to that room opened, and Patty came out, carrying the then 16-year-old Min Pin (don't worry—he still had four more years left in him). There was a grassy area under some palm trees by the side of the hotel. I walked up behind her and said, "Oh my God! It's one of the Andrews Sisters! Miss Andrews—can I have your autograph?" She looked at me, shocked for a moment, and then realized why I was there. Tears sprang to her eyes. She grabbed me and said, "You remembered...You remembered your promise!"

Then she sat down on the grass and full-on sobbed, repeating in disbelief, "I'm not alone anymore."

In all fairness, WW was pretty happy to see me too, especially because now he could take my Budget rental car (a yellow Chevy Nova) to his various 12-step meetings around town instead of the Cadillac. He always said it made him fit in better. I didn't care. I drove the Cadillac all over Southern California.

So that night, after WW went to gambler's or over-eater's anonymous, and Patty cried for her dead sister, I threw out the Librium Jane had been feeding me daily since I was seven years old and began my life in California.

My best joke is: I came for a week, and stayed 40 years!

Tomorrow, "THE PAM SHOW" will pay tribute to LaVerne, on the 53rd anniversary of her death. Today's photo is the last picture ever taken of The Andrews Sisters when all three were alive.

Sing This Note...

How strange it is to feel such an affinity for somebody who has been gone almost 50 years. How odd it is to feel so connected to someone whose time when you were both on this earth was so fleeting. And yet I have always felt, with every beat of my heart, that in some serendipitous way, I was living life for you which you no longer could. Certainly the one thing that bonded us the deepest was our overwhelming pride in the Andrews Sisters, and that the people whom we each loved most in the world were your two little sisters.

I spent the day last weekend reading all your old letters back home to Mips from before and then after the fame. And I found myself laughing at the little things you did, and "mother-henned" over Maxene and Patty. Especially since I know that I myself had often done the same. Maxine, as you know, could always take care of herself, and when she couldn't, Lynda did. But the baby...OY the baby. All I can promise you on this day, your 105th birthday, is that I took good care of the baby. The best I could. I made her smile, laugh, and be herself, and most of all, I made her happy. And she loved me. You know how hard it was for her to trust anyone, to love anybody, besides the wrong men. She loved the three of us. Maxene most of all. And so on your day, I want to share a little story Patty once told me about you.

It was early on in the days of the Larry Rich Kiddie Review, maybe 1932, and Larry Rich sent you and Maxene into the city (New York) to pick up something, escorted by one of the stage hands. Patty was left behind in White Plains, where you three were on the bill in some theatre. An Orpheum, I assume. As you and Maxene passed the Paramount Theatre, you looked up at the marquee and saw they were featuring Bing Crosby and the Boswell Sisters in person. Neither of you had any money, but were determined to get in, just to see it, and them—to be in the same room with all that fame and talent. As luck would have it, you and Maxene were swept up with the crowd, and just kind of pushed along with everyone else into the theatre. After the show was over and you were back on 45th Street, Maxene said to you, "Close your eyes, LaVerne, and imagine that someday our names will be up on that marquee, big and bold and lighting up Broadway." You turned to Maxene and said, "Oh Maggie, you and your crazy ideas!" When you got back to White Plains and told Patty (who also believed as Maxine did) all about your amazing day at the Paramount, seeing Bing And The Bozzies, and that nutty thing Maxene said to you, you added, "Where the heck do you think she comes up with these pie in the sky ideas?"

Thank you for beginning the life that I will continue for the rest of mine.

For hitting that piano key 90 something years ago, and saying: "Maxene—sing this note."

Then "Patty—sing this one."

And starting the legacy...

With all my love, and admiration

Happy Birthday Aunt LaVerne.

Yours, Pammy

"Abbott & Costello in the Navy" *(1941) Bud Abbott, Lou Costello, and the Andrews Sisters - Maxene, Patty, and LaVerne*

Daddy

Since I don't do "THE PAM SHOW" on Sundays, this is my post-Father's Day program.

I realized with great horror yesterday, that when bio mom Jane signed those custody papers, she didn't just sign them to Patty. So if I'm going to call Patty "my mother," I have to, (gasp) call WW "my father"! I'm just kidding. I always celebrated Father's Day with him. I was so young when my real father died that really, for better or worse, Wally was the closest thing I had to a father all those years.

However, today's show is about my natural father, Bill. If I have one regret, it is that my Daddy didn't live long enough to see cable TV, and especially the ID Crime channel, evolve. He was fascinated by murders and murderers, and somehow had a knack of finding himself in the wrong place at the wrong time. He was once standing outside watching me roller skate, and suddenly the cops were there in full force taking him to the police station for questioning because he fit the description of an on-the-loose murderer in our neighborhood (of course they let him go a few hours later).

Also, I'm not so proud to admit this, but he was among the 36 people who heard Kitty Genovese screaming the night she was murdered in 1964 who did not call the police. This was a very famous murder case, because so many people heard her screaming as she was being stabbed to death at 3 AM, and did nothing. My father was walking home from the Kew Gardens Train Station, after spending the night "cleaning out" the gold Atlas Fountain in Rockefeller Center. Sadly he, too, ignored her cries for help.

I don't know what attracted him to murders. Perhaps it's the same thing that brings me back time and again to my own obsession with Lizzie Borden. When I was about 9 years old, he took me to the Coney Island Musee de Wax which, let's just say, did not contain wax replicas of the likes of John Wayne and Clark Gable (or if they did, that is certainly not what I remember about it). I just recall room after room depicting some bloody, gory crime scene: Leopold and Loeb, who murdered a 14 year old boy in 1924 to see if they could commit the perfect crime (obviously they didn't); Bruno Hauptmann and the Lindberg Baby kidnapping/murder; Richard Speck, who killed 8 nurses in one apartment in Chicago; and the Boston Strangler, Albert DeSalvo (we'll go back to DeSalvo later.) It was pretty traumatic for a little kid to learn what evil the world contained by seeing these horribly replicated, incredibly graphic savage killings. If my cynicism didn't start there, it certainly grew by leaps and bounds after that lovely experience.

But about my father—of all the murders he followed, nothing attracted him nearly as much as that of Alice Crimmins and the Crimmins kids in the summer of 1965. Mrs. Crimmins, a sexy, divorced cocktail waitress, raising her 5-year-old son Eddie and her 4-year-old daughter Missy by herself, reported them missing on a hot July morning in 1965. Missy's little body was found pretty quickly in some bushes by the highway across from The New York World's Fair (which was in full swing at the time.) Eddie's body took longer, about five days, until they found him in an abandoned lot. Their mother, Alice Crimmins, was arrested and charged with their murders. I don't know why, can't even begin to speculate, but my father had a full-on thing for Mrs. Crimmins. He began taking me to the Queens County Courthouse daily to watch her trial. And we would stand across the street when the court broke for lunch every day to get an even closer glance at Alice and her lawyers, as they walked by to and from a nearby diner where they went to eat.

Alice was eventually convicted of first degree manslaughter, but after a bunch of appeals, wound up serving only about three years. But my father didn't live long enough to see her released from prison. Unbelievably, she is still alive today, and lives in Boca Raton, Florida, and also on Long Island New York. Thankfully, she never had any more children!

And now back to Albert DeSalvo, the Boston Strangler. In the mid 60s, DeSalvo was making wallets in jail and selling them via ads in the newspapers. Of course my father had one. I have no idea what ever happened to that thing, but I'd love to know. Hopefully my sister Marilyn has it.

This Magic Moment

I wish I could tell you that the first time I worked for Patty was a difficult one where I learned about all the the sacrifice, and time, and dedication that goes into the inner development of a Broadway show. The roar of the greasepaint, the angst and the suffering of live stage performers, from not only The Andrews Sisters, but also from the ghosts and the souls of the shadows of the legends who walked these halls and floors for the last hundred years. But it wasn't like that. It was really easy.

At that time, I had a photographic memory, so remembering where Patty should be, or what she should say or carry on stage at a given moment, or her costume changes, and entrances and exits, and marks didn't require much of me as long as I could move quickly, and zip up, and pull in, and tell Patty when her cues were coming up. There was so much action, so many people moving in so many directions all the time, topped off by John Travolta's arrival by bicycle every night, just late enough to make the Andrews Sisters nervous, and give the producers ulcer pains. Several well-known stars came out of that show, *Over Here*. Treat Williams, Marilu Henner, Sam Wright, John. But nobody knew them yet. They were little more than chorus kids then.

Patty had this one song in the show that she did as a solo called "The Good Time Girl." She, dressed as a nurse, would sing it to Treat, John, and a couple of other young actors who also played soldiers. Every night she would come off after that number grumbling and complaining how that 20-year-old snotty Johnny kid was trying to upstage her.

There was always something going on, and there was Wally to make feel important, as he sat passively on the couch in Patty's dressing room night after night doing *The New York Times* crossword puzzle and reading *The Wall Street Journal*, while we rushed around.

Although there was really no time for any actual conversation between Patty and I once production got underway, she managed to convey to me from day one that keeping Wally's ego boosted and intact was the most pertinent part of my job. Oh, and reminding him when it was time for him to clip on his tie and go down to the orchestra pit in time to play the piano for the third act, which was really the after-show, when The Andrews Sisters sang a medley of their hit songs.

That was always my favorite part of the show. I was supposed to sure to be in the wings when Patty came off. But I loved that part so much, watching them sing the old songs, that every single night or matinee I positioned myself on one of the props—a life-size real Army tank from the 1940s which, when not in use, was stored on the side where I stood, and waited for a few lines of "Roll Out The Barrel" when the star was placed in the Hollywood Walk of Fame.

This third act was the last time the Andrews Sisters would ever sung together publicly. I was so in awe of my "boss," of my job, of her sisters. I was still a kid trying to be a grown-up and I thought nothing could ever get better...UNTIL...

About a week after I started, my telephone rang at 7:30 AM. Today, that is the middle of the day for me. Back then, I was pissed. This was before the big "Friend Bailout of 1974" and everyone knew that I didn't get out of that Shubert Theater until after 11 PM, and usually didn't get home and asleep before 1 AM. Who would have the nerve, the audacity to call at such an ungodly hour? I begrudgingly picked up the phone, resisted the urge to yell, and said very curtly and abruptly, "Yeah? What?" and I was woke up and fumbled, and very abruptly: "Yeah? What?" (This was long, long before caller I.D.)

The voice on the other end did not identify herself. She didn't have to. Even if I hadn't worked for her for eight or ten shows by then, even if I had never met her, it was unmistakable. No "Hello," no "How are you?" Just..."Do you want to go to Bloomingdale's with me?"

This was big! I mean way big! We were about to change this relationship from, "You and Maxene are on in two minutes; I just heard the cue over the loudspeaker." To what, I didn't know yet. I'm glad I didn't. It would have overwhelmed the hell out of me, and probably Patty, as well. It was good that it happened gradually.

When I got to her apartment (which was really a hotel suite on East 64th street, between Madison and Park, where Maxene also lived—but 3 floors up,) I was absolutely thrilled to learn that Wally wasn't going with us. Just Patty and I. Just 16-year-old me and one of the Andrews Sisters! Two weeks earlier, I'd sooner believe the preaching of the rabbis (or even the rabbits) before I would believe this!

Of course, it had begun to snow. But that didn't deter Patty in the least. Remember, she was from Minnesota. So we trudged the five blocks and two avenues through what I considered a blinding snowstorm, but she called "a light dusting." And we talked about every day, ordinary people stuff. That's the thing that first struck me about Patty—away from the stage, and away from Wally—how real she was! How little we talked about show business and her career, and her sisters (that would come later). And how much we talked about clothes, and the styles that were current at that time (huge belts and platform shoes). And I thought how strange it was that talking to her was not much different than talking to any teenager my age.

When we got to Bloomingdale's, me shivering and freezing despite the fact I still had my flannel footie pajamas on under my clothes, and Patty, invigorated by the cold and (as I was to learn in time) the freedom of being away from her husband, were ready to shop. Very soon after we arrived, it occurred to me that someone was lying to Patty, or she was lying to herself, about what size she wore. We were obviously in the wrong department. But I did not want to embarrass her, and so I went along with the lie (as I was to do for the rest of her shopping life). I threw her in the dressing room with the largest thing I could find in that Junior Department and ran downstairs to the Women's Department and brought up everything that she seemed to like,

BUT in the right size. I don't know who was fooling who, but as I said this was the beginning of a game we would play for the next 30 years.

I would have been happy to stay in Bloomie's for the rest of the day—for the rest of my life. But it was a performance night, which meant that Patty stopped eating by 3, so everything was nice and digested when the curtain opened five hours later at 8 PM. And she wanted to go to a restaurant to have lunch before it got too close to her cut-off time. We went to a little burger-type restaurant a few blocks up Lexington Avenue (this was years before I stopped eating meat because of the animals and she stopped eating meat because Wally was convinced it would kill us all and would not allow anything other than chicken in the house. I can't believe what we ate in those days. Disgusting things that my ex-sisters-in-law still eat, like lamb stew, pickled cow's tongue, red meat with strips of thick white fat running through it, liver and tripe (look it up). And the not-so-Jewish foods, though equally grotesque: pork, veal, venison, ribs. We were freakin' Neanderthals.

*Singer Janie Sell with Patty and Maxene Andrews
in* "Over Here" *(1974)*

The Kids — WOW

Anyway, when I woke up this AM, my first thought, as it is most days, was......what am I going to write about for today's show? I know you like to hear Patty and Andrews Sisters stories, and although I can't conjure one up every day, I try to do it as often as possible. My story today is not a big deal, I guess, if we were a couple of teenagers perpetuating the act...But I was the only teenager. The other, Patty, was nearing my age now. Which of course highlights the absurdity of our lives back then.

As I've told you before, Patty did not have any access to any money. Wait, I take that back...if she was able, she got into Wally's wallet in his pants pocket and took out a few bills while he was in the shower in the morning. He controlled every cent. If I or Patty were to go to the market, it was with a check pre-written out by him, the amount left blank, to be filled in by the manager of

Gelsons (the market). The amount of the check had to match the receipt, and believe me, he'd check, item against item.

If she couldn't get into his pants pockets, it was up to me to provide whatever cash we needed to go to lunch., or whatever we did. Now you may ask, "Why didn't Patty just ask him for some money? After all, she earned it..." She did, every once in a while, and he would flat out say "NO!" and a gigantic fight would ensue.

My father had died, a few days before *Over Here* closed. (What a week!) So yes, more often than not, lunch was on me. I never minded. I was confused. It made me question giving control of one's money over to another person, and consequently I have never, ever, had a joint bank account with anyone.

But again, I was still a kid, and screwed up sometimes. It was a different world then. No such things as ATMs existed. If you needed, or wanted, to withdraw money from your bank, the banks closed promptly at 3 PM, Monday through Friday. That was usually my big screw-up—not taking out enough for the weekend, or the evenings.

How embarrassing to have to tell you that on nights when Wally was gone on his 12-Step Circuit, and Patty and I were hungry, we had this most awful plan on how we would get food...Should I have shorted out by then? And she couldn't talk him into taking another shower before his meetings started.

Everyone who owned a business here in Encino knew Patty and loved her. Encino is a very small town. Although it goes way up into the hill, and canyons, the actual main drag is only about two miles long. And she had been here so long, well...Al Jolson was the mayor of Encino when she first got here, if that gives you any idea.

Nobody in town loved Patty as much as the Italian Restaurant. They were forever giving her freebies, especially when people called in an order (mostly pizzas) and didn't pick it up. "You take, Miss Andrews—you take home with you!" almost inevitably whenever we went in there for a meal.

As you know, Patty was talented, she was funny in addition to the singing, and she could do great imitations and accents. So if we were hungry, and it was late at night, and we had no money... Patty would call up the Italian Restaurant, and in someone else's voice (usually her sister LaVerne's) she would order a pizza. Then a couple of hours later, I would go into the Italian Restaurant, and ask to use the bathroom. When I came out, there would be a nice big box and bag for me, by the door, and the owner saying, "You take to Miss Patty!"

At 18 years old I used to think that was so funny. In my 60s, I see how horrible it was. And I don't know who I am more angry at...the man who held onto the money so tightly his wife couldn't even eat.... or the wife who earned all the money, and let him do that!

Do You Believe in Magic

A few weeks ago, someone from Europe wrote to me these words that when translated came to read: "To be Patty's Andrews' Daughter—that would be magic!"

Magic. Imagine finding yourself in the Polo Lounge of the Beverly Hills Hotel. A place so steeped with Hollywood History that you could see the ghosts of Mary Pickford, Charlie Chaplin, Jean Harlow, etc. in every corner, at every turn. To have sat in these rooms where the likes of our idols, my Gracie, your Clark Gable, passed so many hours, where so many incredible movie deals were made on this very spot. The most classical of classic films that we so love began right here, over a drink, a salad, and a pen.

And yes, imagine finding yourself here, sitting indeed across from Patty Andrews. Patty loved the Polo Lounge. And she especially liked eating on the outside patio. I must say, I agreed with her. The patio was small, so anyone who was anyone was usually out there.

And remember the "Little Person" who used to do the Philip Morris cigarette commercials in the 50s? His name was Johnny, I believe, and what he used to do in the ads was walk around with a telephone, and yell, "Call For Philip Morris!" Well by then, he had a new gig. He walked around the Polo Lounge, and would announce calls for the different patrons, such as, "Call for Jimmy Stewart," or "Call for Lucille Ball" and bring the telephone over to their table.

Pretty surreal, huh? And you can't believe it could possibly get better than this, but then Patty started talking, telling me some story about Vaudeville with Larry Rich and his Kiddie Revue, and then about costumes from the Leon Belasco band burning up, and leaving them stranded in Chicago, or driving around the country from place to place with her parents in the back seat of a Model T with LaVerne, while Maxene navigated from the front seat between her mother and father. She is focused on me so completely that no one would dare interrupt her. Well, almost no one.

The door from the lobby opened up, and in walked Lynda Wells, followed by Maxene. Before we knew what was happening, Lynda shot into the seat next to me, and Maxene squeezed in beside Patty.

After all the greeting and the hugging and kissing finally stopped, and Maxene and Lynda ordered their lunch, Patty, not being derailed from the story she was telling me picked up where she left off.

And THAT was when the real magic began. Patty got as far as maybe one sentence into the story, when Maxene picked it up, and back and forth, they told Lynda and I story after story, childhood tales about their summers in Mound, showbiz stories, Junior High School stories... Sometimes they spoke in unison, just as you would imagine in the movies and such. Sometimes one would start a story and they would tell it, trading off line for line, sometimes even word for word, while Lynda and I sat mesmerized, not moving, not talking, barely breathing. I don't think the sisters let go of each other's hands for the entire time.

This would be only one of many afternoons we spent lunching, shopping, and listening to these two treasures sharing their lives with us. Sometimes planned, sometimes not, but always wonderful.

And that was truly MAGIC!

Lynda

I heard the main character on a TV show in the middle of the night talking about her dying brother. She said. "After he is gone, there will be no one left who remembers my childhood."

Being an only child, that thought never occurred to me. To have someone who actually lived it all—the good, the bad, the sad—

with you... What a novel thing. I guess that's what having a sister or brother is all about.

Cue to theme of *The Patty Duke Show.*

Some of you are so young that I should explain. *The Patty Duke Show* was on television, starting in about 1963,until probably 1966. In it, Patty Duke, very believably, played identical cousins, who although they looked alike, were the exact opposite in every possible way. Cathy, complete with a Scottish accent, was refined, and cultured...Patty spoke like a New Yorker, and ran wild through the streets of Brooklyn Heights.

Happy Birthday to my Cathy, from the other Patty, to my not so identical cousin.... Lynda Wells.

Talk about opposites!

My Cathy is older than me, but looks a hell of a lot younger. Her accent isn't Scottish exactly, but rather a Southern drawl. Not surprising, since she is from someplace called Helena, Arkansas, and later Greenville, Mississippi. While I, true to character, have a strong Joan Rivers accent (no matter how hard I try to lose it) and—like Patty—ran the streets of New York, not too far from Brooklyn Heights.

And what brought the Lane Girls together were siblings, whom like us, we can called a parent, at one time or another. And loved very much.

There is no one else in the world who can remember the haunting sound of Maxene's frantic, yet defeated footsteps as she climbed up the stairs of the Shubert Theatre, from the basement, after learning that our beloved "Over Here" was being cancelled, and not going on the road. I will never forget her words, as I'm sure Lynda could recite them in unison with me—"Where's Patty? Oh. my God! They are screwing the Andrews Sisters!" Patty was onstage alone, singing the old songs, so Maxene could find out about a secret meeting that was indeed "screwing the Andrews Sisters." I was in my usual spot backstage watching the third act.

Who else shares the same claim to fame, as being the first car ever to be allowed to park in Shubert Alley? Who else shares the feeling of standing in the wings every night, listening to that hauntingly beautiful compilation of the hit songs that Patty and Maxene sang after the show? Who else knows what the words "the third act" means? And who else was so loved by one of the Andrews Sisters?

That was my childhood, and this is the only person alive who shared it with me.

And then we came to California, all of us. And sometimes it was bad (thanks to you know who), so bad we don't even talk about it. Perhaps that's why we can't write about it yet.

But sometimes, most times, it was wonderful. And the four of us just enjoyed each other so much. There have been circumstances, and people, who have tried to come between me and my not-so-identical cousin. But they didn't. They wouldn't. They couldn't, because in terms of minutes, or rather seconds, I knew Lynda before I knew either of the Andrews Sisters.

44 Birthdays! Thank God, I'm not the one who has to find someone famous to sing "Happy Birthday" every April 19th. But not to worry...I'll be calling, and doing it myself later. So in advance...Happy Happy Birthday, and lots more with years of good health, happiness, and from every single viewer on here, these sentiments...Thank you for making Maxene so happy. For taking care of her, and the Andrews Sisters, and me through very scary times, and for always being the one who kept her cool, no matter what (and there were a lot of whats!).

I love you... Happy Birthday.

As always,

Your Little Big Mouth, PAMMY

The Boogie Woogie Bugle Bus

Yes indeed– I actually did drive around the country in a multi-colored Econoline van with the words "Boogie Woogie Bugle Bus" painted on either side of it. Almost like *The Partridge Family* bus, but so much worse!

You see, I am a horrible driver. I admit it. Always have been, always will be. The state of New York failed me five times before I finally got my license (and that was questionable). My friends call me "Magoo" when I drive, like in Mr. Magoo who, as you know, is blind and drives around and narrowly misses hitting people and cars, and driving off cliffs, into mountains...etc.

The cute little 1969 red Camaro with the black top had made it through almost the whole year of the Broadway show. Every night, it was parked in Shubert Alley next to Maxene's Rolls Royce (we were the first people in the history of the Shubert Theatre who were allowed that privilege, and I don't know if it's ever been granted again since).

But now it was 1975, the show had closed a few days into the new year, and I wanted a van. Not just any van. A brand new '75 van with orange carpeting. I don't know how, but I talked my Grandmother into getting me one. Problem was, it was white, and a bad driver in a white car is not a very good mix.

The first day I had it, I was speeding down Park Avenue with Patty, of all people, in the passenger seat, when I took the door off of a taxi. Oh my god, the screaming that went on that day—Patty in one ear yelling, the taxi driver with a thick Russian accent in the other ear. And now my nice new van was streaked with yellow taxi paint. As time, and winter, went on, I skidded into a Stop sign, and crashed into a green NYC bus, along with my usual scraping of the walls and posts and curbs. By the time that van got to California, it was a mess! But since this was the psychedelic period, I came up with a brilliant idea. I would paint the van.

However there was no Earl Scheib in the picture for me that time. I decided to do it myself. I would go to the hardware store and buy a can of spray paint, use it until it was empty, and then go back and get another color, use that one up, get another color, and so on until the van was covered in multi-colored spray paint. Then to top it off, I painted the words: BOOGIE WOOGIE BUGLE BUS on both sides of the van. That was the outside. Inside, there was a bed—that same coffin which my father kept for some reason in the living room throughout my childhood, and Mr. Heldenmuth's World War 1 army trunk. Mr. Heldenmuth lived directly downstairs from me when I was a kid in Queens,. He was a German refugee, who had a metal plate in his head as a result of injuries in the First World War, and probably some sort of PTSD, because every little noise bothered him. I bothered him, and perhaps also my practice of putting strong magnets on the floor to see if they would connect with the metal plate and pull him up to his ceiling. The day I told him that I was moving to California, he cried. Tears of joy! And he ran—quite good for a man in his 80s—down to the basement of the building and hauled up that 1917 trunk with his name stenciled across the sides with some German writing, and told me to take it with me, so I could get all my stuff out and never have to come to Queens, or the building, again.

I forgot to mention that to top it off, the van had bright orange shag carpeting. And to answer your question: YES THEY DID! Both of them (at different times), but Patty on a daily basis. Even I, at that age, couldn't believe they would climb into the passenger seat of that heap, and drive around with me. I don't know, maybe they secretly took some pride in The Boogie Woogie Bugle Bus. But we sure looked like *The Beverly Hillbillies* carting around town in that thing.

Still, the most fun we had in that van had nothing to do with the Andrews Sisters. For my L.A. friends, please bear with me while I explain this little practice of ours to those in other states and countries. I don't know if it is still done, but every Wednesday night from the 1950s to at least the 1990s was "Cruise Night." Every kid in town would drive up and down a street called Van Nuys Boulevard. It was the teen thing to do, and you would park for a while and hang with your friends. A big deal to say the least.

So of course I did Van Nuys Boulevard every single Wednesday night, and the friends whom I had made out here (besides Dutchie) were a bit younger than me, still in High School, and each played a musical instrument (drums, guitar, keyboard, trumpet; I think there was a kid who lived in the hills who played the sax.) But I had quite a little band assembled in the back of the Boogie Woogie Bugle Bus. We would throw open the back doors and blast away.

But if you remember from previous "PAM SHOWS," I told you how Patty didn't like to be alone, and I would stay with her until

Wally got home from his assorted 12-steppers. Sometimes by the time he got done counseling a hoarder, or a victim of racial profiling, it would be after midnight. On those nights, I would just throw Patty in the car and take her with me. Two thousand teenagers and Patty, and do you know that she was never out of place? It was amazing!

And those 12-step meetings of Wally's turned out to be a good thing, when it came time to get rid of the Boogie Woogie Bugle Bus. One of his buddies from Narcotics Anon worked in a car dealership, and actually took it as a trade-in! So see, you never know!

Movies with Maxene

Many of you have seen a smidgen of the films I am about to talk about today. And I am happy to say that although not in my possession, these movies still exist today.

It was a party at Maxene's house. Or maybe it was just a group of us who went back to Mackie's after dinner for dessert, and one of those board-game-playing evenings, where only Maxene knew the rules (because they changed with every roll of the dice). How I wish I had written down Maxene's rules for backgammon, Monopoly, even checkers.

Well on this particular night, after Mackie had beaten everyone, at every game, and the talking had returned to a quiet lull, Maxene went into another room and pulled out... the movie projector. And many, many reels of film. I don't remember how many people were there. Lynda, of course, my ex-husband, Uncle Louie and Jeannie (his wife of our Aunt LaVerne) family, and friends, an odd assortment of neighbors, and people who would never have been brought together if not for the common denominator—Maxene.

Sadly, I could not get Patty out of the house from under the thumb of her ruler. But how she would have loved that night. How I loved that night. Maxene put on reel after reel of her home movies. When I say that some of you have seen a smidgen of them, it's because Lynda allowed the use of some of them in the BBC documentary of the Andrews Sisters. Here and there, something might pop up when you least expect it. So watch the show again, some of you are in it, and you will see a bit of what I'm talking about.

Reel after reel after reel. The three of them laughing, pushing Patty into the pool. Couldn't have been LaVerne—she was terrified of water after seeing her mother almost drown in the lake in Mound, Minnesota. Dressing up, doing imitations, the famous friends visiting. (For all I remember Doris Day could have been among them) and Dutchie (Aleda) and Peter in the Halloween parade at the Buckley School, standing beside a certain Miss Minnelli, decked out in one of her father's movie costumes (miniaturized) while a certain Miss Garland sitting beside Aunt LaVerne cheered and clapped. A school Halloween pageant, one of the last places in the world you would ever expect to find LaVerne Andrews, dressed as beautiful as ever, sitting on the bleachers with Judy Garland.

Maxene kept changing films. I was sitting on the floor next to her, handing reel after reel, making neat little piles of what we had already seen and what was yet to more. They were so beautiful, there was so much love immortalized on that celluloid. So much laughter, so much joy. I was crying, overcome with an abundance of emotion.

Finally at about 2 AM, Maxene flipped on the light switch, and we discovered that besides us, everyone else in the room had fallen asleep. Right about now, Lynda is going to interject that she was awake. But that's not how I remember it—Honey, my ex-husband was snoring.

I looked up at Maxene. The tears were streaming down her face, too. In that moment, I never loved her more.

When she could find her voice, she whispered to me: "I loved them. I loved them so much..... I love her so much."

I knew exactly what she felt. Patty could turn on a dime on any of us in that room, at Wally's request, and she had. But in those movies, long before Baby Boy Weschler made his first appearance all bundled up against these harsh Californians winters, at the piano. That's who Maxene missed, and knew, and loved. And that was the person I knew, as we sat in the hills, or restaurants, or the closet at night, listening to those old 78s.

That evening bonded Maxene and I in a way I can't really explain. But I was so lucky to have her to run to when things got awful, and to share with when things were great. In my whole life, I've never felt that closeness to another person. I doubt I ever will.

Stage Clothes Shopping

My three most favorite days of the year with Patty were always Dec 29th, 30th, and 31st (bet you thought I was going to say my birthday, her birthday, and Christmas.) And while I admit it was awfully fun to walk through the stores with her during the holiday season and hear the Andrews Sisters and Bing Crosby's Christmas songs blasting through the mall (just like going to the Brown Derby with one of them, and insisting that we sit under their picture), this was even better.

Patty and I would get all dressed up and go to the best stores in whatever city we were in. Usually we were in Los Angeles, so we went to Neiman's and Saks in Beverly Hills. Patty had a credit card, and spent freely on clothes, provided they looked like stage clothes as opposed to everyday outfits that could be worn on the street.

So we would shop and carefully go through every item in her size (or not) in the store. I say "or not" because sometimes I didn't want her to feel badly that she really wore a bigger size than she thought she did. So I would venture into other "larger" departments and come back with piles of designer clothes and tell her these things were in her size. The reason I could get away with this so easily was because she didn't like to wear her glasses out in public, and this was about as public as one could get.

For hours she would try on everything with sequins and beads and, oh yes, feathers. We laughed and joked, but she worked hard trying on all those clothes, then sorting through them, earnestly trying to decide what would look best on her on stage, color, comfort, and trend-wise.

Now, these fancy stores, have restaurants, which they don't call "restaurants" but "tea rooms." Eventually we would wind up in one of these tea rooms for lunch, where they gave you a little food for a lot of money. And while you were eating, they would have something that Patty called a "Style Show." Models would walk around the tea room, and try to interest the customers in the latest fashions. How Patty loved those Style Shows! How, I'm sure, her sister LaVerne did, too. Me—not so much. They made me nervous. I was having a hard enough time trying to do the whole manners thing right, without having to be aware of that going on, too.

We would continue shopping until the late afternoon. Those three days of every year, Wally didn't mind having to find his own dinner. Thankfully, the tea rooms only served lunch, so Patty and I usually went to a drive through on the way home, only to go back early the next morning to do it all over again.

Then it was New Year's Eve, and what the Weschlers lacked as far as I was concerned at Christmas and Thanksgiving time, they more than made up for on New Year's. Wally especially. And his kindness carried over into the first day of the New Year as well.

But then came January 2nd. To most of the world, it is the second day of the new year. To Maxene, and my bio mother, it was the day before their birthdays. And to me, although it took a couple of years for me to catch on...it was "Return Day" in Beverly Hills. I would feel so badly for Patty, because she put so much gusto into the shopping and choosing that I really believed that she must have really believed that the day would come when she could actually keep some of the outfits we bought. Not in my lifetime, and since she died before me, not in hers, either (after WW came into her life full-fledge anyway). Early morning January 2nd, while she was still in her bedroom sleeping, Wally would gather up all the new clothes with the tags still on them, put them in my car, and send me back to Beverly Hills so that when the stores opened, they could all be returned and credited back to his charge account.

Meanwhile, he had receipts dated the previous year for costumes and stage clothes for deductions when tax time came around in April.

That is why, if you notice, when I talk about the costumes, jewelry, stage stuff, etc. that I have from Patty, very little of it is from after the 1950s. I can really only think of two things: her "Victory Canteen" shoes (which don't really count because they came from the theater company) and that lovely white, green, orange and black number from "Here's Lucy."

But whatever WW deprived Patty of, I made damn sure that one way or another she had whatever it was that she needed or wanted. And I will go to my grave being proud that I could always figure out how to pull it off for her. Even as a young child, I did it, because I knew if anyone deserved it, it was Patty. She could have been married to the Elephant Man, and to me, it wouldn't have made a bit of difference. It was ALL, always for Patty.

Spying on Maxene

If there is anyone out there who thinks that the first time Wally Wechsler had me find someone to tape Maxene's show was when I dressed Emma up as me, and sent him to West Hollywood (when he ruined the tape by gushing over Isabel Sanford (Weezie Jefferson from *The Jeffersons*, who was sitting next to him), you are crazy.

That man was as paranoid as they come, this side of Bellevue, and had me find someone to tape as many of the shows that Maxene did as was physically possible. In a few minutes, I will be telling you about the very first time, in New York, at the Spindletop in 1975, when Mackie made her solo debut.

But maybe Cousin Ernie can help me explain something, since he has been a long time employee of Radio Shack. Bugging a phone (even your own) is illegal here in the state of California. So the next best thing WW (Wally) could resort to was having these suction cup gadgets from Radio Shack attached to the telephones. Perhaps Ernie can tell us what they were. I remember that with these things, he could tape all incoming calls, but not the outgoing ones (that's why Patty had to be the one to call me at 3 or 4 AM for our nightly chats—plus, even if the house wasn't bugged for all incoming calls, if I rang the phone in the middle of the night, it would have woken him up, and in addition to being taped, he would have been listening on the extension).

Okay, so WW was obsessed trying to catch Maxene doing what? She certainly had the right to sing any Andrews Sisters songs she wanted to in her act. She was, after all, one of The Andrews Sisters. He said that he wanted to make sure she wasn't doing any of his material. This from a man who claimed he wrote "Way Down Upon The Suwannee River." There was no use trying to understand or make any sense of it. It was just easier to do whatever crazy thing he wanted so I could hang out with Patty to my heart's content. Secretly, I would pray that when Maxene performed, there would not be any birthdays in the audience which she might have felt inclined to acknowledge. Because, after all, everybody knows that WW wrote "Happy Birthday" (okay, that was lame, even for Gracie, but nevertheless true!).

So when Maxene made her solo appearance for the first time, I was too involved to be able to just sit there, with a hidden tape recorder, and record the show. I needed someone else. Someone unsuspecting...Andy's Hungarian mother. She would be perfect. And she would do whatever she was asked, go wherever she was invited, as long as her son was with her. I got them tickets and explained to her that she needed to bring a bag large enough to hide a tape recorder.

"I bring my knitting bag," she decided, and put the recorder under something she was knitting for the Hungarian refugees.

When they showed up, I put them right down in front by the stage.

Maxene came out, She looked lovely. I remember she had these specially designed sequined tennis shoes. That is about all I remember. Because neither my mother-in-law nor my idiot ex- husband thought to put a fresh tape into the recorder...

Sooooo, of course Mama Wohl hit the PLAY button, instead of the RECORD button, and as Maxene belted out "Bei Mir Bist Du Schoen," the tape recorder belted out "Hava Nagila"!

Maxene, ever the pro, just shrugged and kept on singing. Later, of course, I told her the truth. And what would sound horrifying to most was just another day for us with Wally Weschler! We laughed about it, and went out for night lunch after the show.

By the way, Maxene was quite a big hit. She always was in her solo act. She had a rich, soulful voice, and sang from her heart, unlike my Bubby, who somewhere along the way after Mr. W. became the arranger, resorted to screaming instead of singing.

Golfing with Patty

So that my sister can stop praying for me for using the Lord's name in vain, and the people who are distressed that I don't support the Special Olympics can stop questioning my lack of compassion, today's "PAM SHOW" is going to be about Patty and I (usually a safe subject!).

The story begins sometime in the 50s, when the Andrews Sisters were performing in Las Vegas. Since it was after December 1951, a certain husband was right along with them, playing the piano and trying to run the show.

Every morning, very early I might add, that husband—Wally—would wake up Patty to have her go with him to the golf course. She was supposed to drive the golf cart while he played the course.

After a day or so, an older lady walked up to Wally, and asked to play a round of golf with him. Wally consented and Patty drove the two of them from hole to hole, chatting with the woman whenever she wasn't hitting the ball. The lady introduced herself as Pauline Hill, and said that she was a Congresswoman in New Jersey. Wally introduced himself and Patty to her as Patty and Wally Weschler from California. No further explanation.

Well, Pauline liked playing golf with Wally, and pretty soon, every morning, they had a standing golf date. And Patty continued to go along to drive the golf cart and chat (it was rare that she had a friend who WW liked).

So after about a week or so, Pauline said to them, "Gee, I'd really love to take you out to dinner tonight to show you my appreciation for playing and driving me around all week. But I have tickets to see a show tonight, and it is with my very favorite performers." Perhaps it was the use of the letter "s"—the plural of "performers" rather than the singular "performer"—but at that moment, Patty realized that Pauline Hill, Congresswoman from New Jersey, had no idea who had been driving her around the golf course all week, confirmed when WW asked her what act she was seeing? And she replied proudly, "THE ANDREWS SISTERS!" Patty and Wally exchanged looks, but neither said a word. They wanted to see how it played out.

That night, as Patty and her Sisters took the stage, the gasp from the audience was audible. As were the words, "OH MY GOD!" which Pauline couldn't suppress upon realizing that her golfing chauffeur was the "lead sister" of her favorite singing group.

So they stayed friends. I do believe Pauline was the only Republican Wally ever let in the house.

Fast forward about 20 years. My friend Ramona was visiting LA at the same time as Pauline. Patty and I decided to combine the sightseeing duties with both of our guests, which meant that while the four of us took a tour ushered by Patty of the movie stars' homes in Beverly Hills, we also spent hours sitting on the bench as the Encino Public Golf Course watching Pauline hit balls.

Ramona and I. That was some combo. We are one day apart (I am one day older than her). Two street-smart Queens girls. She and I met in Kindergarten. We drove out here from New York in two days (with 18 speeding tickets—but that's another show.) A Republican Congresswoman, and an Andrews Sister. But somehow it worked. Pauline really liked Ramona, and by then, Patty and I could read each other's mind.

One day (to avoid the golf course) Patty suggested that the four of us go to The Farmer's Market (that was the place where at another time we had lunch with Charlie Chaplin). We had a nice meal, went into some of the shops, and then, all of a sudden.... Patty disappeared.

As a group we looked all over the place (and it's pretty big) for her, and still could not find her. So we decided to split up. Me and two people who lived back east and had no idea of the layout of this place. As they said once in a song, "We looked for her uptown, and crosstown, and downtown (and if I continued the song, we'd be in New York instead of L.A.). Three hours passed, and still no Patty. Then, in the distance, I saw a building. One that would have been Patty's salvation, after a week of golf courses, screaming Queens accents, Republican politics, and too much eye make-up. The Wine Tasting Gallery! I pulled Patty out of there, and let's just say that she didn't at all mind sitting on the bench in the Encino

Public Golf Course that afternoon. Come to think of it, she didn't mind anything that day.

We never did find out of what became of Pauline. Suddenly the phone calls stopped. And finally when Patty attempted to call her, the phone was disconnected. Patty wrote letters. They came back. Since she was at least 20 years older than the Weschlers, it seems pretty obvious what had happened.

That's The Chance You Take

8:20 PM. How I waited for that minute to arrive. It seems like almost every night, for years, and years. Wally would go off to a few of his 12 step meetings, and we headed for that secret place, way in the back of the big walk-in closet in Patty's bedroom. How I remember falling asleep in that closet, so many times. But I'm getting ahead of myself.

Wally Weschler hated The Andrews Sisters. He was jealous of his wife's talent and success. He would not stand for her sisters. He would not allow us to play any of their music in the house. Not even Patty's solos, nor the ones he claimed he wrote.

But in the back of Patty's closet, buried beneath rows of costumes, old purses, gloves, scarves, and props, Patty managed to hide an old Victrola. It was so old, we had to wind it up with a crank. And even though it probably was, I never considered that record player to be an antique. Just a wonderful box, that produced the most beautiful sounds and emotions that two people could ever share.

The things I heard coming out of that box. A recording of 7 year old Patty singing with her mother in 1925. Air takes, ad checks, and mistakes, and conversations that were never meant for outside ears.

It was in that closet, that my best memories, of my years as Patty's adopted daughter were made. Such raw emotions, (when Patty would sit, eyes closed, (tears sliding down her cheeks) grasping on to my hand so tightly, it hurt. (But in a good way.) As she listened, really listened to the amazing sounds that came out of her, and

Maxene and LaVerne. She really just did not know how great they were, how great she was.

And it was in those stolen moments, while Wally was standing in the heat of a 12 Step Meeting, lecturing about how he overcame a defect, or addiction which he never really had...that Patty was able to really feel, to really understand the enormity of what it was. To comprehend what made the people wait for hours to see them at the Paramount, or some theater, to get what it meant, when they stood on docks all over the world singing "I'll Be With You In Apple Blossom Time" as ships full of naïve young boys sailed off to war, some never to return alive again.

But for some reason, her favorite part to play in the closet was her solo rendition of "I'll Never Enter My Mind." Over and over we played that while she cried with pride for herself, for The Andrews Sisters, repeating and saying "Oh my God, That is me!" and things like "I was never vocally better than this." She had another solo song she loved called- "That's The Chance You Take." She told me that when mother recorded that song, she thought to herself, "If I ever had a daughter, this will be my song to her." Hence, "That's The Chance You Take" became my song. And for hours, she would sing it to me.

Sometimes, Wally would come home early, hitting only 2 meetings, instead of his usual 3. And we would scramble, as Patty would run downstairs to distract him, and I would re-hide the contraband under the costumes and shoes. Then I usually fell asleep in the closet, under the heap, alongside those treasures.

Today would have been my Bubby's 102nd Birthday. If she was still alive, I know exactly what we would be. (Eating lunch at our favorite Chinese Restaurant here in Encino, and lying that her birthday cake was 100 years old. (Even for me.) But instead, for Patty's 98th, I'm sharing my most precious memory, and I would venture to say, one of hers too.)

As for me the Birthday, I'm not too worried. Nobody could throw a party like LaVerne, with Maxene a very close second!!!

Happy Birthday Bubby.

I will cherish you always.

Unforgettable

So every so often, Patty would get these creative surges when she wanted to paint something. She actually was a very good artist, but on this particular day, that was not the kind of painting she wanted to do. She wanted to paint furniture. Now the only color of paint she had was that God-awful forest green. You know-—the color city benches were painted in the 50s and 60s. But she thought it was a beautiful color, so we began sanding and painting an old dresser, old end tables, etc. After a couple of hours of this we were covered in green paint—it was on our shoes, our clothes, even in our hair. But we were both hungry and decided to take a break and go—of all places—to McDonalds.

So we are sitting there, eating French fries, looking like a couple of Martians out of Roswell, when a man come over and very politely says: "Oh Miss Andrews, I just want to tell you, I've always loved your work..."

Now I can see that Patty is totally embarrassed at being caught looking, well, not like Patty Andrews.

I couldn't contain myself. I had to ask him, "How did you know who she was?"

And I will always remember his answer. He said, "Once you've seen her, you never forget her!" Well, sir—you were right!

The Great Depression

I hope I can, in some way, with some words, impact as many people as possible. In part, that is why I do "THE PAM SHOW." While it's fun to squeeze out little tidbits about the Andrews Sisters, and Hollywood, I bare my soul and secrets to you each and every day, in the hope that somehow, someway, what I've gone through will help one of you reading this.

I once had to get an operation, in the 70s. It was one of those "female" things you did not talk about. I told nobody, not even my

California friends... so, while staying at my grandmother's in New York...I drove myself alone to the hospital. The whole drive out to Long Island, I listened to Judy on the 8-track singing "You'll Never Walk Alone" over and over. She and that song got me through the surgery, and the three long days by myself in the hospital after. What I'm trying to say here is, if a song or a person gets you through what seems impossible, then by all means use it. Use the Andrews Sisters. Use them often. Use them loud! They would be so proud if their songs, if their beings, if LaVerne drying lettuce with a fan, or Maxene punching Shemp Howard in the nose, or Patty falling under that huge apple tree gave one person some salvation, a reason to live, to believe it gets better, then all those years and tears, and even Wally Weschler, was worth it. And I know that as hard as it is to believe, it is true. That's what they lived for. For you, and you, and you, and you.....

I had never before been prone to depression so severe that life was not worth living. I didn't believe in shrinks so I'm pretty sure (self-diagnosis) in looking back, that I had a nervous breakdown when I was 20 years old. There are two, maybe three things that happened during my duration with the Andrews Sisters, that I will never share with you unless Lynda and I sit down and write our elusive book. But I will tell you that if I did have a breakdown, it was caused in part by the conclusion of one of these events, ending with a certified attorney's letter instructing me that I was never to have any contact (and it listed various means of contact that were prevalent in the 1970s) with Wally (who the fuck cared?) or Patty (my heart was broken). It went on to tell me that this was irreparable, and I was never refer to the Andrews Sisters, primarily Patty, again.

I was 20....I did not know any better. I thought my life was over. I was nervous, and shook, and cried all the time. I couldn't eat. I did crazy, crazy things like run up a $1000 phone call to my ex-husband who was in Hungary that summer. Can you imagine? One phone call, $1000? And in 1977! Nobody knew what do with me. And to make it worse, Patty was on that awful *The Gong Show* weekly, so as I might not to, I still saw her on TV once a week. Wednesdays, if I remember correctly.

Finally, with three of the four originals (my father was dead by then) who had wrestled and lured me into that Elmhurst Hospital

Teen Ward some years earlier showed up for an intervention (I was now over 18, and could not be taken against my will, unless I was a danger to myself or others), it shook something inside of me. No, I did not want to die. NO OTHER PERSON. NO MATTER WHAT THEY DO, NO MATTER HOW MUCH THEY HURT YOU, NO MATTER WHO THEY ARE, is a reason to give up your own life! You never know what the next day will bring, or the next. Something better, perhaps, something different, perhaps....but it is so worth sticking around to find out.

By the way, I received this life-altering letter in late July or August of 1977. And in fact I did spent my 21st birthday (March of 1978) with Patty and Wally. I don't remember exactly how this was fixed, except the wording of the letter said I, Pam Dubois, was to not have contact with the Weschlers. It did not mention my then-87-year-old grandmother.

Now there is a moral to this. What once seemed so terrible, so life-threatening, turned out to be nothing.

The second time I got a similarly worded certified letter from the Weschler's lawyer was right after I wrote the liner notes for the MCA Andrews Sisters 50th Anniversary CD (Vol. 2). This time around, I crumpled the paper that was oh, so close to the one that nearly ended my life a little over a decade earlier and threw it at my dog, Joey. Joey and I played catch with that letter for about 20 minutes, and then I threw it in the trash...

...and went inside to complete my liners for *The Andrews Sisters Capitol Collectors Series...*

My Friend Gayle

So I have a friend that I have known since 1960. The fact that we go back so far accounts for why I put up with her nonsense. Anyway, her name is Gayle. Now Gayle has always been a large and portly girl. Hell, what am I saying? She's tremendous! Weighed more at eight years old than I do now.

Many years ago, Gayle got herself on a morning talk show which filmed in Toronto. For the life of me, I can't remember the name of the show, but I do remember the topic: was "Losers in Life" (I don't know if Gayle was fully aware in advance of what the subject matter would be; she just told me that she wanted to see Canada for free).

Well, it turned out that "Losers In Life" really did want to help her and they arranged a month- long stay in a weight loss psych rehab here in California, about 200 miles from where Emma and I lived. I don't really know know the details, but after two days, we received a call—first from Gayle, telling us that she had been kicked out of the program for not following their rules and her return airline voucher to New York wasn't until four weeks from then and her parents refused to pay the difference to change the ticket. Could she stay with Em and me?

And then, before I even had a chance to discuss this with Emma, the phone rang again. This time it was the weight loss rehab hospital, informing me that they would send Gayle by limo to my address, as long as she vacated their premises within the next half-hour (God only knows the commotion and scene she must have caused).

Several more phone calls followed, not only from Gayle, but from the hospital wanting to know where they could "deposit" her. What were the rules she didn't follow? Well it seems Gayle got kicked out of the program for a number of violations, chief among them hiding numerous candy bars around the hospital room. And so, since her return ticket to New York was non- changeable, and it was scheduled for a month away, my sister Emma and I got Gayle.

We had many crazy adventures with Gayle staying with us...

We had to remove the door to my bedroom when she locked me out.

We got a priest at Denny's to get in my car at 2 AM to talk to her because she was so upset.

But nothing was worse than when Gayle came to me with the following request: SHE WANTED TO MEET ONE OF THE AN-DREWS SISTERS!!!

Now, I knew Patty would not have put up with her, and her opinions, and her questions, for more than three minutes.

Generally, when we took someone to meet one of the girls, we took them to Maxene, as she was more tolerant, warmer, and not as impatient with strangers. So I told Gayle that I would take her over to the rehearsal studio where she could watch Maxene rehearse her solo act, and then maybe we would go have lunch with Maxene and Lynda after. The only rule was that she could not make a sound while Maxene was practicing, as Maxene had limited use of the studio, the piano, etc. and couldn't take time away to deal with any nonsense.

So off we go to the Debbie Reynolds Studios in North Hollywood, with me repeating and repeating how she had to be quiet (if you know me, you know that I tend to repeat the point over and over again.)

All started out pretty well. Then Maxene launched into "Bei Mir Bist Du Schoen" and next to me, I hear the sobbing beginning. As it rose to full on wailing, Maxene stops and says, "What's going on out there?!"

Before I could say anything, Gayle—all 350 pounds of her— toddles up to the stage and says, "Oh, my Daddy loved that song. He used to sing it with me when I was a little girl."

By this time, I'm so embarrassed I'm praying for an earthquake to happen. Anything to shut her up...

But you know what Maxene did? She said to Gayle, "Well, why don't you come up and sing it with me, then?" So Gayle did, and stayed up there on the stage with Maxene through God knows how many more songs, until finally I got her off (which was no easy task!).

I never forgot Mackie's tact or kindness during what could have been an awful scene. And yes, we did go to lunch afterwards...

Liner Notes

1987 was a banner year for the Andrews Sisters. It was the 50th year since "Bei Mir Bist du Schoen" propelled them into worldwide fame virtually overnight. MCA, the parent company at the time Decca Records released a 50th Anniversary CD with their top songs which was so successful that it was followed up with a Volume 2 (which we will talk about in a moment). And as a final culmination—MCA/Universal wanted to at long last get the Andrews Sisters a long- deserved star on the Hollywood Walk of Fame.

Maxene was on board all the way, but Wally puppeted Patty into making ludicrous demands. She would only come if Maxene didn't, or Uncle Louie, who was to accept the honor on behalf of his late wife LaVerne. I would listen to them firsthand at Patty's, and then laugh about them later with Maxene.

But MCA/Universal did not find any humor in the situation. They had paid for the star, and guaranteed the appearance of the two living Andrews Sisters. Frantically they called Maxene and asked her what to do. Either she or Lynda suggested they talk to me, as I really was the only one who knew how to play Wally.

Suddenly I became a much sought-after person in this deal. A couple of different Vice Presidents began picking my brain, taking me out to nice lunches in Beverly Hills, having me up to the office at the Universal lot... It was great, it was fun, I felt like a big shot for a while. But ultimately, it was Maxene who hit on the answer. One of the VPs at Universal called Wally and Patty and just came out with it: they were sending a limo for Maxene on October 1st for the unveiling of the star. Did they want a limo to be sent to Patty, as well?

Of course they did. And as it turned out, we were all there. Even Vic Schon, the genius arranger behind the Andrews Sisters for all the successful years, before.

Apparently somebody—somebody? of course it was Maxene, Patty never would have praised me—told those Powers That Be at MCA about the fact I could write pretty well, when she could have pushed Wally's accolades on them. Anyway, one of those Vice Presidents called me up and told me about the upcoming CD sequel—The 50th Anniversary, Vol. 2. He asked me if I would be interested in writing the liner notes for that compilation, and offered me a surprisingly large sum of money to do it.

Liner notes, for those who don't know, are the little booklets that come with a CD with a biographical background on the artist, or artists, and sometimes a bit of insight into the songs on the album.

All I knew then about liner notes was that they were something Wally was just itching for the opportunity to do for many years.

Maxene and Patty on the day the Andrews Sisters received a star on Hollywood's Walk of Fame

Not a book but a booklet, just long enough for him to denigrate Maxene and LaVerne, boast up Patty, and elevate his importance to the trio. I was quite aware that if I did write the liner notes, someone (I did not know who yet) was going to be really furious at me.

But then... Grandma died.

And when the MCA Vice President called me not long after her passing to find out if I would write the notes or not, the first place my mind soared back to was the utter humiliation at the La Mouche nightclub so many years before, when all I wanted was for a little old lady to see that her granddaughter had a bit of writing talent. Fair and square, I did write that song, and they couldn't even give me that. No, more important—they couldn't give my 90-year-old grandmother something that would have made her so happy, so proud... something that didn't happen very often in that family.

"Yes, Jeff," (we were on first-name basis by now), "I would love to write the liners."

And so I did. With Maxene telling me stories, and Lynda editing my habit of using too many superlatives and some other mistakes.

It was one of the few secrets I ever kept from Patty.

A couple of days before the CD was to drop, I got a couple of advance copies. This was it. The I moment I looked so forward to, and the moment I feared most.

I made sure to get over there when Wally was at one of his "anon" meetings and Patty would be alone. "Hey, Bubby," I said, a little too exuberantly, "I have a surprise for you!" I took the still-sealed contraband from my jacket pocket and handed it over to her. "Read the liners. Did I surprise you?"

It seemed like it took her forever to read that little booklet. Of course, she also stopped to check out the very cool pictures which MCA inserted around my sentences. Nearly thirty years later, I can still remember her every move, her every gesture, her every word.

"You sure can write, kid. But you do know—Wally is going to kill you!"

Yeah, Bubby, I knew. All too well.

When Wally got home from Smokers-Anon, or Overeaters-Anon, or wherever he was that afternoon, Patty pushed me towards him and whispered, "Show him!" All I could do was hand him the new CD and mumble, "This came today..."

He stood there in the kitchen reading the liners, sometimes shaking his head, sometimes even laughing when he came upon a funny story. I really think he liked it...until he came to the very last line. Well, actually, the last five words:

LINER NOTES BY PAM DUBOIS

And then the furniture started flying. He went absolutely bat-shit berserk! In-between throwing the chairs and dishes, and tossing the table upside down, he screamed at me about his chance to destroy Maxene and (posthumously) LaVerne being so close to his hands, and I selfishly kept him from it (as if any record company would publish the ridiculous lies he wanted to spew out).

Finally, Patty—in fear of not having any kitchen left at all—yelled at me to go, to run out the front door. As I did, I heard the sound of wood splintering against the door jamb on the inside.

There was a long stretch of time where we didn't speak. I don't remember how we ever did resolve it. But I certainly can't forget how Wally tried to put fuel on the fire during that duration and make it even worse.

Since I did have the published MCA liners now on my credits, I thought, "Maybe I can get some of the other record companies to pay me to do this..." It was not difficult to do a short bio on anyone from that era. Chances are I must have crossed paths with the person at some point. So I sent out an introductory letter and a copy of my liner note booklet to all the labels I could think of which put out artists' music from the 40s and 50s.

I only got one phone call from one recording company. But it was Capitol. And that was really, really good. Yes, they liked my work, and yes, they had a number of collections coming out the next year— The Pied Pipers, Jo Stafford, Judy Garland...

That was all I had to hear! I was practically begging and pleading with this VP—Wayne something—over at Capitol to let me write the Garland one. I was so eager I even told him that I would do it for whatever amount they wanted to pay me, no arguments, no wheeling and dealing. Just set the terms, and I would comply.

But the arrangement he had in mind had nothing to do with money. Too bad— because I probably would have done it for free.

No, no, no. His deal was—I could write the liners for Judy, that was fine.... But only after I wrote the liner notes for something coming up before the Judy project.

THE ANDREWS SISTERS–CAPITOL COLLECTORS SERIES

I kid you not!!!

Well I didn't say "No," but I didn't say "Yes," either. I called Maxene.

Mackie suggested that I do them. Patty and Wally weren't speaking to me, anyway. It couldn't possibly get worse.

And then it did!!!

Well—not at first. I wrote the Andrews Sisters again (if I had to start one more story with the words: "One typically cold mid-November day, three tall, skinny girls of Greek-Norwegian heritage walked unnoticed into a New York City recording studio...").

And I wrote the ones for Judy Garland, as promised.

I was paid really well for each of them, and everything was progressing as scheduled. And then, in 1992, Capitol Records had a 50th Anniversary Party.

How the hell in my wildest dreams could I have predicted that Patty would ever persuade her lovely beweddded to actually go to this shindig? They readily accepted invitations, but unless it was Thanksgiving or Christmas, usually wouldn't go. Wally would either pick an argument or feign illness at the last minute (remind me to tell you what he pulled when there was a party at La Scala in Beverly Hills waiting to celebrate their 50th Wedding Anniversary). Never in a million years, though, did it occur to me that they would be there. But here's how it went down...

Apparently Vice Pres Wayne Something went up to them and introduced himself and said that *The Andrews Sisters Capitol Collectors Series* CD was coming out, and it was going to be great. Beautiful photos, wonderful liners....To which, of course, Wally asked, "Who wrote them?" When he told them, Wally and then Patty following suit pretended that they had not ever heard of me. And they asked if Capitol could send them the liner notes in advance since they had never heard of this PAM DuBOIS chick.

OH YES! THEY REALLY DID THAT!

And wait—it gets worse.....

The next thing I knew, I was getting a telephone call from Capitol telling me (I swear to God) that they couldn't use my writing—because Patty Andrews said it was inaccurate!

I don't remember if Maxene just called Capitol, or if she had to go down to Hollywood and meet with them as well. But because Maxene was the nicer of the two sisters and didn't have Wally's hand shoved up her ass like a puppet, somehow she convinced them to go with my writing. So they did publish my liners on The Andrews Sisters.

And although they had paid me for it—they never used my Judy Garland work, and basically told me, "Don't call us, we'll call you!"

Of course I never heard from them again.

Nepotism. Now that's a laugh. Whatever I did, I did not because of Patty, but in spite of her and her twisted hubs!

A 21-Gun Salute

Anyone who has ever played with a Tonka truck, has seen the little oval label on both front doors, which bears the words "MOUND MN" under TONKA. Mound Minnesota is known worldwide for its mass production of metal toy trucks. But, long, long, long before, it was Patty, Maxene, and LaVerne's stomping ground. Their uncles lived there and ran the general store. All the summers of their childhood were spent in Mound. It's a beautiful little town right on the shores of Lake Minnetonka.

Patty told me stories about those carefree days in Mound. They were among the happiest of her life. Their two bachelor uncles—Uncle Pete and Uncle Ed—didn't provide much supervision, Patty said, and as a result she, or perhaps all three of them, ate a bologna sandwich with orange soda for breakfast, jammed their pockets with penny candies from the uncles' candy counter, and went swimming in the lake, etc., until dinnertime.

Of all the many fascinating countries and places the Andrews Sisters had seen throughout their years of performing, this little town 20 miles west of Minneapolis was the one she loved most. Maxene told me Mound was her favorite place in the world! And LaVerne... well, we can only speculate that she felt the same. Even as the years went by and their fame rose to legendary heights, there was always a clause in their contracts—two weeks off in the summer so they could vacation in their beloved Mound and visit their uncles. Their grandparents had lived in Mound and are buried there. By 1925, out of a family of nine (seven children), only the girls' mother and her brothers, Pete and Ed, were still alive. In all the years, I never heard anything but wonderful happy memories of this magical place on Lake Minnetonka.

Tonka Toys later came and went, and built its factories on land that did indeed belong to the two brothers.

After Maxene died in 1995, Lynda took some of Maxene's ashes to sprinkle along the waters of the Minnetonka, and all the other little places which were so significant to Mackie. It was a touching heartfelt gesture, and when my time came, and Patty passed away in 2013, I thought I might do the same in her memory.

The idea started out simple enough. Emma and I were going to fly to Minneapolis, rent a car, drive to St. Paul to see Baby Angelyn's final resting place, then drive out to Mound and spread some of Patty's remains in the lake and the various places she had talked about with such love and joy.

Then, before I knew it, Emma had shared our plans and one-by-one the fans and even my ex- husband asked if they could join us. And it grew to so many people wanting to participate that we made it an Andrews Sisters event which thankfully Lynda, too, agreed to partake in.

Now a whole group of us were staying in various hotels and motels within the area of Mound. I was lying on the bed in the hotel, getting ready to watch a repeat of my favorite show, *My 600 lb. Life*, while awaiting the arrival of the fans and Lynda.

I got Wi-Fi password from the front desk (still had a few minutes before the program was to start) so I turned on the computer to check my emails. There were at least 50 messages (and a lot on my phone as well) telling me that I HAD to be at the Westonka Historical Society by 7 PM to accept a flag in the Andrews Sisters' behalf. I got out of bed, turned off the TV, and yelled at Emma to get dressed while I got ready. He was going with me to this flag presentation, as were my ex-husband and Gavin, my then cameraman. Hey!—I thought it would make a good "PAM SHOW."

We got there a few minutes before 7. Emma looked around and there was no one there. After about 10 or 15 minutes of waiting, I sent my ex-husband out of the car to make sure we were in the right place. Suddenly the sky lights up, it's booming something crazy outside, and my ex- husband is running back to the car, screaming (with New York mentality), "They are shooting at me!" So we all huddled in the car for another 15 or so minutes, only to find out that they had the military out there doing a 21-gun salute to The Andrews Sisters. And I missed it!

But I still got the flag, and to walk along "The Andrews Sisters Trail." Not a trail of places they enjoyed, but the City of Mound actually built a walking trail named for them. As the group of us hiked along the trail, I couldn't help but think (and laugh to myself) that if they were only here now, Maxene would have loved it, LaVerne would have been anxious about her designer shoes getting dirty, and Patty would be complaining, "My bunions are killing me!"

Va-gee-na Man

QUESTION: Did you ever make or get prank or obscene phone calls? You must have been pretty funny!

PAM:

Em and I used to get The Green Sheet, or The Buy Lines (precursors to Craigslist) every week and Emma, in his best LaVerne voice, would call up all the people who had a Kelvinator refrigerator for sale. And by the time he got done confusing them, he made them feel guilty for getting rid of their Kelvinators. I used to laugh so freaking much I would be crying.

As for me getting obscene phone calls, of course there is a story in that...

After Patty smashed her knee at the end of 1999, she spent weeks in the hospital, until they threw her out of rehab for refusing to do the exercises. The only solution was to get her nursing care at home.

Now it didn't take long before Wally, jealous of all the attention Patty was getting, decided that he, too, needed a nurse, a male Filipino nurse, to take care of him. Neither at this point, nor for the next seven years, was there were attached wrong with him. But it didn't matter. Patty had a nurse, so he wanted one, too. So he called the agency that specialized in nurses from the Philippines and ordered himself a male nurse.

Enter Dixon, pronounced Dee-Jon...like the mustard. Dixon was born the exact same day and year as me in Manila and had not been in this country very long. He had no place to live and slept on the floor at the foot of Wally's bed. Wally used to dress him up in his old tuxedos and band uniforms, and pretend he was a butler rather than a nurse—his very own Mr. French.

Dixon was so polite and attentive that Wally was just basking in all the attention, and really left Patty and I alone. No longer was I having to run crazy errands for him. No longer did Patty have to listen to endless rants about her sisters, both of them long gone by then. It was wonderful, except Dixon had a bit of peculiar habit—he used to make obscene phone calls to me at three o'clock in the morning.

Now you may wonder HOW did I know the calls were coming from Dixon? Well, to cut a long story short, it was probably the only time in my life when I heard "that" part of the female anatomy referred to as a "Va-gee-ma." And also, along with the sex calls, Patty's number would come up on my caller ID. I thought about it, talked it over with Patty, and she said, "If Wally finds out, he'll fire him! Would you rather have to run around downtown L.A. looking for old magazines from the 40s and 50s that one of my sisters maybe commented in, so I can then have to listen to him go on and on about LaVerne's boyfriends in 1942? Please, please let this Filipino nut case mispronounce sex words to you in the middle of the night." She was right. We dubbed Dixon "The Va-gee-ma Man" and I just let him call away. Eventually, he got bored and moved on to someone, or something, new.

Dixon lasted an astonishingly long time. Then one evening he called me (on the level, for once) and told me that Wally was throwing knives at him, and he thought he (Dixon) was having a heart attack. By the time I got over there, Dixon had disappeared into the dark night, never to be seen again.

Before I dared tell Wally that his beloved manservant had quit, once again I went to Patty first to talk it over (thank God, those two ALWAYS had separate bedrooms!). Patty suggested that I track down the nurse who took care of her father after he had his kidney removed.

"Wonderful nurse, just Wonderful!" she bragged, "Perfect for Wally!"

Something didn't sound right.

I asked Patty, "When did your father have his kidney removed??" She replied, "1940."

This conversation was in 2010.

It was then seventy years since Patty had last seen that nurse. If still alive, she would have been pushing 120.

When Wally Met Patty

As most of you know, I have been writing a "Tell-All" on Joanna's ex-husband, Alex Cord. Basically I have been sharing either legal papers, or newspaper interviews, or articles, or other published materials. The story of what went on behind those closed does back then is not mine to tell. It is Joanna's. She and Damien Zach lived through the horror. Damien Zach is no longer here. He is forever 26 years old. So it is now Jo who can speak for both of them. I have every confidence that she will.

However, many of you are telling me that you are sad, bummed, angry, etc. at the abuse that Alex Cord perpetrated and never went to jail for, or suffered any legal ramifications due to the era, the statutes, and such.

This is something I can address through my own experiences. Sometimes KARMA can be worse than any prison sentence. I cite this as a perfect example.

The Andrews Sisters were at the height of their career in the 1940s, the top musical act in the world. They had more gold records and hit songs than anyone before then, and pretty much everybody who came after. THEY WERE UNTOUCHABLE, UNSTOPPABLE! Nothing or no one could invade their solid bond as sisters, not their success entertaining.

THEN PATTY MET WALLY WESCHLER.

In fairness to Patty, she was definitely on the rebound from her then husband, Marty Melcher, who was having an affair with their neighbor, Doris Day, whom he later married. As well as I know Patty—and I know her better than anyone—I never could understand her need or attraction to controlling, bossy men. Neither could Maxene. It was always quite the conundrum. She was talented, pretty, witty, and had half the leading men in Hollywood chasing after her—sometimes literally. Yet, she only had eyes for these weak, insecure men who hid behind power-filled illusions and personas they created to fool people.

I've heard varying stories of how they met. Patty told me that when the trio held auditions for a new piano player, many pianists showed up to try out. Partway through the auditions, Wally walked in, and Patty gazed at him lovingly and whispered to Maxene: "I'm gonna marry that man someday!"

Mackie's version differed greatly. She said, "He was a second-rate piano player, who was brought in as a substitute, until we hired a real one." And she was absolutely perplexed as to why he would play the piano dressed in full winter gear. She would look down in the orchestra pit and see him with a winter hat, a scarf, and a muffler, playing the piano with snow gloves on. For in her telling about Wally's total disregard of his father from the war stage. She would look down in the orchestra pit, and listen to his wild with a hat, a scarf, a muffler, playing the piano with snow gloves on. Knowing him the way I did for the last 36 years of his life, I am quite sure Maxene's version was the more accurate one.

A vulnerable opportunity cropped up one night, and let's just say that was the last time that man ever did a thing to earn his own money. For a $2 investment (in a marriage license) he got millions in return.

And the indestructible Andrews Sisters were no more.

Within 2 years, he drove a hole right into them the size of the Grand Canyon. He made Patty sue LaVerne, and ultimately Maxene, because he didn't like the fact that LaVerne inherited a larger portion of their parents' estate. He decided Patty would be much without the dead weight of her sisters if she did a solo act. He pulled her away from, and out of, the Andrews Sisters completely. One man, one insignificant shallow man was able to do the unthinkable. He broke up America's wartime sweethearts.

That is not to say that I, too, as an extended family member, was not affected by him. He molested and sexually abused me when I was 16 or 17. Not once but several times. As I was later to learn, he also did to Aleda (Maxene's daughter) and several other close family members when they, too, were that age.

I've given you somewhat of a background about the man he was. There's so much more—a book load, but I'd like to get back to my original point: KARMA.

For a long time, it seemed as if Wally Weschler could plow his way through life screwing and kicking aside anyone or anything that disrupted his plans of destruction.

Then just like that, one day KARMA reared its head, and nothing was ever the same.

I first remember it was January 2007, in a Chinese restaurant in Encino, where I lived at the time. Patty had a nurse because she had shattered her knee cap, and needed help getting around.

In January of 2007, we were in the restaurant having lunch— Wally, Patty, and me at one table— the nurses speaking their native languages at each other. Or should I say, nurse and butler, because up to that day, Dixon did not use a bit of his nursing knowledge. Wally started choking and was taken from the restaurant by ambulance a few blocks to the hospital. He was diagnosed with a condition called DYSPHAGIA- or more specifically:

Oropharyngeal dysphagia

Certain conditions can weaken your throat muscles, making it difficult to move food from your mouth into your throat and esophagus when you start to swallow. You may choke, gag, or cough when you try to swallow or have the sensation of food or fluids going down your windpipe (trachea) or up your nose. This may lead to pneumonia (which it did several times).

I believe there was some sort of surgery Wally could have had to strengthen the throat muscles, but he procrastinated his way to a permanent tracheotomy in his neck hooked up to a ventilator. Over the next 3-1/2 years, and who knows how many bouts with pneumonia, he managed to obtain a feeding tube in his stomach, a bladder tube, and a bowel tube. The nurses—first Dixon, who hung on as long as he could before calling me from the hospital where Wally was once again on death watch to tell me that Wally was throwing and hurling things at him, and he (Dixon) was having chest pains and couldn't do it anymore. Exit Dixon and Enter Arnold—a blessing from God. He hung in there for the duration of Wally's life, cleaning him, pouring some kind of liquid goop in the feeding tube, and vacuuming out the crap (yeah, you read that correctly—VACUUMING) that accumulated in what was left of Wally's lungs every four or five hours. Wally suffered more than an inmate waiting to go to the electric chair. It was a slow, agonizing demise, a prolonged, painful death in which he lost control of every single function. Yes, his body betrayed him. But in the most ironic twist, his mind didn't, and he was aware of every single thing which was happening to him, and that there was nothing he could do about it.

After watching this unfold from the sidelines, I can absolutely tell you—the gas chamber would have been more preferable. And in death, when he could no longer bully everyone by dangling Patty in front of them, he was given as much respect as he truly deserved. The nurses went back and forth preparing Patty's dinner. The lawyer and I walked through the house making various decisions. All of us passed the hospital bed where Wally lay, rigor mortis starting to set in, as we waited for the mortuary to pick him up. I had informed Patty earlier of his passing, biting hard the inside of my cheek in the hopes of squeezing out a couple of tears.

But ten minutes later, she didn't remember, and asked one of the nurses how he was doing. I guess that's what evened the score for me at the end of his life. How truly insignificant he really was. Everyone (nurses, lawyer, me) carried on, doing the things we always did, almost oblivious to his corpse rotting away right in front of us. And eventually, over time, Patty didn't remember him at all. But up to the moment she herself died two-and-a-half years later, she never forgot Maxene, and LaVerne. She never forgot THE ANDREWS SISTERS.

So that's why I say WAIT. Wait till the story is over, till the fat lady has sung, till Alex Cord inhales his last breath of Texas Cow Shit. KARMA will come through. It always has. It has never let me down—yet!

A Forgotten Birthday

Well once again, Patty forgot my birthday. This was a yearly event (the forgetting), although you'd think it would have been easy enough to remember. Like her, and her two sisters, I was born two days after a holiday (March 19). And it became a game for me, year after year. Not a good or funny game, but rather a sad and hurtful one. I think once I hit about 35, I stopped testing her and would just write it in big letters on the calendar she always kept in the kitchen. But before that, the pain, the hurt I would feel every year when she did not remember, really ruined a lot of birthdays for me.

I remember one in my 20s when I waited all day for her to say something, and then at 11PM, I heartbrokenly told her, "Today was my birthday," and let her feel as guilty as humanly possible for not remembering. I don't know why, exactly, but back then I used to play a hell of a lot more attention to those who forgot than to those who remembered.

Now, on my 18th Birthday, she did not forget, and bought me a beautiful silver spoon bracelet that she had engraved: "Happy 18th Birthday, 3/19/75, Love Patty." For years, that was my most treasured possession. I never took it off.

But all that changed on one of the forgotten birthdays in the 80s. For whatever reason, I was particularly devastated that year by Patty's inability to remember that my birthday was two days after St. Patrick's Day. I lived with my sister Emma at the time, and I know that I told him I was so upset, I was going to the beach and throw my fucking bracelet into the Pacific Ocean (okay, so I was a bit dramatic back then). I did go to the beach. I was listening to Cyndi Lauper on the radio. I know this because before she became famous, Cyndi used to run a vintage clothing store near my Grandmother's apartment. We just knew her as that kook with the pink hair (now I've got pink hair, and "that kook" has a hit Broadway Show, *Kinky Boots*).

But anyway, I drove the canyons over to the beach, with the intent to throw that bracelet into the ocean. But once I got there—Malibu, I think it was—I couldn't do it. I could not make myself throw away that bracelet. Thank God. But I also couldn't bring myself to go home and tell Emma that I wasn't strong enough to do it. So I put it in my storage unit, and lied to Em, and told him that I had indeed thrown it way out into the water.

A few months passed. And of course the farther it got from March, the less important it became, and I missed wearing my bracelet (plus Patty kept asking me where the hell it was). So I came up with what had to be the stupidest, most far-fetched story of my life. I told Emma that I was going to the beach to look for my bracelet, in case it had miraculously washed back on shore...which is exactly what I told him it did. In reality, I went to my storage unit and got the damn thing out.

What made this crazier was that for years, Emma actually believed that I had actually found the bracelet in the sand, seven months after I supposedly threw it into the Pacific. He believed me until I finally told him the truth.

In Remembrance of Maxene

L ast week as I watched Joanna mourn the passing of one of her dearest friends, a thought flashed across my mind. I wondered if in grieving the loss of Toni, Jo was also fearing her own mortality. I know that this is an emotion I experience whenever I learn of the passing of a celebrity near my age, and certainly when I have lost somebody I have known and loved personally.

I have already outlived my father's life span by two months. His last coherent words were, "I'm not afraid to die." Well, Daddy, you were a better person than I am, because I certainly am. Still, no matter how much it frightens me, the reality is one day the sun will rise and set, and the moon will glow, and I will not be here to see it.

The fact that these phenomena have gone on for thousands of years before we were here, and continue long after we are not, seems to be lost somewhere in the comprehension, and translation. Really, even though we see films and clips and, in my case, the Andrews Sisters, famous for twenty years before I was born, we honestly give little credence to the actuality that there was an existence before us. Oh, of course, we are aware on a historical, factual level, but emotionally, this is a hard concept.

Sometimes I think about all the conversations Patty and I had— "Bing Crosby died," "Groucho Marx died," "Uncle Louie died," "Grandma died," and the worst of all, a Saturday in October, nearly a quarter of a century ago: "Bubby—your sister died." And that second of silence, after which she gasped, as if not quite believing me, and then she whispering, almost prayer-like, "Maxene."

I spent the next three weeks with Patty, pretty much around the clock. Wally had a terrible "accident" and was in the hospital.

Anyway, one night soon after Maxene's passing, Patty and I were watching, I believe, a news program, and they did a tribute to Maxene. They showed the *Buck Privates* clip, the *Hollywood Canteen* clip, and a few others, after which at the end they pointed out which one was the fallen sister. We were both aware that this was a montage that was prepared long ago. Obits, death notices, and remembrances of famous people are done years before and archived in the Associated Press files. We also both knew that I was watching her watch what would inevitably be her own memorial piece one day, just with the arrow moved to point towards the middle. This film would be the exact same one they would use to announce her future death.

How odd that must have felt, not only the gut-wrenching sorrow of losing the person you most loved in the world, but in essence watching your own memorial that will be shown after your own passing. I stared intently at her face as she viewed it, looking for a clue, any indication of how this was affecting her. She gave no visible reaction. Her expression never altered. So I asked her. I did. I said, "Bubby, how does this make you feel?"

She snapped back at me a well-deserved, "How do you think it makes me feel, Paaaaaaaaam?" How could I know? How could anyone ever really know?

And yes. They did indeed pull out the same damn film strip when she died in January 2013, with the arrow focused this time on the middle. All the nurses and I saw it on the mid-day news, while Patty was still in her bed awaiting the mortuary pickup.

DEATH. It comes to all of us, just as easily and as often as BIRTH. Everything that begins must someday end. Even that 1,000-plus-year-old oak tree in Encino.

What exactly are we afraid of? That the world will go on without us? That we'll be forgotten as this giant blue ball spins and spins into eternity? That beyond this...there is nothing more?

Many years ago I discovered the most intriguing, foreboding burial site, or rather headstone in the graveyard beside the ancient Trinity Church (yes, George Washington did pray there; there is even a pew dedicated to him with a plaque saying it's the one he always used). The grave, which is actually an above-ground crypt, so worn and battled by age and weather, so decrepit that you are able to peek through the crack and see the two tiny brown coffins which have rested inside for 225 years. Their father, embittered by the fate that had befallen his family, could hardly contain his anger and grief as is evident in the following epitaph:

Here lie the bodies of two infant brothers:

VALENTINE MORRIS WILKINS
and
ISAAC WILKINS

The first departed this life
on the 24th September 1793
aged 1 year and 5 days
the second on the 18th Feb 1794
aged 5 years and 2 months
We were born to die;
'Tis but expanding thought,
And life is nothing.

But what if Mr. and Mrs. Wilkins were wrong? Of course there are no justifications for the death of a child who has not ever had the chance to live. I still question Stewart's death 33 years ago when he was 17. So when I ask, "What if the Wilkins' got it wrong?" I don't mean to denounce their bitterness at their terrible loss. They had every right to mourn their babies.

What I guess I am saying is, the last engraved line: *AND LIFE IS NOTHING*

But what if it is not true?

What if LIFE, no matter how short or how long, is merely the gateway to something more? Something more outstanding than we could ever imagine?

Look at it. When someone we love dies, we soothe ourselves with phrases like, "Well, he is in heaven now watching over us" or "She is in a far better place."

Are those really just words of solace? Or do they seriously hold the answers to all the mysteries of the hereafter?

When I was a very young child (the last time this happened I was six, and remember where I was exactly), every so often this strange feeling would sweep over me. I don't really know how to explain it, except to say that I felt the insuppressible need to reassure myself that I was me, and that this was my being now. Almost like a tangible disconnect between soul and body, as if the inside of me, whatever contained emotions, and shame, and guilt, and also joy, etc... was not in the same place it had once known. Sort of like two separate entities trying to meld together. I've never had any kind of regression therapy, but I've heard that those most apt to assimilate to a past life are below seven years of age. Don't get me wrong—I have absolutely no recollection or memories of ever living before this time. I'm just throwing the "what if" out there.

And what if... what we tell ourselves, and others to comfort during a time of great loss is really true? And it just might be.

Common knowledge was that the earth was flat, until somebody proved it otherwise.

And the notion of "A better place where we would be reunited with the people we have loved and lost," The concept to see my father, and my grandmother again, and all four of the Andrews Sisters, and Sandra, and Stewart—to throws eggs at Bio for all eternity...

If we only knew for sure, then dying would be nothing to fear but rather to embrace whatever it is that comes next, after our rides around the sun on this planet come to an end.

Letter to Patty on Her Passing

My Dearest Bubby,

I can hardly believe it has been over six years since I let go of your hand, and they took you away. In your last hours on earth, you couldn't speak to me. Were you frightened? You were always so scared to die. But yet I think you were ready. Just a day before, you were calling out dance counts to Maxene and LaVerne. Perhaps you were getting them ready for the ultimate Andrews Sisters reunion. You went so peacefully. Just took a few deep breaths, and I told you to go be with your sisters, and you went. Just like that. It was quiet, yet the nurses were playing your music in the background. Maybe you went to Heaven finally realizing just how great you really were. I hope so.

All those years, when someone whom we loved died, and you held me, or I held you, and we cried along with each other, I never thought, never truly believed, that there would really come a time when I would be here without you.

You were so much a part of who I was, who I am. You defined me. And I miss you so. I miss sharing a sandwich from Jergenssen's Market with you, and having my own place at the dinner table, even if we did eat chicken every night.

I miss our talks. I miss knowing someone who could, and would, keep every secret I told her. I miss the shopping, the lunches with Lynda and Mackie (or, as you insisted on calling her, "Maggie"). I miss your humor. I even miss your "blasting," as you would so adequately call your yelling. But most of all, I miss the nights of just us, you and me, listening to the 78s on that old record player in your closet, and you singing along, singing just to me. And it was so emotional; tears would roll down your checks. And as always, in times of intensity, I would hold your hand. How I miss that hand. How I loved you. How I understood with every fiber of my being—why the caged bird sings. I have done my best to keep the Andrews Sisters legacy alive and going strong. Lynda has, too. I have made a lot of new friends on the computer. They love you and your sisters, too. It is through them that I am able to remember you (as if I could forget anything).

Happy, happy 101st Birthday, Bubby—you can finally eat your birthday cake without us having to lie to W. about the frosting!

Always, and always,

Your Mean Kid

The Rose Parade

B ecause that's what I want to talk about today on this non-PAM SHOW "PAM SHOW."

If anyone thinks that my need to strongly voice my thoughts, feelings, and ridicule on any given subject in pursuit of "Attention Whore-ism" began with the advent of the internet, no no no—this mouthpiece has been ranting my immoveable opinions for years!

Long before blogs, and MySpace, and Facebook, and "THE PAM SHOW," I used my writing abilities, desire to evoke shock, and my filter-less beliefs to write long Op-Eds in the newspapers.

Someplace in one of the storage units is a large box, overflowing with newspaper articles clearly stating my views on everything from Jerry Lewis bilking that Labor Day Muscular Dystrophy Tele-thon for years to gas rationing on odd and even days. In the late 1970s, it was easy to get published in *The New York Post*, or *Daily News*, or *The Los Angeles Examiner*, or *Valley News*. But I gotta say, I was quite proud when I made into both *The Los Angeles Times* and *The New York Times*. And that is wherein the answer to this question lies.

One of the things I was most vehemently opposed to was the New Year's Day Pasadena Rose Parade.

And I let it be known.

How companies could donate millions of dollars for stupid floats made out of flowers that would be dead within a week was way past my comprehension, especially when there were so many other causes and charities that money could be better used for. Year upon year, as it got closer to Rose Parade time, out would come the pen, or typewriter, and off I would go!.

I had some very prevalent points besides money. TIME! What a waste of time, right after Christmas. Hours upon hours of glu-ing pedals and seeds, and asking for volunteers to come and work without pay endlessly on something so stupid. I carried on about this for about twenty years.

And then one New Year's Day, my phone rang and the friend on the other end said, "Did you see who just went by on the Rose Parade?"

Channel 5 ran it over and over all day, but this was apparently the first broadcast that morning. In response, I launched myself into my usual tirade about how I hated the damn Rose Parade, how I wouldn't watch that crap, how if the Nielsen Ratings were keeping track they'd see I didn't even want it to register on my TV.

My friend was taken aback by the harshness of my response. But he asked me if I could do him a favor and on the next rebroad-cast, just watch about ten minutes in.

I agreed, half thinking that my friend Cassandra—Mrs. Gre-enthumbs, the Garden Lady—was going to make an appearance, and I was getting angry at her in my head for not telling me that she was in California! So I turned on the replay, and sure enough, about 10 or 12 minutes in, there was no Cassandra, but there WAS the most beautiful float depicting THE ANDREWS SISTERS! So intricate, and so detailed. It honestly took my breath away. I mean, they really captured the three of them. I called Patty, and I think Maxene, too, and said, "For God's sake, watch the Rose Parade!" They probably thought I was joking, after all the years I'd spent griping about it.

After seeing it—they wanted pictures. I wanted pictures. Friends in New York wanted pictures.

The next couple of days—January 2nd and 3rd—the floats were put on display on Colorado Boulevard and, for an admission fee, you could get up close to them, snap photos, and see all the love and craft that had gone into making them. Both days it was pouring rain, but I dragged my wet ass down to Pasadena.

I do believe that this was the only time in my life that I ever flipped so contradictorily on anything I have ever had an opinion on.

Oh, I may sway. For example, the horse racing that I loved so—about 45-50 years—is now to me a cruel abuse to animals.

But this was really the only time I've ever done a complete 180-degree switch on anything.

Usually right or wrong, I'll keep fighting to prove my point.

But this time... this indisputable truth was in the pudding.

No—not "PUDDING," but rather "PUTTING," as in "PUT-TING" the flowers together to create a beautiful depiction of Patty, Maxene, and LaVerne!

For Patty

I thought that I knew everything there was to know about death. Lord knows I've been through it enough times. Seven years ago today, I lost you.

With you, I carefully kept memories. I always knew the second something happened, which moments with you, would be the ones I'd remember forever. The ones that would carry me on when the time came that you were no longer with me. You were 39 years older than me, so it was kind of inevitable in the circle of life that you'd pass first.

The funny thing is that most are such silly insignificant times not even you would remember, are what made these impressions that are sealed forever in my heart. An instant, so many years ago, when we were driving on the Hollywood Freeway, and the sun hit the Hollywood sign in a way that you reflected against it. And you looked so beautiful, so magical, and I wondered, in that tiny space of time, how did I get so lucky to be here with you, to live this life you had given me? Our nights parked in the hills looking down at the bright lights of Los Angeles, talking, just talking, about everything, about nothing. And in the same way, our drives through snowy Central Park for hours and hours, after your Broadway show was over for the evening. The seconds in time when I learned the truth about you, and you about me, when you let your guard down, and confessed all your secrets to me, the ones you never told another soul. And I can truly say with all certainty that I knew you better than anyone in the world.

So now when fans (and boy, do you still have lots of them!) ask me questions about shows, or songs, just like you had to, I too find myself having to refer them to The Andrews Sisters Experts. No, Bubby, I'd never remember on my own what you recorded on January 2, 1941. ("Boogie Woogie Bugle Boy"), but I'll never forget how you ate those black and white "cow" ice cream sundaes at Swenson's any chance you got.

And of course my very favorite: the music in the closet. But hey, your birthday is in a few weeks, and I have to save some things for that.

As I was saying, I thought I knew everything about death, and I did, up until that moment I held your hand, and told you that it was okay to go join Maxene and LaVerne. And you went... But unlike all the others who had died, you were not gone. Your body, maybe, but you are a legend, and when a legend passes, they simply go into another universe. Kind of like another room, another studio, another theatre. Here on earth they live on. And here on earth in that moment when you went to your sisters who you truly loved all your life, with all your being, I became... I was going to say your voice, but everyone's heard my voice, so I couldn't do that to you! I became the keyholder to your life and your legacy.

I knew you wanted to be remembered. How you wanted the Andrews Sisters to be remembered. I knew also what you never wanted known. But as the "Latch Key Kid of Your Immortalization," I had to share it. The people who worship you had to know the truths, the truths you told me so many years ago during our private nights in Central Park, or the Hollywood Hills, or at home, whenever we were alone. The truths I watched unfold for forty years. And the words you said to Lynda, and to I, just weeks before you died: "I loved my sister Maxene more than anyone else in the world."

You were a really private person, Bubby. Best secret keeper that ever lived. But the people had to know about the chaos, and who and what caused it, and what really went on after the last chorus of "Apple Blossom Time" was sung, and the curtains closed, when the magic was gone, and we had to go back to living in the real world. You knew it, and I think you knew that when the time was right, I would do with it what you couldn't.

I love you Bubby.

I always will.

POEMS

"A clicker – a clacker
An animal cracker"

A cellophane slit – a slash or harpoon
Set the cog wheels in motion like a raging typhoon
You may lie to yourself – but no one's ever immune
A celestial zeppelin – a bespectacled raccoon
A red blazing dragon – a vanilla saloon
Celestine rainbow crystals which slid off of the moon
Or the chrome murky puddles of an abandoned lagoon
Like a clock spinning backwards – is it nighttime or noon?
Did I trade with the devil my December for June?
Is the calliope playing or just a soft gentle croon?
I am twisting and turning towards unspeakable ruin
Once revered as a dreamer – now just a rambling buffoon
An impatient cricket who jumped too high way too soon
Somebody stop this old spiraling Disney cartoon
But wait – have some fate – when the dice are all strewn
I'm compelled to excel just by changing my tune
Here it is – hear the fizz leave the rancid balloon
Say goodbye – butterfly's in a brand new cocoon.

KEEPING UP WITH THE NARCASHIANS

Always spinning in circles is such an ordeal
Behind the flash and the sparkle – there's so much to conceal
The cracks in the sidewalk beneath chalk drawings – surreal
You don't have to confess what you refuse to reveal
So you build your own bunker which you'll never unseal
As your brain starts to fracture (and) your mind begins to congeal
And you live to be praised as a soul who's not real

You're a circus magician – a fraud with bogus appeal
A balloon that's inflated with too much ego ideal
Obliviously sheltered in your gilded Bastille
Where you cast all the judgment and you make every deal
Never giving a shit about how others may feel
A self-centered coward with a heart made of steel
A chameleon presenting as sweet and genteel
Gaining trust – only just routing – Achilles heel
Promise-making – you're faking – every word you'll repeal
Any questions or suggestions – you'll simply lie, scream and squeal
A racing hamster chasing nothing on a rusty old wheel

PINBALL BLIZZARD

It started quite subtle – A whipped cream illusion
The facts and the faces blurred – masking any conclusion
Then a fluttering touch – jellyfish-like translucion
As the pressure of nothingness added to the confusion
Yet tranquil I floated on the sea of seclusion
'Til panic broke out – what a chaotic intrusion
They smashed me and bashed me with well-planned collusion
Too violent to be just a strange misconstrusion
I was flung, I was tossed, I was lost in abusion
I hit wood, I hit walls with hard rubber inclusion
There were lights – neon brights from some hidden diffusion
And loud whistles and bells in abundant profusion
Apocalyptic pinball couldn't be ruled an exclusion
As scarlet red blood oozed from a crayoned contusion
What to say – wisp away all the flips and their fusion
Wish I knew – what to do – to stop these dips and protrusion
Wait!!!!!
This time – save the dime – and cut the electric infusion
Now I hide that mad ride as a mindless suffusion
And the raw splintered see-saw – just a drunken delusion

THE SURREPTITIOUS PEZ SCORPION
(SIMON SAYS – SATIN OR SATAN)

This web may look fragile – an embroidered lace weave
The illusion these threads are meant to achieve
But look close at the delicate silk you receive
At the iron-clad stitches which are there to deceive
A camouflaged crypt of cryptic misconceive
Monarch butterflies perched in a day lily cleave
Beauty masking the truths all our lives we should grieve
Blindly smoldered perceptions – we've been taught to perceive
The rippling foam courts the shore – so naive
With no inkling of depth, tides, and potential upheave
Clueless to the devastation left when they leave
No regret, no remorse, no repent, no reprieve
Moving on to the next prey, the next soul they will thieve
A scorpion dressed in black tie and white sleeve
Just keep walking. Stop talking – it's all make-believe.

IMMERSED IN A DIVERSE UNIVERSE

Marshmallow moons tinge an aqua stained sky
An island of whipped cream slowly floating awry
On a sea of green Jell-O or is it-key-lime mint pie
An alternate world or a world—I belie
In the distance—Iridescent cellophane balloons cry
Passing stars made of marbles—Rainbow, Clay and Cat's Eye
And though I don't understand as to the reasons why
My mind's a free space where the rules don't apply
Then the butter sun rises—Vanilla custard clouds fly
Suddenly it's a new day and there's snow in July
A Ferris wheel spins—A parade marches by
Just go with it—Flow with it—And don't justify
The sand is a-blazed—With red searing deny
While tranquil turquoise ocean waves taunt it in reply
See the shells on the shore—Gifts from those who already did die
Look at them carefully—Come on—Just give it a try

STEWART

Last night
I dreamed about you
About us
As we were.
In a time long gone by
When I called you:
"My Daddy Boy."
And pushed you on the swings
A life time ago.
When I pretended and wished
You were my brother.
In a way you were—sort of
For a little while, anyway.
On the day after you were born
I held this perfect child
A special baby
And wondered what would become of him
Knowing—even then—
How terribly unique
You were
And so very beautiful
Especially when you smiled
Seems as if
You always smiled
Back then
Just like in my dream
And in my dream—
I wanted so much to tell you
How I loved you
How I've always loved you.
And how proud I was of you
But I never got the chance

As I was dreaming—you were dying.

I think—Stewart
that you deserved so much more
That this world could ever have given you than anyone could—
And although
I will never again hold you in my arms
My heart will always hold its own place
where the happy remembrance of a little boy—
running quickly and freely through life,
will last forever—
Good-bye, my precious Daddy Boy
I'll miss you so
You did it just right, Stew
And that is why
wherever you are tonight
Somewhere,
created from crayons
and from all the memories
and wonderful things
you meant to so many people
I would like to believe
that a colored banner waves —
once more welcoming you home, Stewart
(This time — for good.)

My Birth

Sometimes—every so often (though not nearly enough), I would look at this woman beside me sharing the morning paper, or a ham and jack cheese sandwich from the corner deli with me, and think, "This is really one of the Andrews Sisters. For real." One of the three women whom I'd been told, drummed into my brain, had been the heart and hope of this whole America World War II. Now, I'm not crazy. Well, yes, I am, but not in that way. Of course I knew who and what she was. That was the whole reason I met her in the first place. But like a bolt of lightning, or a wave splashing you unexpectedly in the face, from time to time...it would hit me.

She really was so talented, such a great performer. My father's boyhood love crush in his youth, and one of the few singers who could ever evoke any sort of emotion from my empathetic-less Bio Mother. I often wonder about them back then, and how they would have felt if they could have looked into the future and seen their own child was being raised by their idol. It's a good fantasy. With my father, I will never know the answer. Less than four months had passed between the day I met Patty he passed. He was exactly six months older than I am now. Scary, but I try not to think about it.

Bio, though, was thrilled to be rid of me. And even more thrilled when she could parade her friends by the theater, come in the stage door, and introduce them to Patty and Maxene.

How Bio and I survived the little time we had together during my childhood is still a mystery.

I was born two days late on March 19th, 1957 (if I had popped out on my due date, my name would have been Patricia), kicking and screaming and trying desperately to stay in there. Even *in utero*, I must have sensed that there was something very strange awaiting me once I slid through that vaginal canal. I take that back—I never slid willingly through anything other than the slide at Steeplechase in Coney Island. Some doctor—his name was Dr. Frank Clark—had to pry and pull me out. The weird sounds and noises and dual conversations she had with herself somehow seemed to penetrate through the womb. I was told that I gave Dr. Clark a good fight.

I was an unwanted child, and a baby wanted for the wrong reason, who soon became an unwanted child times two. My father thought that his child rearing days were long over. He had a son and daughter in their 20s and he was already a grandfather. Honest to God, I have a couple of nieces out there who are older than me.

But Bio Dearest looked around her, and all she saw were pretty little babies being pushed down Queens Boulevard in their big old English prams. Those ornate baby carriages had a wild rejuvenation in the 1950s. And after all, that's what nice postwar wives who lived in Queens did—have babies. Unfortunately, Bio's only experience with children/babies was admiring them from afar. She had no clue that babies cried, and shat, and made messes, and needed things. I really believe she was genuinely shocked to discover that she couldn't just take me out and play with me like the Patsy Ann's of her own childhood and then put me in the toy box and move on to something else (Patsy Ann was a very popular doll made by the Eff-En-Bee Doll Company in the 1920s).

Truth be told—I'm not the only person who concluded that Bio suffered from some form of mild autism. She had been a very much-wanted child who had taken ten years to conceive. Her father doted on her, buying his first home movie camera 1928, and documenting her life on film until 1934 or 1935. Of course I have those films, originals and transferred copies, in all formats and all the original devices to play them on, including Grandpa's 1928 movie projector and camera (hey, would you expect anything less of me?) In the films, as in motherhood and adulthood, Bio could not stand any physical contact. She was the same robotic, unfeeling little girl as she was when I knew her, till the last day she screamed at me before she died.

Anyway, when she was about seven or eight, they were at the beach (Coney Island I think, because later on in the movie they take her on the rides). Someone else was filming as her father bent down to kiss her, and she kicked him in the face. And no, she was never molested. I asked her point blank and she said, "No, I just am not affectionate."

When I was older, I would turn to my grandmother and say, "What the hell happened?" Grandma would put her hands in the air, shrug her crooked little shoulders, and just shake her head. Back then, there was not yet a word for it. She knew that her daughter was uh, odd...different.

My grandparents believed that with their intervention, they all could raise a reasonably normal child. But that was not to be. Grandpa weighed 300 pounds, and that heart attack took him down when I was a year-and-a-half. The following year Grandma got cancer. Thankfully, she recovered and lived many more years. Without her, I would have not grown up at all. She was the one stable thing in my chaotic world. Until Patty.

Well...I guess you could not call my relationship with Patty stable. It was as up and down as those merry-go-round horses back at Steeplechase in Coney Island. But there was a sense of peace that I had not known before. No matter what happened, we both were secure with the unspoken knowledge that no matter what, we would always somehow find our way back to each other. We knew way too much. She knew all my secrets, and I knew the real Patty, the one she hid from everyone, especially herself. And forever in my life, my greatest memories will be of the nights we sat in her closet, listening to the Andrews Sisters, and her solo records, while she sang along just for me, crying sometimes because she could not that she actually sang so well.

We listened on a beat-up old Victrola which she had hidden away from Wally under some wigs, or hats, or gloves. He did allow Andrews Sisters music to be played in the house. But on those nights, he would be gone. 8:20 PM was my favorite time of the day. That was when for sure Wally would be gone to spew his lies at some 12-step meeting. Most of my viewers never met him, but for those who did...imagine those poor people trying to get sober, or detox, or stop an addiction for the first time, and being greeted by that? (Somewhere in the desert, Lynda is reading this and laughing—but it's true). With absolute certainty, I could swear that the success rate at all types of Anonymous self-help meetings in the San Fernando Valley hit an all-time low during the 70s and 80s.

Patty liked the night. Sometimes we would drive and drive until we settled in some remote canyon, usually way on the top of a hill, overlooking the whole city. That's when I got to know the true Patty. All alone just with me, not judging her, she was herself, and she told me stories of her life and her feelings and her thoughts, and dreams that she had never before shared with another person.

Shimmy Shimmy Coco Pop and Other Games

Since it's been confirmed and you guys know that I like to reminisce on the "PAM SHOW" about childhood days long gone by, even before my would became Patty...in retrospect, the mind is selective, and we can feel the joy, and freedom, and fun, without the disgusted ever- present reminder, that somewhere up in that miserable apartment on Pershing Crescent Street, the Bio must have had a hidden calendar where she would secretly mark off the days until somehow she could be rid of her mistake/disgrace. I like remembering things which didn't involve her, like sitting on the stoop on cool summer New York evenings with the other Pershing Crescent Street Kids, using the streetlights as our clocks and waiting for Morey or Steve to arrive (the Good Humor ice cream men). I always had a dime tucked inside my Keds for a tiger-striped popsicle. If that popsicle dropped on my clothes, it used to throw Bio in a tizzy something awful. But for some reason, she didn't mind dirt, so if the popsicle dropped, I would smear clumps of soil over the stains to keep the peace.

I like bringing back to life the image of playing Box Ball with Sally, or Flip the Penny with Ellen (sidewalk bouncy ball games in which the lines on the concrete served as markers, or miniature courts). Or Chinese Jump Rope, a large round elastic chain made from tying rubber bands together and twisting the finished product around two players' legs on each end, while a third child did intricate dance steps and moves in the middle. I liked the middle. I liked being the "Monkey in the Middle." I like being "It." I liked, "A—my name is Alice, and I come from Alabama..." I liked "Miss Mary Mack," and "The Lady with the Alligator Purse." I liked "The Tulips and Twilight Forever" and "Shimmy Shimmy Coco Pop."

Put your hands flat up against mine and I can still do every clap-ping move right smack in rhythm.

I liked it when Rock, Paper, Scissors, Eeny-Meeny-Miney-Mo, Odds or Evens, or The Potato decided who got to take their turn first. I liked it when the worst chalk-drawn hopscotch game, where the "3" might be one foot long but the "5" jagged and uneven might be only 6 inches, and despite the differences, those bound-aries were respected and adhered to as a solid rule. I like playing Skully. I'll bet you have not thought about Skully in fifty years, if ever. Skully was interesting. You took a bottle cap, melted a crayon into with the sun (to give it weight), drew a lopsided chalk square with a few Safety Zones, and then tried to flick your opponent's bottle cap out of bounds. Kind of like marbles, or agates. Did you know that Maxene was the Marble King of Hannepin Avenue in Minneapolis in the 1920s? She beat all the boys. And then her fa-ther beat her with his razor strap, for playing with the boys.

I have shot marbles with Maxene, and Damn! She was good!

In other states and cities, in other towns, did you play Red Rover Red Rover, Red Light Green Light 1,2 3, and Simon Says? Did you play knock hockey, or Follow the Leader? Did you line up along a metal gate with lanyard strips clipped to the gate, the crazier the color combo the better, and braid an intricate vinyl necklace to hold one's skate key, or latch key? Or was that just a New York thing?

Did I ever tell you about my stilts? My skateboard with the mask-ing tape? The unicycle that Jeff Flamholz made for me by sawing apart an old tricycle? Eventually my father always got around to stealing the "right" properly-made item from someplace in Rocke-feller Center. But each of these things always started out as "home-made." I was blessed with an incredible sense of balance when I was young (before these boobs got so large that they knocked me off-kilter). I loved to walk on walls, on fences, on window ledges, the higher and longer the better. Those flying Wallendas had noth-ing on me. I built myself a pair of stilts by nailing a square of wood into two long boards, and then practiced until I could walk up and down Pershing Crescent Street, seven feet up in the air. I painted those stilts red and white striped, if I remember correctly.

Now the skateboard thing was tricky. So many kids were getting concussions and turning their brains into mush because of skateboarding accidents that they were completely banned in New York City in 1967. I don't know why it never occurred to anyone, especially the powers that had been, to slap a helmet on our heads, and maybe some padding, and let us ride. But nobody wore a helmet back then, except maybe to play football. So skateboards were taken off the market. But I wanted one. I really, really wanted one. So I made my own.

I found a small board in the trash and broke up a pair of roller skates. I got rolls and rolls of different colored masking tape from Woolworth's 5 and Dime (who recalls Woolworth's?) and taped the board, though slightly slanted, to the tops of the roller skates. Now remember, these were the flat roller skates that clamped onto the bottom of your shoes and you tightened them to the exact fit by inserting and turning a skate key until it was secure and wouldn't fall off. I used so much masking tape that, unbelievably, that piece of wood never came loose from the skates.

And then I taught myself how to ride it, first down "Buckwalter Hill" (until I couldn't outrun Stanly Buckwalter anymore, who was pissed that I was trespassing on his property), and then down "Chatham Hill," which was quite steep. I actually had more control of that flimsy taped-up thing, and could do more tricks, than on the real one, which my father finally found in one of the empty NBC studios while making his 4 AM "rounds."

I never did learn to ride a unicycle, and the only person who could have taught me was three years old at the time and didn't know how himself, yet.

Now, I don't know if you would call this FUNNY, or PATHETIC. I chose HILARIOUS-OVER THE TOP- FUNNY. In addition to her lack of mothering skills, Bio's housekeeping skills were not much better. For one, we did not use the bathtub for the purpose it was intended. Bio never did any laundry, so she would put the dirty clothes, etc. in the bathtub. Eventually, she would put my stilts, the unicycle, a cot, a shopping cart, and any other items she couldn't be bothered to find a place for, in the bathtub, too. I know that on weekends my Grandmother would come over and pick through the piles in the bathtub and wash the clothes I would need for school and play for the upcoming week. But to this day, I don't how or if the rest of the rest of the laundry was ever washed. I cannot think of a single time when that bathtub wasn't filled with clothes and junk. So consequently, nobody could take a bath or a shower. I remember standing at the sink nightly on a towel, washing myself with a washcloth and soap, and my Grandmother (again) washing my hair on Sundays before she left. But nobody in that apartment ever took a bath or a shower! Nowadays, Bio would be hauled into court, and my father not too far behind her, for allowing that insanity to go on (among his other capers).

Childhood Memories

If you could obtain a magic ticket to go back in time to the day of your 18th birthday, and as a once-in-a-lifetime miraculous gift, receive a second chance to restart your life—would you? Could you? With a whole new blank slate of endless possibilities spread out in front of you (like a bucket list in reverse) what would you do? Would you take the ticket? Would you go in an entirely different direction, pursue other dreams that you thought were unattainable the first time around? Would you throw caution to the wind, or would you be more in control of your destiny? Would you live and be your authentic self?

I wish my answer could have been "yes!" that I'd opt out for the do-over, but the key word here is "18." By that time in my life, I already had been with Patty for a while. My most wonderful, my most impossible, my most beyond measure, my "these things don't happen in real life" had already come to be, and even now, I can't think of anything that would have been great enough to pull me in a different direction. But believe me, it wasn't always easy. After one too many times of ditching plans and friends because I was off doing something more fun with Patty, a group of about twenty of my nearest and dearest sat me down in a circle in someone's basement, and long before there was a word to deem this act, I was the recipient of what would someday be known as an "Intervention."

But they were not asking me to choose between them and drugs or alcohol. They gave me the ultimatum: "PATTY or US?"

And so for a while, I was pretty friendless. Still, remember that the glass is always half full, and when the time came, it only made the move to California that much easier. My whole life has been a series of "OR US's", like Wally's constant barrage of "Maxene or US!" So I would lie to him, park my car in some desolate, remote spot, and climb through random people's yards, over fences and gates and gazebos, until I could zigzag my way over to Maxene's without being seen. I know he used to check up on me, looking to see if I was parked in front of Maxene's house. We would see him in his shit brown Cadillac driving slowly by Maxene's, looking for my car. That was well over 45 years ago.

Unbelievably I still have "OR US's" in my life today. But rest assured, I believe that, as I did back in the day, I'm still choosing right.

Now, do you want to hear more about the Pershing Crescent Street Kids? If there was a magic golden ticket to go back and revisit that time, those early 1960s, I would love to grab onto that.

Did I ever tell you about my best Pershing Crescent Street Friend, Laurie Liebowitz? She was a trip. I used to be so jealous that she was born on Judy Garland's birthday—June 10th (never mind that Judy was born in 1922, and Laurie in 1957). Laurie was the oddest, coolest little kid. Friendly and fearless. The exact polar opposite of what I was like as a little girl (remember I was very shy until 1969). Once when we were about six years old, sometimes after the broken arm incident, my Grandmother had taken both of us on the subway for some reason; I think to go to the Central Park Zoo where Jackie Kennedy had just donated her daughter Caroline's pony, "Macaroni." And we went to see it. The outing was wasted on Laurie. Her favorite animals that she saw on her visit to the Zoo, she would tell people, were the pigeons. But anyway, back to the subway, Laurie managed to wrestle herself away from Grandma, walked up to a complete stranger on the train, a well-dressed woman with a very high coiffed hairdo, and inquired in earnest curiosity, at the top of her lungs, "LADY! LADY! ARE YOU WEARING A WIG?" When the woman didn't answer her, Laurie persisted, "LADY! LADY! ALL THAT HAIR ON YOUR

HEAD LOOKS LIKE A WIG, IS THAT A WIG, LADY?"

Grandma was mortified. I found it hilarious, even when I was six. What was not so funny when I was five years old was that Laurie came home from school one day and told me that, "OOOOOO-HHHHHH! A BOY IN MY CLASS SAID FUCK!" I had no clue that there were such things as "bad words" that were actual words never to be said (honestly, 56 years later, and I'm still a bit fuzzy on that one...) Anyway, Bio had a few important Queens ladies over one night later that week—the president of the PTA, the head of the Queens County Republican Club, somebody who met Totie Fields in an elevator... I don't remember who all was there. But I was bored, and started kicking the leg of the table saying, "FUCK, FUCK, FUCK, FUCK" for no other reason than the fact that I liked the sound of the word, especially when pronounced with a hard "K." Bio turned purple, and my father came raging out of somewhere with a belt doubled over twice, so that he wouldn't miss my ass with it, and said that I was being hit for saying a "JAIL WORD!" (again, still fuzzy). And that the police would come and lock me away if I ever said it again. A fine, excellent bit of parenting skills those two had, if I must say so myself.

When I learn about days gone by, long before my time, I am most interested in the subculture, or rather the daily act of living, existing in those days. I wish they would teach a class on, say, the daily goings on in a Victorian household. Not the facts, but the things and behaviors that seem to have gotten lost with time. Could you imagine overhearing a conversation between a Boston family in 1793? Nobody could teach you that!

I have a friend on Facebook who is fascinated with the 1960s. Hippies, and the 'Peace and Love' illusion in the latter part, the Kennedy properness, and progress in the beginning of the decade. I wish I could tell her / show her what the 1960s felt like, what they really looked like. Unlike the drab 21st century, the 60s was full of color. The cars were bubble-topped and two-toned, with great paint combos, like pink and black, red and yellow, blue and white. My father had the latter. There were no such things as seat belts. Very, very young children sat in car seats that clipped onto the front bench seat. The rest of us rolled all over the front or back seats.

Once I even fell out the window while Gayle's father was driving along the highway. Gayle's father and mine used to follow the garbage pick-up schedule. They were just ahead of the trucks, so they could get the first good picking before the trucks took the refuse to the dump. On this day, I was with them, sitting on my father's lap in the passenger seat. They were running late, and in order to beat the trash truck, Gayle's father was driving extra fast. He hit a bump in the road and out I flew! I remember sitting on the side of the highway, unhurt, but gearing up to cry for a toy or something for my "trauma," while waiting for them to get off at the next exit and turn around and pick me up. In the meantime, I amused myself looking at the vast amount of billboards lined up one after another in the grassy central part of the highway, advertising everything from Chesterfield cigarettes to Coppertone sun tan lotion—all the things that are taboo today. It was never the product that mattered. I don't think I could even read yet. It was the color. I am glad that I can envision my childhood in color. Sometimes, pictures depict that world as the gray and dismal place it is now. It wasn't always like this. Not until the new millennium began.

Grandma's Wig

Well, as most of you know, I've never been the most mild mannered, even tempered person in the world. As a matter of fact, I've even been called "volatile." Can you believe that?

Now combine this personality with a 4ft 8in 68-lb very old lady, and you think it would be no match. Wrong... My little old Grandma would get bored, and to stir up some action, she would stir up me. Along with Patty (neck and neck) I loved that tiny woman more than anyone in my life, but boy, when she wanted some entertainment, she sure knew how to provoke me.

This was how it went. She would say one of the "trigger" phrases to me, and I would get so angry, I'd throw her gray wig out of the 6th floor window onto 90th Street. It was hilarious to see the people on the stoop or the street below watching as this gray thing came floating out of the sky. They assumed it was a dead pigeon.

But more upset than Grandma about her wig flying out of the window was my poor little "Toto- Cairn Terrier" dog, Joey. You see, this gray wig sort of resembled Joe, and he had kind of fallen in love with it. Whenever it was off Grandma's head, or not flying down to 90th Street, he would take it under the couch, and kiss it, and cuddle it, and growl at anyone who dared to come near it.

So one day, after one of these episodes, I took Joey with me to go downstairs to retrieve the wig. Joe was very well trained, very well-behaved (or so I thought) that even in New York City, I never put him on a leash. As I bent down to pick up the wig, I saw Joey staring at some poor woman and her baby who were sitting on the stoop. The woman had on a white jacket, and...Well, you know the rest. Joey, thinking the woman had stolen his wig-baby, was pissed, and lifted his leg, and pissed all over the back of this lady's beautiful jacket.

After that, Grandma started storing the wig at the neighbor's, Mrs. Meadows, apartment across the hall, and Em and I started filling up condoms with water and throwing them out of Grandma's windows instead.

Mission Position Impossible

Well, Happy Birthday to my Grandmother. MAYBE. I say "maybe" because she was born in Poland, in 1886, and nobody bothered to record the actual day of her birth. So it's either today, or tomorrow, 129 years ago (these Grandmothers of mine are getting quite old!).

Anyway, onto "Mission Position Impossible Part 2." I've decided to spare the children of the person involved any further embarrassment due to their parent's behavior. I have come to this conclusion based on the story I will tell you in a minute, and also because I love the children more than I dislike the parent. I will handle "Mission Position Impossible Part 2" privately, making the situation known to those whom I feel appropriate, while sparing the children any more humiliation than they have already endured. That said, however, "THE PAM SHOW" still welcomes any ideas or suggestions which might help my dear friend with his penile erection problem and chubby chaser fetish (because as funny as it may seem, it is hurtful to his main squeeze that he can only get a rise out of that thing by looking at very fat women).

Okay, so it was 1965, and I was in the third grade. Like all the other Dubis' (DuBois'?) that came before (and many after), my father had a drinking problem. But what he had was something called "periodic alcoholism," which meant that he could go years without drinking, and he did, but once he started he could not stop and went on a bender that went on and on until he wound up in a hospital.

I've heard that his first time it happened I was a baby in the playpen and he fell on top of me. After that, nothing for seven years. Suddenly though, one evening, he disappeared for and was gone for three days. Jane probably figured it out. I, of course, knew nothing. Then on the fourth night, at about 3AM, we were awakened by the constant ringing of someone leaning against the doorbell. Daddy was home! Drunk as a skunk, but home, nevertheless.

I remember Jane sitting up all night watching to make sure his lit cigarette did not fall out of his hand and burn the house down. Very considerate gesture, indeed. But then she made for his mistake, which obviously still stays with me fifty years later—she called the police, and the state mental hospital—Creedmore, I think it was called (how that woman loved mental hospitals!). While her action was right, as there were no such things as rehab or treatment facilities in those days, her timing sucked big time. Why she couldn't have waited another half hour, or even fifteen minutes more, is still, a half century later, a mystery to me. But just imagine being an 8- year-old girl standing on the stoop of your building with the seven other little girls whom you walked to school with every day while your drunken father rolled around in the grass behind you, surrounded by police and men in white coats. And of course...Daddy was wearing a straitjacket, to boot.

After about a month in Creedmore, Daddy came home, but he eventually left for good. As far as I know, for the next nine years that he had left in life, this never happened again. But who knows?

And that, dear readers, is why I choose to keep "Mission Position Impossible Part 2" only among those who I feel have a need to know!

My First Antique

Today, I'm going to tell you about my first antique. It's a great story considering how young I was.

My father first got me interested in antiques when I was seven or eight years old. He would take me downtown to the antique stores, and to the Antique Toy Show at Madison Square Garden, once or twice a year. And I would try to imagine the people who touched these items before m̈. the children who played with these amazing toys in years long gone by. Who were they? What were their lives like? It excited me. I knew it was my passion even then.

Although we've discussed this before, let me refresh your memory as to the rules of childhood in New York in the 1960's...

At 4 you could play outside, and ride your bike unsupervised.

At 6 you could cross any street, and of course walk to and from school alone.

At 8 you could take the bus alone (not only the school bus, but the regular New York City bus). At 10 you could ride the subway alone.

And finally at 12, right before you became a teenager, you could go to the beach alone. By alone, I mean with no adults supervising. Perhaps with a friend or two your own age, but maybe just by yourself.

And we all grew up according to these rules.

Now 10 was the big one for me. I loved taking the train into the city and walking around Central Park, the Zoo, the Planetarium, even down to the Staten Island Ferry (I don't think we had an age limit on that, taking the ferry). Anyway from my subway stop to the park, I used to pass by the most amazing antique toy store I've ever seen, to this very day. It was called "Chick Farrow's Fun Antiques." Mr. Darrow was a nutcase for sure. He was all over the place, bouncing off the walls, playing with his toys...he reminded me of Monty Hall on *Let's Make A Deal.* Fun Antiques was overpriced as hell, but he sure had beautiful things.

One toy I could not get out of my mind. It was in Darrow's window—a metal, vibrantly multi- colored wind-up Coney Island Ferris wheel. It was pretty large, not like the toys of our time (60s) and Mr. Darrow had it wound up and spinning constantly. It really was a window display quite comparable to one in a very famous toy store a few blocks away—FAO Schwartz.

One day, I think I got the nerve up to ask Mr. Darrow how much it cost. "A few hundred dollars," he answered. So all I could do was look, and dream. This went on for about two years.

Then one day in 1969 my friend and I discovered a new and wonderful place—Greenwich Village. People did things there, well, like you've never seen before. They had riots going on that summer about something called Stonewall. We didn't know what it was exactly, but we liked getting caught up in the excitement. (For those who don't know, Stonewall was a gay bar in the Village, and the police kept raiding it and hitting the patrons with their billy-clubs. Finally, a few days after Judy Garland died and turned the gay world upside down, they began fighting back. This became the beginning of the Gay Rights movement. The rainbow-colored flag was designed in Judy's memory.)

Now being 12 years old, we never had any money besides our subway tokens and the emergency telephone dime in our shoe. As we headed up 7th Avenue to see what chaos was going on one Saturday afternoon, we passed a flea market on the street. I glanced over at it, and the first thing that caught my eye was the exact same metal Ferris wheel as Chick Darrow's Fun Antique" had in the window. By 12, I was a bit more courageous, and went in to inquire the price.

"TWO DOLLARS!"

Two dollars, the man had said. So little, yet so much for a young kid who only had a token, and a dime in her shoe.

We grabbed the first stray piece of paper we could find (I think it was in the garbage can) and borrowed a pen from a local pizzeria, and made a sign that read:

"2 LITTLE GIRLS STUCK IN THE CITY—NEED 2 DOLLARS TO GET HOME!!"

In no time, the nickels and dimes came pouring in, and I was the proud owner of a Chein Coney Island Series Ferris Wheel. At 12 years old, I had made my first good deal (the real value in the 1960s for a Chein Coney Island amusement park ride was lower than Darrow's, but certainly a lot higher than I paid for it).

I don't have to tell you that......I still have it today!

Bargain Basement Barbie

So—today was a thrift store day. And I'm usually pretty good. But I knew this Barbie board game which originally came out in 1959 or '60 was also reproduced in 1994, so I passed on it. After all, five bucks is five bucks.

Many hours later, I was sitting on my bed with my two girls on either side of me, playing on the computer, with a fatties marathon on TLC on the TV, in my PJs, which (certainly not Mel's style!) consist of my old Coney Island T-Shirt, and shorts turned inside out, as it's more comfortable that way. My version of Heaven.

When a nagging thought started...."It's a thrift shop, for God's Sake. They never have any clue what they've got. What if it was an original?" So I started looking online, comparing what I saw to the repros. The repros were pretty expensive, the original was even more!

Let's just say I got plenty of strange looks from the other costumers, with the inside out clothing, And none of the daytime workers who know me were there. The night manager looked me over and felt sorry for me. Probably thought I was homeless, or crazy, or both. Anyway, she said, "Three dollars!" Which I happily handed over, and took my game home.

1959 BABY! 19 freakin' 59 ORIGINAL!

I do have a few good "money" stories. Once a store in New York accidentally gave me a 120- year-old two-and-a-half dollar gold piece, mistaking it for a penny. And no, I did not tell them about their mistake. Actually it was from 1856, so it is now 163 years old. And yes, I do still have it.

Then there was the time in Canoga Park, California at the 7-11. I used to go to the 7-11 across the street every morning and get a large chocolate chip cookie and a cup of coffee. The employees never minded that once I paid, I would plop myself on the floor, spread out the morning newspaper, drink my coffee (with thirteen sugars) and eat my cookie. It's amazing what people will let you do, if you are bold enough to attempt to do it.

Anyway, one day, I was sitting on the floor of the 7-11 reading *The San Fernando Valley Green Sheet* when a heated argument started at the counter. The clerk was accusing some customer of trying to pass a counterfeit $20 bill. The man (customer) was swearing up, down, and sideways that the bill was real, that he got it from some relative who would never cheat anybody. Blah, Blah, Blah... And then I (who was basically staying out of it) heard the words that piqued my curiosity—the 7-11 man screamed, "Liar, I'm calling the police. I have never seen money that looked like that before!"

And I thought to myself, "Was it possible?" After all, I was a kid when the Coinage Act of 1965 came into being and the U.S. Mint stopped making dimes and quarters out of silver and instead used a cheaper combination of copper and nickel. My father (who was still doing his 4 AM raids in his fishing boots in the Atlas Wishing Fountain in Rockefeller Center) would tell me not to take any of his silver money, to use only the dimes and quarters made after 1965. Of course I didn't listen, didn't care, and well into the 70s I was still spending his valuable silver coins. Could this guy be doing the same thing? Using something rare and obscure from someone's numismatist collection (or whatever it's called when it's paper money)?

I left the coffee, and the newspaper, and the half-eaten cookie on the ground and inserted myself right smack in the middle of the disagreement, just close enough to see which fuss was all about. It took every ounce of control in me to act casual, kind of as a peacemaker. I told the two of them, "Look, I've got a new $20 bill. I'll give you that, and I'll take this funny one. That way everybody is good!" They thought I was nuts, but nevertheless, we made the exchange, and in my haste to leave, I knocked over the coffee and stepped on the cookie.

I might have been spending Daddy's silver collection in the 60s and 70s, but by the 1980s I knew damn well what a 1928 twenty dollar gold certificate was.

You might think it would all end here, and under normal circumstances it would have. But if there is anything you've learned from these past 4-1/2 years of "THE PAM SHOW"—my life is anything but normal.

That night, Emma, who was still a teenager and living with me, wanted to go to Hollywood to Gay Roller Skating Night. When he was finally all primped and sparkly and ready to leave, I was so engrossed in my favorite TV show of the day, *Cagney and Lacey,* that without thinking, I told him to take some money out of my wallet for his admission and whatever.

I was asleep when he came home, but woke up when I heard the door open, and realized that I had not yet shown him my prize find. I got up and looked all over, and could not for the life of me find the gold certificate bill. So I asked, Em if he had seen a funny looking 20 with an orange seal on it?

It turned out that that was the money he took out of my wallet earlier that night.

So I thought "Okay, this is going to be easy. All I have to do is call the roller rink and track it down."

But it was far from simple. Emma got into Gay Roller Skating free that night. Maybe it was All People With May Birthdays, or some special promo thing which he fit into. But at any rate, the money wasn't spent until later that evening, at an X-rated bookstore on Hollywood Boulevard. Now Hollywood was very seedy, really dicey back then, and this was about 3 or 4 o'clock in the morning. But that made no never mind. I drove to the bookstore, and if I must admit, gave a performance that rivaled that of the great Katherine Hepburn or Bette Davis. I got the tears going, and despite the sounds of men groaning and moaning in various stages of sexual arousal from behind little curtained booths, I got the proprietor of this joint to believe the story I made up. Unrehearsed. Just whatever spilled out of my mouth. I came up with some nonsense about how my father gave me his "Lucky Twenty" on his death bed, and it was the only thing I had to remember him by.

And just as somebody's climax was coming to conclusion, and he yelled out "BEAT ME DADDY—EIGHT TO THE BAR!" (not really, but something equally as ridiculous), the owner of the dirty book shop handed me back my 1928 20-dollar gold certificate. And yeah—I still have it.

Teacher of the Year?

I first figured out that I must have had some sort of writing talent when I was in the 4th Grade, and my poem "The Little Snowflakes in All Different Shapes are Coming Down in Their White Capes" was published on the cover of the PTA Christmas Bulletin at PS 117 Queens. As I grew up, I used to amuse myself writing editorials and articles for the city newspapers. Then the paying stuff came in, like poems, or little stories in magazines, liner notes, and things about the Andrews Sisters, and Judy Garland...etc.

Oh, but I almost forgot...There was one other paying gig, ALMOST, when I was 15 years old.

I was in High School, and had the most unconventional French teacher that there ever was. She was young, maybe 25. Her name was Barbara (she kept the second "A" unlike a certain other Barbra, whom we all know, and love!). I always called my teachers by their first names, even though we weren't allowed to. Somehow, I always seemed to get away with it, even with the older ones. Anyway, Barbara would sit behind her desk, and if you mispronounced the word in French, or conjugated a verb wrong, she had a full water pistol or two in her desk, and she would "shoot" you. Not particularly thrilling when it was 3 degrees out, but I digress. This lady was fun, and made learning fun. She really made me love the language, and certainly was my inspiration to plan to become a French teacher, had my life not taken THAT very different path down Shubert Alley.

And so, when I read in one of the most popular national tabloids (not a bad one at all!) that there was a contest for high school kids from across America to submit an essay on why they thought that one of their teachers should be the "Teacher of The Year for 1972," I wrote one about Barbara. I no longer remember what the prize was for the winning teacher, but I will NEVER forget that the prize for the winning submission was $1000 and a trip to Puerto Rico.

$1000 certainly would have been great for a kid needing a car in a year or so. I actually already had a car. I saved all of my babysitting, birthday, and assorted schemes money for two years, and bought myself a 1928 Model T. I thought it was sooo cool. But then after I owned it, crank and all, I realized that an antique car was not exactly the best thing to drive around in when you actually wanted to get someplace (I kept it until my father died—I think he liked it more than I did—then I sold it to Andy's cousin).

Then there was the prestige of beating out thousands of teenagers from all over the U.S. Boy, that was something my shattered self-esteem certainly could have used at that time in my life.

Okay, so you know where we are going with this. I did indeed win. First place. I was so excited, so proud of myself. School was out for the summer when the winner was announced. But as soon as they called me, I called Barbara to tell her the amazing news. There was a long silence, not exactly the reaction one would expect when they just told someone that she was now "The 1972 Teacher of The Year," thanks to your entry in a nationwide contest. Then she said, "I don't want to be associated with THAT newspaper." And that was it. Nobody, not her colleagues, not the head of the foreign language department, not even my sweet old grandmother could get her to change her mind. So I had to turn down the prize. Talk about disappointment!

But as you know, even then nothing ever kept Pammy down for too long. When school started again in September, Barbara was gone, opting instead to take a job in one of those swanky art galleries on Madison Avenue. And during winter break, I did indeed get to go to Puerto Rico for a week. To come back to New York in the middle of winter with a tan and a white shirt was just about the coolest thing one could do back then. In those pre-cellphone, trusting days of the early 70s, you were allowed to make a phone call from a public phone, and tell the operator to charge the call to your home number. They did it on the honor system. And I fully put that practice to good use. I called all my friends in New York, several times a day, long distance from San Juan.....And on my still 15-year-old honor, charged every single one of those long-distance calls......................to THE ART GALLERY!!!

Of course, Grandma eventually had to pay for those phone calls, but the damage was done. The Art Gallery on Madison Avenue did not want any employee associated with THAT kind of a person. So they fired her.

The last I ever saw of Barbara was in late 1974 or early 1975, when I was walking down Lexington Avenue with the most famous person (one of the two most famous people) on the Broadway Circuit that season, and I saw her, very pregnant in a phone booth, fittingly, talking on the phone. I tapped on the glass, waved with one finger, and then ran to catch up to Patty.

Car Date and Narrow Escape

Every teenage girl in the world remembers her first "car date," when you finally had the boyfriend who was just a few years older than you, who had his driver's license. What joy, what freedom, to be 14 years old, and be able to go anywhere.

My first "car date" boyfriend was a 17-year-old boy named Ronald. He drove a little yellow Honda. That was when Hondas were really tiny, almost like clown cars, but people certainly looked twice when they saw that car coming.

Ronald had an interesting job. I don't know why I'm bothering to tell you this, except that it answers the age-old question as to who is the voice in the department store who tells you, "The store is closing in 10 minutes," or "There's a special in the women's department—3rd floor." Now Ronald was a nice boy, but he was very, very possessive. One night, I had enough. But rather than back out of our date and hurt his feelings, I constructed this scheme—ten minutes after Ronald came to pick me up, my friend Diane and her mother Gladys were to arrive, (empty) suitcases in hand, and pretend that they were my long-lost relatives from Tuckahoe (upstate New York) coming to visit for an unknown period of time.

Well, Ronald was disappointed at my "relatives" sudden visit, but decided anyway to go alone to the amusement park arcade that we had planned to go to that night.

He never made it. A semi hit the little Honda on the Whitestone Expressway, killing Ronald instantly. He was dead. Gone. He was 17. And I was supposed to have been with him in the car that very moment.

I guess I could say that some guardian angel was looking out for me that night, but more importantly, the lesson learned from this, I believe, is you just never know. So live life with no regrets, and most important—excuse the pun—

...Enjoy the ride!

Stewart Kidman

He could have been your son, or mine. He wasn't. His name was Stewart Kindman, and tomorrow, he should be celebrating his 44th birthday. He was a Briarwood boy. Some of my PS 117 friends may recognize the last name. His mother was one of the kindergarten teachers. Stewart was so beautiful, and smart. When he was in the third grade, they sent him to take college math classes. I used to dress him up in John-John suits (shorts and a bow tie) and send him on stage with flowers for Maxene after her shows. I held him in the hospital on the day he was born. I never dreamed that just 13 years later, I would be spending nights sleeping in a chair next to him in the pediatric cancer ward in another New York hospital. Never imaged they'd amputate his left leg. After that I told him, "You lost your leg, not your life." Of that I was wrong. Stewart died just one month after his 17th birthday, before he learned that he had been awarded a full four-year scholarship. He died before he started the 12th grade. Of all the losses in my life, both canine and human, this is the one I've never been able to come to terms with. I preach about saving the animals, but we have got to save the children, too. St. Jude's is a good place to start.

Happy Birthday, Stew. I've never stopped loving you.

****

Yesterday Kate asked me the reason for my antipathy. I had to think about it. This is my answer: Stewart was the closest thing I ever had to a baby brother. So I make no apologies for it. It's hard still, 30 years later, to come to terms with the fact that he was gone at 17, while the state paid me to watch someone masturbate for seven hours straight twice a week! Sorry if I sound bitter. I am!

STEWART HECHT KINDMAN is honored as an outstanding student who persevered with a healthy spirit after developing osteogenic sarcoma while in Junior High School. Although Stewart missed many weeks of school while undergoing cancer treatments, he remained an excellent student, a member of the National Honor Society, and a National Merit semi-finalist. He was co-recipient of the first William Alexander Memorial Award, and received the Bruce Cutler Memorial Award in 1987, a year after his death. Stewart learned to understand quality of life. In his college essay, he wrote, "While in the hospital, changes began to take place in me. I met incredible people who were much sicker than I was and still had a positive outlook...I was shocked into a realization of what is really important in life...I found an inner strength that I had never before needed."

Those who knew Stewart said, "His warmth and humor in the face of his illness were a true measure of his courage and dignity" and "Stewart found happiness in every single day and took advantage of it," and "His illness was not the focus of his life." He was accepted into an Ivy League School on full scholarship, but passed away before ever learning of it.

Memories of Dad on His Birthday

Today, unbelievably if still alive, Marilyn Becker's and my father would have turned 103 years old. We lost him way, way too young, only 62 years old. If he hadn't been so sick, and ultimately dying, he (more than anyone) would have gotten such a kick out of the whole Andrews Sisters thing, and what transpired (and yes, he would have signed those papers, too).

My Dad was a trip. And as you've figured out by now, was born in 1912, thus making him a young adult (and father to Marilyn, and our deceased brother) during the Depression. Everyone I know who came out of that Depression came out a bit scarred and overly precautious. My father was no exception.

While some people prepared for the next crash by overstocking food (like my grandmother and the Weschlers), my father did it by hiding money all over that apartment in New York. I guess he didn't trust the banks all that much. So there was always a little money here, and a little money there, mostly in closets. But his big, main "safe deposit box" was right behind the door of the little heating grille in the living room. There he kept a couple of thousand dollars at all times. I don't remember a time when I did not know about it, nor the fact that under no circumstances were we ever, ever to touch that money.

When I was a kid, this was no big deal because, as I've told you before, he worked at Rockefeller Center, and one of his favorite pastimes was putting on fishing boots and cleaning out all the coins in that gold Atlas fountain at 4 AM. So there was always plenty of change lying around, or in piles in the couch (having fallen out of his pockets). And nothing really cost very much back then, nothing that change couldn't handle when you were small.

But then I got a bit older. It was the late 60s—1967, to be precise—and I wanted to dress like all those cool kids who were somewhat older than me: big bell bottoms, tie-dyed shirts, suede fringed cowboy vests (the longer the fringes the better), PEACE medallions (PEACE, everything)...

But more than anything, I wanted a maxi-coat. For anybody under 50 years old, a maxi-coat (no, not a pad for your period) was a full length, down-to-the-ground "granny coat" to go with the "granny" glasses we wore. I remember the maxi-coat cost $48.00— a small fortune for me. But then I got the idea that a few bucks out of the "Emergency Next Stock Market Crash Fund" in the heating grille would not be missed. And it wasn't. And voila! I became the best-dressed junior hippie in Queens, New York! Sometimes being neglected had its advantages...neither of my parents ever noticed the new look (the one new look my father ever did notice came a few years later, when we were protesting the Vietnam War, but that's another show in itself.)

After that, it became easy, but I was always careful to never get greedy, and help myself to so much money that it would get noticed. What I did not know, could not know, was that at the same time as I was striving to become the most mod junior hippie in Queens, Jane—the bio mom—had fallen for the exterminator who came to kill the roaches in the building, and she, too, was striving for a more appealing look for the bug man. And she, too, was dipping into the "Emergency Next Stock Market Crash Fund" in the heating grille.

Without knowing what the other one was doing, we managed to deplete the entire stash. When my father discovered what we had done, he went crazy. And when he went blind crazy like that, his favorite thing to do was to throw things out the third floor window. I know my little box turtles went out. Pictures off the wall. Small pieces of furniture. Of course the portable TVs flew out. Clothes. Kitchen stuff. I think I even remember the toilet plunger going out the window.

But at least I had my maxi-coat to wear to go down in the snow with the bio mom to retrieve whatever wasn't broken, ruined, or dead.

Happy Birthday Daddy.....maybe I'll throw something out the window in your honor today!

Rockefeller Daddy

Now I did not know "Daddy" for very long. He died when I was a teenager. When I lost him, he was just 4 years older than I am now. I wasn't there when he passed away (working on *Over Here* that night), and wasn't aware how seriously ill he was, but Marilyn and her mother (my Dad's only real true love) were with him. Marilyn told me that as he was dying, he proclaimed, "I'm not afraid to die!"

For all his craziness, I am still in awe of his bravery in the last moments of his life. This was a man born in 1912, nine years after the Wright Brothers created flight, who was terrified of airplanes. He used to look at me in amazement and ask me how I could get on one of those things? I think he both admired me, and thought I was nuts.

Marilyn got Daddy when he was barely 20 years old. I got Daddy when he was in his late 40s. And I believe that both times were the wrong times for him to be raising kids. But he was quite colorful, and he instilled a life-long love of antiques in both of us. She owns, and lives above, an antique store in Upstate New York. I just live in the antique stores wherever I am.

Daddy worked at Rockefeller Center. I'm not exactly sure what he did there. I know he sometimes drove the Zamboni machine across the ice rink. (He also taught ice dancing at the rink. However, one of his favorite things to do was to put on his fishing boots, and "clean out" that gold fountain at 4 in the morning. Perhaps I should explain that the Rockefeller Fountain is a wishing fountain that draws thousands of tourists every year, throwing money into it. Daddy probably made more money from that Fountain then he did from his job there.

Also, Daddy knew that growing up I liked all things French and Spanish. See the flags in the picture of all the countries surrounding the rink? Well, one day in the 60s, the flags from France and Spain mysteriously disappeared, and I suddenly had two new bedspreads. I remember sitting on my bed singing "The (La) Marseillse" while people frantically hunted 30 Rock for the missing flags. I never said Daddy was ethical, just colorful. That might also explain why, all through the 60s, Jane walked around in a mink coat that had the name "HAPPY ROCKEFELLER" engraved in the lining. And maybe why I had toys before they came out on the market (NBC Studios NY is part of Rockefeller Center—need I say more?).

So on the subject on languages, Daddy came to me one day with a problem. In those days, NY had a heavy Puerto Rican population, and Daddy wanted to be able to tell them something, either "excuse me" or, to the girls, "you are very pretty." I don't remember which, but he asked me how to say the words in Spanish. As a joke I taught him to say this: "Quiero tener sexo con usted" which translates into "I want to have sex with you." Daddy couldn't figure out why every Spanish woman on the subway beat him up every time he tried to talk to them (see—I was a hellion, even then). The poor man would sit on the couch for hours, stare at me, shake his head, and keep mumbling something about "The Bad Seed." I

always thought he wanted to go see the movie with Patty McCor-
mick, but somehow, I have a feeling that's not what he meant...

Antiques are My Life

QUESTION:

How did you come to like antiques so much? How old were you
when you started collecting for this hobby?

I love this question. I was eight years old in 1955. My father
loved antiques, and would take me to downtown Second Ave in
Manhattan where there was a cluster of antique shops in the day.
He would hand me antique toys and objects and tell me to imagine the children who played with them and touched these items
long ago. Because since I was close to my Grandmother, who was
born in 1891, and heard many stories of that simpler but wonder-
some time, I already had a connection, an affinity, for the past.
Unlike her daughter—the Bio Bitch who had the sentiment of a
gnat, Grandma held on to things of personal and historical signif-
icance. She had the foresight to see the value of her present to the
future. For example, when my Grandmother was just 18 years old,
In 1909, the U.S. Mint decided to change the long-standing Indian Head penny (sorry, PC peeps—that's what it was called) and
commemorate the 100th anniversary of Abraham Lincoln's birth
by putting his likeness on new pennies. The government hired an
engraver named Victor D. Brenner to design the new coin. Brenner placed his initials, "VDB," at the bottom of the reverse side of
the one cent piece between the wheat ear stalks. Never before had
Grandma heard of the designer putting his initials on US currency. She assumed that someday, these coins would be worth something, and saved two hundred of them.
    As it turned out: widespread criticism of the initials' prom-
inence resulted in their removal through 1909. I still have my
Grandmother's hoard today.

When the famed zeppelin the Hindenburg made its maiden voyage in March of 1936, my grandfather (father of the Bio) thought that a piece of mail that actually traveled on, and was postmarked by, the dirigible on its first flight might someday mean something. Grandpa wrote a letter to Grandma and Bio, saying that this might someday be of historical importance. This was thirteen months before the famed explosion; the Hindenburg disaster at Lakehurst, New Jersey on May 6, 1937 brought an end to the blimp. Thirty-five people on the airship and one member of the ground crew were killed by the crash and the fire, although miraculously 62 of the 97 passengers and crew did survive. I still have that letter, which the grandfather, I was to know for only less than 2 years, wrote and speculated about so many years ago.

But back to my father, and my real passion for antiques. I remember once a year he would take me to a huge antique toy show at Madison Square Garden. The exhibitors would look at us apprehensively. Who wants a young child around these precious vintage collectables? But I was good. If I dared to touch anything, it was always precariously, with one finger. I loved those antique toy shows at eight as much as I did at 58 and beyond.

Yet, as with everything in life, there was a downside to our mutual love of vintage objects. Daddy had a habit of bribing me, usually for good school work. He would say something like, "If you get 'A' in Economics, I will buy you the Velocipede (a bicycle with a large wheel in the front and a small one in the back which we saw on 2nd Ave) at the end of the semester."

So I would work my ass off for months and get that 'A,' but then he would find something else, something random, to punish me for. And, of course, the punishment was that the promised antique would be taken off the table. After the third or fourth time this happened, I gave up. But it really screwed with my head (there is comfort in the fact that at least he knew).

It took me a few years, but one day I woke up in my little room at Patty and Wally's and realized that I was no longer in a position where I needed my Daddy to buy me anything (not that he was alive to do so). That's really when it started. I went out and, little by little, found and bought myself every single antique that my father promised me over the years but ultimately flaked on—the Veloc-ipede, the cigar store Indian (sorry again, PC peeps, that what is was called), the calliope, etc.

Interestingly, I was the product of my father's second marriage. When he was very young, he and his first wife had two children—a daughter in 1933 and a son in 1936. His son died many years ago, but my sister Marilyn is alive and well, living out Daddy's dream in Hawaii. She is 86 years old. And do you think this was her life's passion? She owned and operated an antique store in Upstate New York for many, many years.

Coincidence? I think not!

My Neighbor, Mr. Heldenmuth

Today on "THE PAM SHOW" you are going to be introduced to Mr. Heldenmuth and his wife..

Growing up, for as far back as I can remember, we lived in apartment #3G, and the Heldenmuths lived in apartment #2G (I think you know where we are going with this). Now, poor Mr. Hel-denmuth was a veteran of the great World War. No, not that great World War—the first one. I can't even tell you what side he fought on. I can venture a guess. He was from Germany, a skinny thing with the biggest nose you ever saw, and a thick German accent, so whether he was with us or the Kaiser is anyone's guess. Mr. Hel-denmuth had PTSD from the war, and also a metal plate in his head (I can't tell you how many times I bought powerful magnets and put them on the floor of my bedroom trying to raise Mr. Hel-denmuth out of bed). He had very little tolerance for a small child living above him, and in those days when Janie Dearest still lived up there with me, she was terrified of him. Most of my childhood was spent with Mr. Heldenmuth shaking his fist at me and scream-ing something in German every time he saw me. When I got older, and Mr. Heldenmuth found out that I had no intention of going to an out of state college, he was more disappointed than when the Hindenburg crashed in 1936 in NJ.. (I know this because he told me so.) Then when he found out that the road tour of *Over Here* had been canceled, he was damn near suicidal (he told me this, too).

However, after I had been in California for a few months and had decided to make it permanent, I went back to New York to collect a few more of my personal items. Mr. Heldenmuth would stand guard outside the building for hours, a remnant of the Winter of 1918, when the platoons stood guard outside the trenches. So when I saw him on his usual patrol, I said, "Good news, Heldy, I'm moving to LA!" Well, tears sprung to that old man's eyes. He must have been in his 80s by then, but you never saw a man (not even Bruce Jenner when he was still a guy and in the Olympic triathlon days) move so fast. He ran down to the storage room in the basement of the building and came back up hauling his World War I army trunk with his name "HENRY HELDENMUTH" stenciled across the top. "Here" he said, "you can take more with this," and he gave me the trunk.

So between Mr. Heldenmuth's World War I footlocker and my father's coffin (wait—I don't mean the one he is buried in; for some reason my father had a real coffin in the living room, where he stored things; when he left, and then died, the coffin just stayed there, part of my inheritance, I guess), and an Econoline Van (which we will talk about in a future show), I managed to bring a lot of my clothes and things back to LA.

Many, many years later, in the mid-90s, I went back to New York on a vacation and, for nostalgia's sake, drove by the old building. At least 20 years had passed since I left. When you "go home again," everything that you remember as being so large is really so small. The houses, the street, the trees, Mr. Heldenmuth....Mr. Heldenmuth? How could that be? But it was! Still patrolling his area in front of the building, he was now over 100 years old (I guess there is something to be said for those steel plates the Germans put in their soldier's heads at the beginning of the last century). I went up to him, and he remembered me. He tearfully told me that Mrs. Heldenmuth had died, and he was all alone, and wished he could join her (which he did, in a couple of years). And then he admitted something astonishing. For the past twenty years he had missed me! I thought back on all the nights he had pounded on his ceiling with a broomstick, all the screaming (like you saw on *The Honeymooners*) out the window up at me, and I realized that all of my childish antics brought some fight and spirit back into that old man's life. It's a shame that a house full of nosy screaming brats didn't move in after I left.....but never again was Mr. Heldenmuth blessed with a child living above him. Only boring old people.

He lost his will to live.

Before you ask the obvious question—the answer is no. I gave it to Maxene.

Two Little Girls on the Subway

I was going to post this story on yesterday's "PAM SHOW" in honor of Gay Pride Weekend, but because it was my father's birthday, and although he does have a small part in today's show, I wanted one that focused more on him.

Remember how I've told you about the 1960s New York age allowances for children to be granted certain privileges, like crossing the street alone, taking the bus alone, etc.? Remember that 10 years old was the all-important age when one was allowed to take the subway without adult supervision? Remember that, because it plays a very important factor in today's adventure.

My first friend in the world was probably about a week or two old when I met her in June 1957 (I was three months older) but I've heard we shared a crib together many times (we still talk today). And certainly the first 13 years of our lives, we were inseparable. One day in 1966, we did the unthinkable. We got on the subway. What made it so taboo was we were only nine. In those days, she was the outgoing, adventurous one, while I was the follower. I remember another time, on the subway with her when we were four (with parents) and she was walking up to different ladies in the subway car asking them if they were wearing a wig.

I don't know what made us do it, or why we wound up where we did—14th Street in Manhattan. I remember that in front of NYU College there was a demonstration going on. People were holding up signs and chanting "G-A-Y, G-A-Y" over and over, while walking in a wide circle. Now in sheltered Queens in 1966, we had no idea that there was any other meaning for the word "gay" than "happy." Through dribs and drabs we were able to learn that a male professor at NYU wanted to wear a dress to teach his math class. We were so young, so naive, that we actually believed that the people were marching because they were happy and gay that he would be allowed to wear what he wanted to school. We hated the dress codes that were still in place in schools in '66 and thought, "Well, if they let this man wear a dress to school, maybe they would finally let us girls wear pants" (although that didn't happen for another 3 years).

So we joined up with the group and marched around for a while shouting "G-A-Y, G-A-Y" along with everyone else, oblivious to the news trucks pulling up one by one and the cameramen jumping out to get shots of this little "celebration." We stayed for less than an hour, got a hot dog from a street vendor, and went back home on the train. We were so damn proud of ourselves, we pulled it off!

But not so fast. My father watched the news every night, and the expression on his face when he saw his nine-year-old child marching in a GAY rally, was priceless! See, even though it obviously was me, his brain could not compute such a thing. He never said a word to me...but from that day on, he kind of looked at me a little differently, as if he was never really sure.

What finally clinched it though, didn't happen until 1970. By that time, it became a statement against the Vietnam War to wear an Army jacket, if you were lucky enough to be able to get your hands on one. Someone whom I babysat for let me have his...so then I began walking around in an oversized men's Army jacket, with a black band tied across my left forearm, again making me very hip with the Junior High School crowd.

My father couldn't handle the Army jacket, though. That's what finally pushed him over the edge, and believe me, it had nothing to do with the Vietnam War protests. Every time I walked by him wearing it, he would put his head in his hands, and mutter to himself something about creating "The Bad Seed." and what had he brought into society?

Perhaps it was a good thing, after all, that he didn't live to see me grow up!

The Schwinn Lemon Peeler Bike

In 1968, I was the proud owner of a Schwinn Lemon Peeler. How many of you reading this remember what that was? How many are too young to have any clue as to what I'm talking about? For those in question: a Lemon Peeler was a Stingray bicycle—bright yellow, of course! So now I will go on to explain what a Stingray was. A Stingray was the ultimate, enormous oval shaped seat. A banana seat! Elongated handlebars that dipped and tipped, and if you were lucky, a Sissy Bar. A Sissy Bar was a long metal backrest that attached to the back of the banana seat, and the higher up in the air it went, the cooler you were. And if you really wanted to make the neighborhood kids jealous, you opted for one with all the bells and whistles, with fluorescent-colored streamers pouring from each of the handlebars, and with gear shifts. That 5-speed thing was a bitch; it never seemed to be in the right gear, and each pedal was hard to work. Secretly, I missed the Royce Unions of my youth, but at 11 years old with a brand new Lemon Peeler, one did not complain.

I always had the best toys, pretty much as soon as they came out, or even before. CONTRADICTION of everything I've told you thus far about my childhood. I mean, how could I be so un-wanted and neglected and yet be showered with the grandest array of toys? Not the way you think...Remember I told you that my father drove the Zamboni machine over the ice rink at Rockefeller Center? And then at 4 AM, he would put on a pair of fishing boots and "clean out" the coins people threw in that gold Atlas wishing fountain? Well, helpful man that he was, he also enjoyed "un-cluttering" the NBC Studios that were situated in Rock Plaza, too. Back then, new products and toys were advertised directly on the TV programs live, and Daddy never understood why the sponsors needed to send so many of the same items. A happy part of my life was that I never knew what I might wake up to find—sometimes toys that were not even on the market yet. I certainly know that I had the first Pebbles Flintstone doll ever produced. Which one, you ask? All of them!

But back to the Lemon Peeler. It was seriously a chore to pull that thing out of the basement storage room, where the tenants stored their "too big for the apartment" or "no longer used" belongings. Even then, I loved that room, filled with the old record players, radios, and bird cages. Even then, I appreciated the beauty of days gone by. The bicycles, peddle cars, sleds and baby carriages were kept in an area with easier access to get in and out of. Truth be told, although it was beautiful to look out, and I of course enjoyed being envied for having it, especially when Carrie Blatt was riding behind me on her sister's 20-year-old bike (with the training wheels on it) huffing and puffing, trying to keep up...I really, truly hated that Lemon Peeler. Riding it up and down the block a few times was the equivalent of working out for, like, two hours at a 24-Hour Fitness gym.

So one Spring day, when we arrived home from school (the Pershing Crescent Street Kids) and discovered three police cars parked haphazardly in front of the building only to learn that one of "those people" (the cop's words, not mine) had broken into the cellar and stolen an array of items—the Lemon Peeler among them!—I feigned a few tears. But...well, you know the truth.

And so I ask the age-old question: how and when did we become owned and defined by our possessions, instead of the other way around? I, for one, am probably the guiltiest of all. Three storage units? Four pinball machines? Three pianos? A couple of Cigar Store Indians (Native Americans), etc., etc., etc.... And I am caught somewhere in the middle of being a "compulsive hoarder" or, as I like to call myself, a "preserver of history." As far back as I can remember, I loved "things." I can still recall every single toy my grandmother kept for me to play with in the bottom drawer of her big Victorian dresser. Okay, to be fair, besides the Popeye Weather Colorforms that rotted away, I still have them. All of them. Yes, the original ones she bought in 1957. In my early life, gifts and shiny trinkets were the way undemonstrative people showed that they gave a shit about you. And eventually though sometimes very burdensome, these items seem to meld into a dimension of their own. Especially if that is really a person's only perception of love.

For example, my Daddy got me the coolest Lemon Peeler bicycle (never mind how he got it) so therefore he must love me more than, say, Carol Blatt's daddy, who had her riding around Pershing Crescent on her sister's old beater (with the training wheels so Carol could balance).

I still remember an early October day, probably around this time of the month, only it was 1961. My Grandmother and I had just returned from playing in the park, and we were a bit late for the start of our (notice I say "our") favorite cartoon—*Alvin and the Chipmunks.* Back in those days, you only had one television set, and it was always in the living room. I ran into the room at full speed to turn on the set (no remotes yet!) lest Grandma should miss Simon, Theodore, and Alvin singing their opening theme song. And wouldn't you now, just at that exact moment, my father was getting up from his nap on the couch. Hey, when you spend your nights stealing from the Rockefeller Center studios, offices, and fountain, and ignoring Kitty Genovese's screams as she was being stabbed to death, you've got to get some sleep sometime. Right? Anyway, as he stretched his legs off the side of the sofa, I ran in and tripped over them, landing on my elbows. And I cried. Not so much because it hurt very badly, but because when you were a kid, you cried whenever you fell down, even if there was no visible evidence of injury. It was kind of an unspoken rule of childhood.

I really have no recollection of any pain, but rather of this miracle that was unfolding there before my eyes. You see, the more I cried, the more things the grown-ups gave me—Oreo cookies an hour before dinner, that ever-present roll of butter rum Lifesavers in my Grandmother's (and in all grandmother's) purse, her green plastic subway token holder (yeah, still got it), a Chapstick (no, I don't still have it)... Anything to make me stop wailing.

And then I saw it, sticking partly out of a bag in Bio's closet—a present for one of the Pershing Crescent kid's upcoming birthday party: the most beautiful red tin Marx Disney car, with Mickey at the steering wheel, Donald in the passenger seat, and Goofy and Pluto in the back. (I saw this same car selling for $700 at an antique store last summer, but I'm getting ahead of myself!). Suddenly I wanted that Disney Marx car more than anything in the world. So I just kept crying and staring up at the package in the closet. Eventually, Bio got the idea and gave it to me ("Aaaahh-hh, what do you want a boy's toy for anyway, PAMMY?") And I abruptly stopped crying.

However, that was not the end of it. Apparently, I did do some major damage to my left arm, including a complex fracture to the elbow, and spent the next week in the children's ward in the local hospital in traction, followed by four months of a sterile white shoulder-high cast, and the dire warning to my parents: "She will probably never be able to use this arm again!" Of course, I was a lefty.

Still, that is not how I remember it. I loved that cast. Not for the special treatment and sympathy it might have gotten me, but for the opposite reason.

See, as I've said before, I did not find my voice and become the assertive "PAM" who you all know today until I was 12. Before that, unbelievably, I was an intensely shy little girl who would do almost anything to not be the center of attention. I would even get questions wrong deliberately on my tests in elementary school for fear of being singled out for achieving the highest grade in the class. At parties, I would "pin the tail" on the donkey's nose, or miss the musical chair so to be eliminated, rather than risk the focus perhaps being put on me had I won the prize. Having been on the far end of either side of the spectrum, or in my case the see-saw, I can tell you without a doubt the three things an introverted painfully shy child fears/hates the most are: birthday parties (except their own), winning a game, and the worst by far—Halloween! Really, what could be more awful than having to put on one of those itchy store-bought Ben Cooper character costumes and a plastic mask of Yogi Bear or Captain Kangaroo with only one little teeny tiny air hole in the mouth area to breathe through? And then having to parade up and down the street ringing stranger's doorbells and begging for candy while they exclaimed how cute you looked? All this done, in New York, at least, while wearing your winter coat, which covered up the ugly, stiff, and I repeat ITCHY costume, anyway.

So that Halloween in 1961 with my cast-covered arm bent in such a peculiar position, I knew it would be impossible for me to fit into any of those Ben Cooper's, from The Carousel Shop on Queens Blvd, where all The Pershing Crescent Street Kids went to get their Halloween attire. I figured I finally had a reprieve. No costume, no trick-or-treating. No stupid Halloween events or parties. Grandma and I could sit home, give out candy corn (nobody gave wrapped candy in those days) and carve a pumpkin (or rather Grandma could scoop the guts out and carve it while I would watch.) But that was not to be.... Somebody came up with the brilliant idea that while I might have to forego the Ben Cooper Character Costume, they could turn me into a "Japanese Lady" complete with the kimono which would cover up my cast. I was the epitome of all things politically and socially incorrect today, right down to the white face, painted eyes, and the chopsticks in my hair. But alas, all was not lost.... Every year, no matter what she went as, Carol Blatt could be counted on to inevitably trip over her costume, or her big feet, and hit the sidewalk with her bag of candy sprawled out all over the place in front of her. No matter how old or young I was, that never ceased to be funny. It's still funny. I'm laughing now thinking about it.

My Three Boyfriends

People have often asked me what I was doing hanging with Patty when I was so young and should have been in high school. It's a simple explanation. I skipped the 8th grade and finished high school in 2-1/2 years. I was 16 when I was all done. And the college diploma is from some bogus University in France, where they gave you credit for your life experience as long as you also sent them $500 (as Grandma did). I graduated Phi Beta Kappa with my life experience and Grandma's money.

However, during my last year in high school, I was very busy. The only boy I ever really loved had broken up with me on my 16th birthday, to go out with a girl whom he met at my Sweet Sixteen party two nights earlier (nice guy, huh?).

So although I didn't like it, I was free to date whomever and whenever I wanted. I was kinda popular and used to getting what

I wanted, so securing a new boyfriend wasn't really too difficult. The problem was, I managed to secure three, all at the same time.

The first one was named Claude. He had a bird named Fluffy. Perhaps that should have told me something, but I was oblivious at the time. I must have been the first (and last) girl Claude ever dated. He was clueless, and thought that dating a girl meant you had to do whatever she told you to. And OY, the things I told him to do—but I'll tell you about that later in the story.

The second was Gordon. He had an afro, very styling, and very appealing to me back in the early 70s. And Gordon was two years younger than me, another asset which I found very appealing. He was adorable, and played the best piano I've ever heard. We would skip school, go to his house, he would play for me, and I would sing away. And he never said one word about my singing, but he must have liked me an awful lot to put up with that for hours on end.

Then finally there was Russell. His assets were, shall we say, a little small, in any and all ways that comment can be taken. But Russell made up for it in other ways. He pawned his mother's jewelry piece by piece to keep me in presents. One, a 1940s Hawaiian Isle pinball machine, which he pawned his mother's diamond ring to buy, is still with me today.

Now dating three boys during the same time period is really not that much work. See, all I had to do was tell each one individually that the others, although just friends, might like me a little, and even though I didn't reciprocate the sentiments, (I only love you, darling) we don't want anyone's feelings to be hurt, so no touching or kissing me when the others were around. And that way, not only could I date three guys, but I could go on one date with all three of them at the same time.

Russell, to make up for his "shortcomings" in other areas, was always the big shot spender, and insisted on paying for these triple dates as his parents wedding silver diminished greatly in abundance, meal by meal, date by date. Me and these three stooges were dining at Tavern on the Green, and The Top of the Sixes (hey, I've always proclaimed that the Bio mom didn't feed me, I never said I didn't eat well). Riding the horses and buggies through Central Park, seeing everything on Broadway that season, anything and everything the city of New York had to offer that year, we took advantage of. So that, plus all the gifts, kept Russell around.

Claude stayed around for our amusement. He was so naïve that when I told him that if he really loved me, he would parade around Queens Boulevard in one of Janie Dearest's old bathing suits from her closet, because that's what boyfriends did, off he went, clad only in Jane's little red- and-blue swimsuit from 1952, complete with the frilly little skirt on it. I think on occasion I also sent him to the candy store in Jane's orange muumuu to buy me cigarettes and gum.

And Gordon, well, he put up with my singing. And as I said before, nobody could pound out a show tune like Gordie.

And so Curley, Moe, Shemp and I kept up this facade for months until the Andrews Sisters got their Broadway show. Apparently, I stood up one person too many in order to do something more fun with Patty, and a group of my friends (including these boyfriends) staged an intervention on me. Talk about being surprised! They jumped on me when I least expected it, and gave me an ultimatum: EITHER PATTY GOES, OR THEY GO (I kid you not). You know what I chose. So I was friendless for a while, but the biggest joke was still about to come out.....

It seemed that while Claude, and Russell, and Gordon were dating me, they were also, (all three) secretly dating each other. That's right. I had managed to snag not one, not two, but three gay boyfriends (and then a husband, to boot). Liza would have been so proud. Come to think of it, so would her mother!!!

Sweet 16 Party

Talking about my three gay boyfriends on yesterday's "PAM SHOW" made me think about my Sweet 16 party on March 17, 1973. Aside from losing the only guy I ever gave a shit about to one of my friends who was also a guest (he was to break up with me on my actual birthday, which was two days later), it was a pretty good party. My Grandmother rented out a French disco called Le CoCu on 53rd and Lexington. She told me I could invite thirty people. I agreed, "Yeah, sure, Grandma," and the final count was 83.

Grandma and I had the biggest argument over whether or not to invite Gayle. I said, "No way!" Grandma said that I had to, since we had known the family practically all of my life. What could I do? She was paying, I had to give in.

The party was fun. I reveled in all the attention I was getting, Attention Whore that I am. We danced. we ate. my closest friends made me memory objects of the party, like a hat made out of the wrapping paper, and bows from the presents, and a water glass filled with some of the items and mementos, and sealed it over with wax, dripping the number 16 in red onto the solid blue wax background.

But there was one present that could not be wrapped. Andy, my future gay husband, bought me a live guinea pig. However, he did not get me a cage or tank for it, so we decided that the best thing to do would be to confine it to a small room. The only thing that would work would be the Ladies' Room on the second floor. I announced over the microphone to everyone that the guinea pig would be in the Ladies' Room, and to be careful going in or out, and also to not step on it. And then we continued to party.

About a half an hour later Gayle and her mother blew in the front door, complaining about the Long Island Railroad and how late the train was. Then with her usual tact and flair, Gayle's mother (who, like her daughter, was a large and portly woman) announced, "I've got to take a piss something awful," and went in search of the bathroom. I was oblivious to all of this because, much like I am today, I was completely absorbed with the gifts I had gotten. And Grandma, along with one of my language teachers, was in the middle of arguing in French over some inaccuracy in her bill. So she did not notice either. Nobody did...

Until we heard a scream, a loud piercing scream that overtook Barry, Bette, or Karen (whomever the DJ was playing at the time). Gayle yelled out, "Oh no! That's my Mawmey screaming! Something must be wrong!" A group of us headed up the stairs in the direction of the terrible commotion and hysterical yelling and discovered—much to my horror—just what had happened.

Gayle's "Mawmey" had come up to use the Ladies' Room. Because the Long Island Railroad was late and they were subsequently late, they had not heard my announcement about the guinea pig running around the bathroom. "Mawmey" came in and saw what she thought was the biggest rat ever to grace New York City. She ran into one of the stalls and somehow got herself in a standing position on top of the toilet, shutting the door behind her, and began to yell and freak out. But that, my dear readers, was not the worst of it.....

After someone explained to "Mawmey" that it was a guinea pig, and one of my birthday presents, she calmed down, and agreed to come down off of the toilet seat and go back downstairs to the party. But when she tried to open the stall door, it opened in and not out, and no matter how far she backed up, "Mawmey" was just too fat to get past the bathroom door. It just could not open enough.

So they had to find a handy man or a plumber, somebody to get "Mawmey" out of there. Because the whole staff only spoke French and barely any English, they could not call anybody and communicate what we needed. Grandma had a plumber in the city, but he was religious, Orthodox Jewish, and this being Saturday before sundown....he would not pick up the phone, much less take the train from Brooklyn to help.

I went back to the party. Not my Mawmey, not my problem. Besides, I had lots more presents to open (83 guests equaled 82 gifts, and the guinea pig), drinks that somebody spiked with rum to drink, and a boyfriend to lose. Grandma sat alone at the bar, yellow pages in hand, desperately trying to find a handyman. "Mawmey" began screaming again, and just like a mother elephant pulls its young out of the mud with its trunk when the baby is stuck, Gayle yelled, "I'll save you Mawmey!" (Gayle, however, was even larger than her Mawmey, and couldn't get through the door of the Ladies' Room).

Finally Grandma got a plumber who made emergency calls to come over to Le CoCu, along with his helper. The helper quickly emerged to let us all know that between the 2 plumbers, Mawmey, and all the tools they needed, there was no room for the guinea pig, and Andy had to come and get it (Andy found the poor thing cowering in the next stall over). The plumbers finally removed the door, and pulled Mawmey out.

By this time, the party was over, and everyone was leaving. Grandma complained that the plumbers cost her more than the whole damn Sweet 16 did, party gifts and dinners included. And for the next almost twenty years that Grandma lived after that party, she never again told me to invite Gayle or any member of her family to anything ever again.

The Flagship Diner

Although I have lived in California for over 40 years I am coming back to New York to be part of the end of an era—the closing of the Flagship Diner on July 22, 2018. It holds such sentiment for me that whenever I did come to New York for a visit the Flagship was always the first place I went to. The memories... my Grandmother and I were there the night it opened in 1965. I was eight years old. By 1968, my best friend in the world and I would have our Saturday lunches at the diner. Lunch consisted of a plate of fries, and two vanilla milkshakes. My 14-year-old boyfriend and I would sneak out every night in the early evening in 1972, after we scraped together enough change to share a bagel and two hot chocolates. It was a place of love, of laughs, of great times, and even sadness. It was at the Flagship Diner at 2 AM where I had to break the horrible news to my mother that my father had died, when I was just 16 years old. It was the place of my 11th birthday, of my 15th birthday, where I celebrated getting my driver's license, and also my high school graduation. But most importantly it was the every Friday night hangout for my beloved little grandma and me. Every Friday, starting in 1965 until I moved to California to pursue my dream job of working for the Andrews Sisters, and whenever I would come to visit Grandma in New York, we would go to the diner until she passed away at 102 years old.

We did crazy things over the years at the Flagship that still make me laugh today. I used to write notes to my Spanish teacher on the walls in the ladies room (she was in that diner almost as often as I was). By the same token, another boy I knew would write my name and number in the men's room whenever he was upset with me, and it stated, "For a good time call Pam." I heard my very first rock song on one of those table jukeboxes. It was ten cents a song, or three songs for a quarter.

One of the funniest memories I have of the Flagship is a dinner with my husband, my mother- in-law, and a rather large rotund friend I had. The big lady managed to squeeze herself into one of the booths, ate a large meal and then was unable to slide herself out of the booth when it was time to leave. The workers had to release the bolts that attached the table to the floor in order to set her free.

I have not eaten meat in many many years. However in com-memoration of that first meal at the Flagship's opening and clos-ing, the Friday night dinners with my precious grandmother, and all of the zillions of memories I have gathered over these past 53 years, I will once again eat a famous Flagship hamburger and fries, and imagine my little grandma sitting across from me when all was right with the world.

Good night Briarwood, Good night my childhood. Good night Flagship.

The Center of My Apocalypse

No matter where you live in the world, you've probably seen this picture: ELMHURST GENERAL HOSPITAL IN QUEENS, NEW YORK. It has been called Ground Zero of the Coronavi-rus, deemed "The Center of The Apocalypse." There have been so many deaths from C-19 In this hospital they ran out of room to store the bodies, so a makeshift morgue has been set up in the driveway. Look closely at that driveway, very closely. Over fifty years ago, where the mobile mortuary now stands, I stood, right in that spot, trying valiantly to wrestle my 13-year-old self out of the paralyzingly strong grip of Gayle's father's humongous hand on my left, and my own father's equally vise-like hold on my right.

This is not something I generally like to talk about. Aside from the stigma and humiliation of a child being locked up, drugged, and molested, and behind a bolted and barred door, this was the day that broke me as a human being, right there on that driveway.

It was on this piece of paved road that I learned to never ever trust another living soul—an issue I still grapple with today, a half-century later. The physical placement of imprisoning me in a facility for messed- up, incorrigible teenagers, and the method by which we were contained, was horrifying to say the least. I think I slept in a hallway for the first three nights, for lack of room.

But it was nothing compared to the lifelong psychological damage which resulted from that one single orchestrated action. The lying, the tricking, the elaborate plan to get me as far as that driveway, where Bio could surrender me to the Elmhurst personnel and be rid of her problem. The hate and betrayal under the guise of concern to anyone on the outside looking in was so surreal, it was as if my mind snapped. My heart grew an iceberg around it, and in some strange way which I can't exactly put into words, I lost something, something most people take for granted. I was to never again feel completely safe in my own skin.

However, Bio was looking for the ultimate way to get rid of me, and unfortunately right after I became a teenager, I provided her with it. I cut school for a total of six weeks starting in January of 1970. Stupid story, really, and any other reasonable parent would have handled it and resolved it with love and compassion. Bio used hate, indifference, and opportunity. As I said, I ditched junior high school for six weeks. It started after a science teacher said something (so insignificant I no longer remember what it was) which embarrassed me. I stopped going to his class. And pretty soon, I stopped going to all my classes as it started to look strange that I would disappear for one hour in the middle of the afternoon every day when I was supposed to be in Science.

If you can believe it, I, who cannot stand to be in weather less than 75 degrees, would leave for school at 8 AM every morning, veer instead in the opposite direction across Queens Boulevard to the Maple Grove Cemetery. I would brush the newly-fallen snow off the green bench by the duck pond and there I would sit, huddled up in my ski jacket, for the next seven hours.

Eventually, the school called, Bio found out, and she, my father, and Gayle's parents snatched me and without a word of reasoning, discussion, or alternatives restrained me until they were able to lock me up. Four adults, two of them extra-large (they were, after all, raising and feeding Gayle) and me. Just 13 years old, having not gone through puberty, and subsequently giving the appearance of a 9-year-old.

Meanwhile, up in the Adolescent Unit, the infringements varied. The main sin was being a knocked-up teenager. That bought a girl at least six months of confinement. Several like me skipped school for a long consecutive duration of time. Some had shoplifted and had progressed to real robbery. We were the prerequisites to the "Scared Straight" experiment, only when it was over, we didn't get to leave. Most of the teenagers (there was a boy's adolescent ward as well) were locked away in there for months, as I'm sure was Bio's intention for me as well. But somehow, someway, in what I like to call a serendipitous miracle, came those random moments of fortuitous circumstances when all the stars are aligned in one's favor.

You see, my father never came to visit me during the 11 days I was held in Elmhurst. He felt way too guilty, having been sent to a remote reform school in the early 1920s for some stupid childish prank. I believe this hit a little too close to home for him. Bio visited, Grandma visited, but not my father, not since he and Seymour had me pinned to the ground of the driveway. The Driveway. You can see it. It's under the morgue.

As luck would have it, though, Bio had been trying to get herself on a local game show as a contestant for years. The call for the audition finally came. Grandma was in Atlantic City for a few days. There was no one to come see me on Visitor's Day. Reluctantly, my Dad caved in and agreed to show up.

He did, and lasted about 10 minutes before he turned white and bolted for the locked door, banging on it furiously until some guard let him out. I sat there confused and crying. This was really bad, or so I thought. Suddenly, my father was back, coming in with great authority accompanied by some important-appearing men in expensive business suits. He said to me, "Get your stuff, I'm taking you home." Sad to say, I didn't have any stuff. I entered that building wearing a pair of green bell bottom pants and a "Lake George" sweatshirt. As the week, week- and-a-half went on, the bell bottoms ripped up both sides of both legs until they were just flaps of corduroy swishing and splitting whenever I walked. I begged Bio to bring me some clothes, but she always "forgot." Needless to say, when Bio got back from her tryout for "Paycards" (which she failed) she damn near had a coronary when she saw me sitting there!

Of course, I went back to school the next day, and went on to skip a grade and a half, graduating when I was only 16, which made the whole Patty thing possible.

Oh, so before I end this, let me tell you why my father got me out of there. We had an old stereo in the visiting room, but we only had one record—a 45 of the Jackson 5 singing "ABC" on one side, and "I'll Be There" on the other. The girls on the floor played it constantly, over and over. My Dad made it up until the first time Michael's sweet voice sang out, "Whenever you need me, just call my name and I'll be there. I'll be there for you..."

sweet voice sang out- "whenever you need me, just call my name, and I'll be there. I'll be there to protect you..."

And he realized, as his ex-wife never did, that you don't lock up children like caged animals.

Some of you may find it ironic that as I sit here, IN MY 60s with my SOMETIMES purple hair, which nobody who knows me seems to give a second thought to, discussing this subject. Today I want to talk about Crazy People. More specifically Crazy Street People. You know, the ones who rant away at imaginary objects, and fight Quixotic windmills. The politically correct wording is probably "mentally Ill." But I've never been politically correct, so I'll just call them: "fucking nut cases."

Now what's even more paradoxical is that while I HATE the crazy street people here in Los Angeles, yesterday I saw one lying half on the curb, half in the street, on his back. I thought for sure he was dead, so I called 911, and then as they put me on hold as usual, I saw his head slightly move, so I hung up. But I have to admit, I was very disappointed. When I think of all the people gone too soon, people who gave and contributed to making the world better, and then see these whack jobs taking up space, on this earth, never mind what I wish.

Here's the paradox...While I HATE LA Street Crazies with a vengeance, I absolutely LOVE the ones in New York. I don't get it, either. Perhaps it's because they are so much more colorful back east, or perhaps it's because I know first-hand how easy it is to live out here, and how hard New York living can be, really in every aspect you can think of. When Liza sang "if I can make it there...I'll make it anywhere...Come on, come through New York, New York," she was speaking the truth.

Three of my all-time favorite New York Street Crazies are: Rollerena, a 6' 4" man who roller skated around Manhattan in a pink tutu and tights. Last year when I lived in New York, I saw Rollerena every Saturday at the Antique Garages, now a little old lady. He apparently likes antiques, too.

Then there is the Peeing Lady of 6th Avenue. She waits until the height of traffic is driving on The Ave Of The Americas and goes out in the middle of the street, pulls down her pants, and, well, pees, as traffic is backing up into Brooklyn. I admire her nerve, her sheer guts.

And finally there's Greta (I'm sure I've talked about Greta before, so if you know this story already, I hope you like it again). When Em and I were living at my Grandmother's apartment, there was this very strange man who used to wear wristwatches all up and down both his arms. Now on the Upper West Side, Broadway is such a humongous street that it is separated by an island, dividing uptown and downtown traffic. In the middle of this island there are benches for people to sit on. The wristwatch man always sat on the benches right by where we lived.

And unlike the other Street Crazies, he never spoke, never said a word. Em and I were fascinated by him, and it became a game, a sort of contest between us to see who could make the watchman talk. For months, we tried everything. We were friendly and nice. We were patient and (believe it or not) soft-spoken. We were teasing and taunting. We were yelling and ridiculing. I even sang to him! Nothing ever worked. The wristwatch man sat on that empty bench, day after day, silently staring vacantly through anyone who tried to talk to him, never making eye contact of any sort.

And then one afternoon, as Emma and I were crossing Broadway, and we walked past the watchman, I very sarcastically said: "What the fuck, do you think you're Greta Garbo? Do you want to be alone?" His face lit up, and he reached out his hand to fist me, and then to Emma, and said with a big smile, "Hello, I'm Greta Garbo, and it's always a pleasure to meet my fans!" And he started chattering away, a mile a minute. From then on, as long as we called him "Greta" or "Miss Garbo," he was thrilled to see us. And we got kind of close to him, too. I remember sitting on that bench, telling Greta my problems, and him sympathizing with me, and he actually gave me some decent advice.

I don't know whatever became of Greta. He was in his 70's in the 1980's, so I'm sure he's gone now. But he was one of the most eccentric, exhilarating people I ever knew. Oh, and by the way, when I asked Greta, why all the watches, he said, like it was the most logical thing, "Oh, in case one stops, I'll still know what time it is!"

Cassandra's Garden

It was really nice that so many of you remembered Cassandra (Mrs. Greenthumbs) yesterday on the 18th anniversary of her passing. More than a few asked me what she was like in real life, and if she was just as funny. Yes, she was. But I think you can really get an insight into Sandra as a human being by this true story.

When Sandra and her husband got married in the late 60s, they moved into this wonderful apartment in Greenwich Village, right on 11th St and 6th Ave. There were just two downfalls to this situation. First off, it was a six-story walk-up (and of course her apartment was on the 6th floor). And the second one was that right adjacent to the building was a huge trash dump, with eight-feet-high piles of old disgusting garbage that did not smell too pretty. Sandra learned somehow that this refuse area also belonged to the owner of her apartment house, and tried to make a deal with him—if she cleared out that entire junk yard, would he allow her to garden down there? (Unheard of in NYC!) He kinda laughed and said, "Lady, if you clean up that mess, you can have the land!"

So she set about the task, day after day after day, until one morning she came upon a strange find—a tombstone dating back to 1805. Perplexed, she kept clearing the mounds of trash, and suddenly there was another grave marker, and another, a whole lot of them, all dated pre-1829. Sandra had unwittingly uncovered what turned out to be the second oldest cemetery in New York City proper, long, long forgotten, as buildings and such shot up in the two centuries to come.

A deal was struck. The cemetery, of course, was turned over to the City of New York, where it is proclaimed a historical landmark. And the only key was given to Cassandra, so she could garden in there and make the long neglected, though once sacred, ground beautiful again—for the rest of her too short life.

Victimhood

Maybe to commiserate with my intense situation—last week I have gotten so much sadness and hopelessness and cries for help in your PMs, emails, and responses that maybe I might try to bring about a different perspective on how to survive this, and any other trying time in your life.

Since "THE PAM SHOW" is comprised of 100% honesty, let me start out by saying that my reason for not filming today is a very superficial one at best. But now I realize that if one has committed (as I have) to being "there" for others... it is not contingent on the antique store's party schedule.

Let's remember that everything is temporary. Much as we hate the vagueness and uncertainty of that statement, as terrifying as change is, it is inevitable. Fear of the unknown is scary. Some of us (I did) stay in a place where we are miserable, because familiarity is at the very least "familiar," which is far safer than facing something strange and different. A lot of this is the way we view things, and truly what we are getting positively and, equally as significant, negatively out of a certain given situation. For example, Patty and me at the holidays. After the first—what? five years? seven years?— why didn't I realize then she and Wally were never going to include me, and leave me to make my own plans? Even if that was sitting with homeless animals in the shelter and keeping them company for a little while, that certainty would have been more productive than watching a bunch of old-time celebrities talking bullshit, and delusional ideas for productions that would never come to fruition. Why didn't I accept that my ex-husband, or ex- roommates were never going to stand up to the "Powers That Be" and insist upon bringing me along to *their holiday celebrations?*

Because, as strong as I am, part of me enjoyed being that victim. There. I said it.

Part of me liked being "that lonely forgotten one on Thanksgiving." And I think, hard as it is for us say this out loud, many of us would get off on that "Poor Me" feeling every once in a while. Maybe we use it as a way to justify those deeply hidden questions inside every single one of us, no matter how confident, how famous, or how successful we may appear. I have yet to meet a person in this world who did not suppress that little voice which creeps up now and again to reiterate that we are just not good enough and for some reason deserve to finally be "unmasked."

The truth is you are good enough, just the way we are. No need to overthink it. We just are. You know, I said in the beginning of this that it is a matter of perspective. So if you are, say, "anti- Trump" for lack of a better example, there are two ways to look at it. Pessimistically: "Shit, one more year of that man!", or optimistically: "Just one more year until we get to change the head of, and the direction of, this country." Most days, I choose the latter mindset.

But we are allowed, and perhaps it's good for us, to once in a while focus on the glass being only half empty, as opposed to half full, just as long as we don't stay in that place for a long time. I do not believe that it is all in the cards you are dealt. I believe the reality is in how you play them.

This is a small but simple explanation of how life changes in a minute. So for today, do your best to hang on, and don't let anything be too serious, because like it or not, each day, each week, each year (41 days until the 20s are back again!) brings change. Sometimes good. Sometimes not. But I guarantee you (that must be a saying in my family), you will never stay frozen in the moment you are in right now.

I'm off to the Antique Store Holiday Party. We will talk again tomorrow!

Love you all. Know that, and know you are very valuable to me exactly as you are!

You are enough.

My Friend Glenn

Recently I reconnected with Glenn Gershan. Almost forty years ago, I was hired to look after Glenn. Glenn has a physically disability—he was born with CP, and is unable to talk. But in every other way Glenn is completely normal, with normal intelligence and humor.

One day, in around 1978 or 1979, Glenn and I are driving down Ventura Boulevard, and I'm sure I was in the wrong at the very start of this incident, being the lousy driver that I am. I'm sure I must have cut off the other car, or gotten too close, whatever. But that was my only faux pas, and no matter what, we did not deserve what happened next.

The other driver started honking and cursing at us out his window. Glenn stuck up his middle finger at the guy and laughed. I, too, liked a good game of road rage, and could probably write a book on it. But this one wasn't funny (like the man who started screaming "elder abuse" at me when I honked and harassed him for driving too slow, and it turned out that I was older than him...).

The other car started following us. That still didn't bother me. It's a type of 'road intimidation' I, too, have played. But then he pulled up on Glenn's side of the car and pointed (I kid you not) a gun at us.

This was one thing I had completely no knowledge of how to handle. The game was obviously over. It had become serious. I told Glenn to duck down on the floor of the car, and I hunched down in my seat, as far as possible to be able to keep driving and perhaps not get shot. I tried losing this man, turned left, right, left off Ventura Boulevard (which is the main street in the Valley). That didn't work. He just followed right along behind me. So I got back onto

Ventura. Never in my life I had wanted to see cop so badly. I started breaking every possible traffic rule I could. I ran red lights, I crossed double yellow lines, I made U-turns (like I learned in NY) from the right lane in one direction to the left lane going in the other. No police, of course, when you need one, and the gunman was still right behind us.

My final solution was to drive through the window of CVS (which at that time was still called Sav-on). That would certainly draw a crowd, and the police. But then I realized that I could kill innocent people who were shopping or working there.

So with no other choice, and I apologize in advance to anyone who might be offended by this, but it did save our lives. I told Glenn to act as "retarded" as possible. Glenn wasn't in the least intellectually disabled, but because of his CP, he could pull it off. And with that, I pulled into the CVS (Sav-on) parking lot, and stopped the car, and just got out (I made sure Glenn had memorized the license plate number of the driver with the gun).

I got out of the car, as did the gunman, and before he could say anything, I said, "Sir, I am so sorry. He is retarded, and doesn't know what he is doing. And I apologize for my bad driving, and whatever problem it caused you. Please, sir, please accept my apology. I am so very sorry, and the poor retarded boy didn't mean to offend you. He doesn't even know what the middle finger mean! SIR!"

He grunted a few times (as did Glenn) and got back in his car and drove away.

Glenn and I got into my car, and drove straight to Glenn's house. Thanks to his good memory, we had the guy's plate numbers. Glenn's mother called the police, and a few days later they came over to my apartment and had me identify the gunman by pictures. They then asked me (and I am sure Glenn's mother) if we wanted to press charges. I did. I guess they did, too.

Now, you would think that even with being the awful driver I am, this would still be a once-in-a- lifetime circumstance. Would you believe, about five years ago it happened again?

A Body in the Park

Fantasy Spinner, exaggerator, always adding a little bit here and there to spice up a story. That was the way I thought of my sister David/ Emma. So I listened to him with a grain of salt, so to speak, never really believing all of what he was telling me.

The Summer of 1980 found us living in New York for a period of time with my grandmother, on the Upper West Side on 90th and Broadway (I'd kill for that apartment today). I remember because that was my summer of *Arthur* and hanging with Liza on the streets of New York or in the Astoria Studios every day. It seemed that Emma's stories were getting more and more bizarre by the day. I chalked it up to maybe he was bored and looking for something to "one-up" my Dudley and Minnelli, Ice Palace, and Studio 54 adventures.

It all came to a head one Saturday night, when he woke me up at 2 in the morning, screaming that he had just discovered a dead body in the park while walking home from a club.

I had had it. I decided that I was going to teach him a lesson, make him stand behind his crazy Quixotic statements once and for all. So I sat up in bed and said, "Show me!" I wondered how long he would perpetuate this farce. He let me get dressed, put on a sweater and shoes, and even went so far as to take me down in the elevator into the dark Manhattan night.

Shit, Emma! I had to get up early in the morning. It was the 6th Ave Antique Market Sunday, and he knew I wanted to get there when they opened the gates.

I also remember thinking, "Okay, he's going to take me to the park and then tell me that he can't find the place where he supposedly saw the deceased."

And sure enough he did take me into the park. It was now 3 AM, and we were probably in the most dangerous place in America. Very few lights in that park in those days; the largest glow came from my tip of my cigarette .

Suddenly he stopped and put his hand over his mouth as if to suppress a scream. And he just pointed. My eyes followed his finger, and there was a lesson learned that night. Not by Emma, but by me.... In a rolled up rug, partially hidden behind a tree, there was indeed a dead body feet sticking out of one end of the rug, head lolling out of the other. We ran so fast out of that park, and I never doubted my sister again.

So a few years later, when we were back in L.A. and he was walking home from a club, and once again woke me up in the middle of the night to tell me that he had once again discovered a dead man—this time, lying on Sherman Way, shot in the head—I didn't think twice. I just dialed 911, handed him the phone, and went back to sleep.

Gayle Part 2: Class Reunion

Okay, Okay, this is probably the last Gayle story for a while... Come with me for a moment, back to the summer of '76 (insert the intro to Michel Legrand's "Theme from *Summer of '42* right about here for effect). New York was ravaged with fear of a maniac who was murdering teenagers all over the city who called himself "The Son Sam," Sam being a 5,000 year old year old dog whom, he said, commanded him to kill. The rest of the country was getting ready for the Bicentennial Celebrations which were now only a few weeks away, and the Long Beach High School Class of '76 was preparing to march to "Pomp and Circumstance" (cue that music).

Now let's get back into our time machine and go forward ever so slightly to New York again, only now we are in 1986. New Yorkers were celebrating the 100th anniversary of the Statue of Liberty in its entirety in the harbor. The rest of the country was mourning the loss of all those astronauts on the space shuttle *Challenger.*

And Gayle was preparing the ten-year reunion for the Long Beach High School Class of '76.

She started early in the year collecting money from her former classmates so she could secure one of the many beach clubs along Lido Beach. I believe she was charging $55 per person, or $100 for a couple. The affair was to be catered—nothing but the best for the Class of '76. Black tie only.

Gayle got a pretty good response. Money was pouring in from classmates left and right.

BUT, as you must know by now, Gayle had a spotty work record, and a large appetite, and the two didn't quite go together. Gayle had just gotten fired from her last job as a cashier in a supermarket, when she lost one of her Lee's press-on nails in a woman's watermelon (did you ever notice how plus-size women seem to always have such beautiful fingernails?).

Well, Gayle started to dip into the Reunion Fund. At first it was only for a couple of Big

Macs from McDonalds, or a few slices of Gino's pizza. But then she needed to pay her phone bill, and her Visa bill, and get her car fixed. As the funds dissipated, she knew she still had to do something reunion related, but what to do? What to do?

The idea struck her as she was driving down the Sunrise Highway, past the Green Acres shopping center. Right in front of the Sunrise Drive-in, she saw it—a twenty foot tall blow-up display of the Statue of Liberty. Perfect for The Class of '76. So symbolic.

She rented it on the spot from the drive-in for the night of the reunion for $300, and with that, and her burgers, and her bills, the reunion money was gone!

With no alternative, Gayle had that 20-foot tall Statue of Liberty delivered to her backyard, and the reunion was catered by her father, Seymour, who was deathly afraid of all meat except for hot dogs and fried Pastrami, but he didn't mind manning the grill while the class of '76 in their tuxes and evening gowns desperately tried to avoid the dog shit and green beach flies which seemed to hover around that house ONLY. And the music played on into the night.

A band, you ask?

No—Gayle's 45s on Seymour's wind-up Victrola.

After that fiasco Gayle went into hiding (which was a good thing because the class of '76 wanted to file a class action lawsuit against her). She couldn't find herself a date anywhere in the Long Beach vicinity, and this being long before the internet or Match.com or eHarmony, Gayle resorted to the personals in the newspapers. That worked out okay—until they met her and ditched her, at a phone booth, in a movie line, on the Brooklyn Bridge...you name it, Gayle probably got dumped there.

But out here in Cali, at the time, my sister Emma was working at an exciting new job. It was a phone dating service. The latest thing in the matchmaking world! How it worked was, you described yourself, your likes, your dislikes, etc. and prospective mates could listen to your message and if they found you interesting, you could get together for a date or a drink. This thing was nationwide, and due to Em's position, Gayle's fee to join was waived. But poor Gayle—her voice has always been her downfall. You see, Gayle has a beautiful speaking voice (I always encouraged her to go into the phone sex business). But within minutes of seeing the body attached to that voice, men were dropping her off all over Long Island.

Emma and I tried to think of a way to make it better—besides which, my poor Grandmother was getting sick of having Gayle sleeping on her couch every time a man dumped her in Manhattan in the middle of the night. Emma listened to her outgoing message and discovered the problem. Along with her liking rainbows and butterflies and long walks on the beach at sunset, etc., she described herself as a Julia Roberts type. Imagine expecting Julia Roberts, and getting Mama Cass. That's what kept happening here.

To help her out, and really for this reason only (yeah, right), Em and I rerecorded her message without telling her. Well, I rerecorded her message, and in it, as I was describing myself (as her), I said that I was "QUEEN SIZE." That was all it took. Every chubby chaser all the way out to Montauk was lined up for a date with Gayle. She loved her new popularity. She was the Belle (or rather Gong) of the ball.

Grandma's Girdle

My Grandmother had to be one of the most liberal thinkers of her time. She was born in 1891, still the Victorian era, for God's sake, and although she still dressed like she was living in the

Victorian Age (undergarments), she never much adhered to their practices and beliefs. Naturally, she was a Suffragette, fighting to get the vote, and for women rights passed in 1920. And she went to Speakeasys during Prohibition. She drove an automobile over a hundred years ago, but stopped completely after she accidentally slammed her two-year-old daughter's hand in the car door in 1925. She and her husband, my Grandfather, had separate bank accounts, unheard of in the year they married (1912), but she was a "saver" and he was a "spender" so it seemed this was the only way they could each be happy. She lived in the same apartment on the Upper West Side of New York for 72 years.

Now the reason I'm telling you this is because, as you know, most of my friends are gay males. I am the original "Fag-Hag," probably before the term was coined, and I would often bring my friends up to the apartment with their dates. I had no clue what Grandma thought or knew about homosexuality. The closest we ever came to discussing it was when she told me about a book that came out in 1928 called *The Well of Loneliness*, which was about a woman who fell in love with another woman. It was considered to be scandalous, and most bookstores either banned it or pulled it off their shelves. But Grandma still had her first edition copy (now in one of my units out here in L.A.) and was proud to be able to "go by her own rules." She may have been born in the 19th Century, but she was the kind of person who easily fit into the culture of the 70s, the 80s and even the beginning of the 90s—except for her underwear. I think she could have lived just fine in 2015 America. Of course, she would be 124 years old, so that might present a problem.

Get your fingers off the phone buttons, it's not time to commit me yet. I am fully aware that I mentioned Grandma's undergarments twice so far already. That is because they play a very important part in today's "PAM SHOW." This is how Grandma got dressed in the morning. First she put on her underwear, which were pink shorts that went down to the knee and had pockets on either side. She called them her "woolies." Then she put on a girdle which needed to be laced up, and heavy wool stockings attached to the girdle by 4 garters on each leg. A bra. Then came the slips. One full slip, and one half slip. And finally the dress, the hat, and the gloves, because no proper woman went out without her hat and gloves. That was truly the only thing that remained "old fashioned" of her throughout her life—nearly 102 years of it.

Anyway, a good friend of mine and his date started to get intimate one night in Grandma's bathroom. There was some S & M going on in there, so between the paddles, the whips, and the moaning, they did not hear her little old lady footsteps approaching the bathroom door.

But they heard the banging on the bathroom door loud and clear. My friend later told me they froze. Obviously this 80 or 90-something-year-old woman could hear what was going on. And what came next after the knock was hilarious. She knocked, and then called out, "Whatever you're doing in there, don't get my girdle wet!" To this day, I am clueless as to what she thought they were "doing in there!"

Vitches

So here in the US, tomorrow is Election Day (and I'm taking the day off). I'll vote. Or rather, to be completely accurate, I already voted by mail. Not since that travesty two years ago have I had the inclination to go out of my way to find a polling place in my district and stand in line to vote. I'm not saying that there would not have been problems that Hillary Clinton got elected. There will always be issues. It seemed though, at the time, there was such a feeling that we were on the precipice of something new and exciting. There was such an air of pride surrounding us that day. The hundreds of "I VOTED" stickers stuck to Susan B. Anthony's tombstone, 96 years after women had gotten the right to vote. We had already changed history. Eight years of an African-American President. We were already on the road to progression. Or so we thought.

Today my "I VOTED" sticker is in the kitchen sink.

The regression and oppression of the 21st Century is now (in my opinion) at an all-time historical high. Nothing is politically correct, anymore. Someone is always offended, or yelling "Racial" or "Sexual," or my favorite: "DISCRIMINATION." People are los-ing their lives, their families, and their careers for something as simple as a joke made in bad taste. Thomas Jefferson, who wrote the Declaration of Independence, and also fathered a few bi-racial children, would be rolling in his grave if he knew how we massa-cred those very words that this country was built on.

Granted, a few sections of that document are a bit outdated, such as the 2nd Amendment. The Right To Bear Arms (in 1776) meant a few musket balls versus the high-powered semi- automat-ic weapons of today that fire off hundreds of rounds at the speed light. As far as I'm concerned the Right To Bear Arms is sufficient enough. But more specifically, I never thought that in my life-time, or in any lifetimes after mine, would the fight for Freedom of Speech be so challenged. We are exactly back to the mentality of Salem, Massachusetts circa 1692. If I lost you here, I am referring to the Salem Witch Trials and the mass hysteria that ensued during the latter part of the 17th Century. Freedom of speech was as sub-jective then, as far as I'm concerned, as it is now. You could accuse someone, anyone, of being a witch, of partaking in the evil or dark side, and those who expressed a different opinion, or an individ-ual thought, And as I've mentioned, we must adapt. Our need for owning an individual thought, of partaking with the overall dark side, and as from one expressed a different point of view, or an individual thought as opposed to the majority, were then deemed to be demonic as well. And usually hung. Today we don't hang people physically, but we shun them. We take from them all their glory and accomplishments, in essence their very beings. Based on what? Thinking or expressing one's own perception of something? I sometimes wonder if the way they did it in 1692 was better? At least, if the scaffolding held, it was over relatively quickly.

I realize that I'm going to lose some readers right about now if I don't insert a "PAM" story soon.

Okay. So a few years ago, I made my ex-husband take me on a vacation to Concord and Salem, Massachusetts; Concord because Gayle had been there once when I was very young and saw Louisa May Alcott's Orchard House, and Walden Pond, and I was always jealous of that. The houses there in Author's Row are very small.

People did not have ether nutrients to grow tall and big in those days (Louisa's days anyway—1832-1888) so houses, doorways, and rooms were considerably smaller. Gayle could not fit in the Alcott House or School today (unless someone used those paddles or poles they use in China to cram and stuff the people into the over-crowded subway cars). Hey, if you'd seen Gayle, you'd know even the pond would be iffy these days).

What surprised me the most about Salem was the lack of historical relics, and over-zealous, over-the-top tourism. Modern day Salem exploits the hell out of what happened there 300-plus years ago. Every block, every shop, features caricatures of witches, drawings of nooses, and the date 1692, with really no explanation as to the relevance. Try explaining this to a Hungarian immigrant who had absolutely no knowledge or interest in American History. Oh yes, Andy brought his mother along!

"Vhy do ve keep going to cemeteries?" she asks.

"Because we are looking for witches," I tell her.

"VITCHES?!" And then she proceeded to chant some ancient Hungarian Voodoo incantation.

We never did find any graves of the accused. Finally on day three, I asked one of the grounds workers where they were buried.

Turns out they never were buried. They were hung, and their dead bodies thrown in the street, for others to gawk at and spit at.

I wanted to talk about voting, but now I think I want to talk about vacations. I am cracking up thinking of all the ones I took with my late mother-in-law tagging along. Besides, one can only hold an audience for so long talking about politics and history.

That is one of the good things about having my own show. I can indulge in my ambiguity whenever I feel like it.

I never went on a vacation with Patty or the Andrews Sisters. Oh, I traveled all over the place with one or another, but it was always because they were working (performing). I even went to Florida once with just Patty and me (Wally was sick). She was in a parade, I think singing, "South Rampart Street Parade." Let's just say, that was no vacation!

When I was born until the time I was six or seven, my Bios (on my grandmother's dime, of course) and I used to stay at the beach for three months every summer. That is how I know Gayle. I remember being aware of Gayle the summer that I was three (1960). But I think I may have known her longer. I'll tell you why. Gayle's father used to rent out apartments in his building to seasonal tenants. When my family went to Long Beach for that length of time, they packed every possible thing into the blue-and-white two-toned Chevy bubble top. It was so bad that there were pots and pans hanging out the windows, clanking and banging, as my father drove. Toys (stolen from Rockefeller Center) and beach chairs and barbeques tied to the top of the car haphazardly blocking the windshield except for one tiny slit so that he could see the road. We looked like a 1950s or 60s version of the Joads from *The Grapes of Wrath* (except thankfully we didn't have to dump Grandma in the desert because she died in transit).

Anyway, back to the summer of 1960.

I recall that when my dad turned down a certain street, I even remember the name of the street— Shore Road. Bio had a fit and screamed at him, "What are you doing? If 'they' (Gayle's parents) see us, we'll have to stay in their rental again!" Since she used the word "again" I assume we must have stayed there the summer, or summers, before.

Long story short, halfway up the Shore Road, the Gayle family either saw us or heard us bonking our way down the road. And we were, as Bio feared, stuck.

But I loved that place. What I vividly remember is that it was right off the Boardwalk, and Gayle's father's building had a large square cement patio that he lined with those classic 1950's aluminum chairs in all different colors. As I've told you before, the 50s and 60s were very colorful. The world was not tinted the gray shadow it is today. Older people sat in those metal rockers trying to "get a little sun." Older kids played and swayed with bright beautiful hula hoops and pinky bouncy balls that they smashed against a vacant wall, or stoop. And even though we were right on the beach, Gayle's parents set up a little sprinkler with a Donald Duck head on it for the younger kids to run through.

There was a nursery school directly across the street from us. The owner let a homeless man with no legs live in it when the children weren't there. It was so different then. People were kind to each other. Of course there was crime. There has always been crime. But we were more trusting then. I mean, think about this... Gayle at two years old, and I at three, were allowed to walk "half way around the block" unsupervised. "Half way around the block" meant our street, and the street that connected it to the beach! Two little babies walking alone to the entrance of the Atlantic Ocean, and then dutifully turning around and walking back to the house.

It's funny how some things stay with you a lifetime. The Fourth of July fireworks bursting over the water in the ebony evening sky. The chalky blue sticky cotton candy that was obligatory once you got up to the Amusement Area. The rides (I can still remember every one of them and what they felt like to ride on—the texture, the shapes—as if I was there yesterday). The skee ball and shooting and throwing games that lined the Boardwalk. Again, a place where I was extra lucky. No, not because of skill, but because a man named "Izzie Faber" had the monopoly on all the arcades and carnival games up and down the Atlantic Shoreline. My father and Izzie were poker buddies, or drinking buddies, and because of their friendship, I was able to play as much and as often as I wanted. Gayle, too, I believe.

So much happened on that Boardwalk. Gayle and I were in a "Little Miss 1960" pageant. Bozo the Clown was supposed to make a publicity visit, which was advertised for weeks, but alas was not to be. Bozo dropped dead the night before his planned appearance.

The following year, when I was 4, I taught myself to ride my bike up there. Most poignant, though I can't exactly say why, was a later afternoon, late that summer. Gayle's father and my father took us up to the boardwalk. I remember wondering why I was wearing shorts when it was so cold and windy up there. Gayle had on long pants but she was wearing her bedroom elf bedroom slippers. We looked out at the ocean. At the low-flying planes that would carry advertising banners behind them, and the boats so far away where the sea and the sky melt. In my three-year-old mind, I used to think that the pink Taj Mahal-style hotel (which my father called "The Fat Lady's Milk Farm") at the end of the walk was the end of the world, and where the rainbow led to. As I said, I don't know why this memory is so prevalent to me nearly 60 years later. But it is. Maybe because it was all so beautiful and calm. Until Gayle had a tantrum over some hot dog vendor. She threw herself down on the boards kicking and screaming, her father helpless to stop it. My Dad and I left them up there, and walked home, just the two of us. He bought me an orange Whistle Pop at the little sundry store at the bottom of the ramp. It was called "Pop's Place."

Alright—back to reality, to the drab world of the 2018 midterm elections. I will leave you with a very true summation of the times. I sit here all day long watching *Leave It to Beaver, My Three Sons*, "Fatties" and *Hoarders* reality-show marathons, and the occasional "Dr. Land Phil." Every ten or so minutes, the shows are interrupted by political ads, or commercials for that magic little blue pill. All day, it's elections and erections, elections and erections. I swear I don't know whether I'm coming or I'm going!

Lizzie Borden Took an Axe...

Sometime in the summer of 1982, when I was 25 years old, and back in New York for a while, my friend Cassandra (Mrs. Greenthumbs) and I were reading an article in a magazine in the waiting room of a doctor's office, when Sandra pointed to a picture and said: "My God, that is exactly what you would look like if this was 90 years ago!" I looked, and I did indeed strongly resemble the strange woman in this elusive photograph taken sometime in the late 19th Century. Now my curiosity was aroused. I had to learn more about her. Who was this person who did something so newsworthy, so long ago. Royalty, maybe? A celebrity, a great singer like Jenny Lind? Someone instrumental in the Suffragette movement? A first lady, perhaps?

Nope. Her name was... Lizzie Borden, and in 1892, at the age of 32, she was arrested for the axe murder of her father and stepmother in their home in Fall River, Massachusetts, the most notorious case of a woman accused of patricide in history. August 4, 1892. 123 years ago, TODAY. That's right folks, that's how the obsession got started, and I have just now lured you into celebrating the anniversary of the Borden Murders with me!

Let me start out by saying that Lizzie Borden was acquitted of the murders. She was found not guilty on June 20, 1893, and lived the rest of her life in Fall River, where she died in 1927. I cannot, and will not, say that Lizzie was guilty of these murders. Although all evidence points to that fact, a jury of her peers (well, twelve men) found her innocent of all charges. Was she acquitted because the punishment in the 1890s for such a crime was death by hanging, and no one could fathom hanging this naïve, unmarried Sunday School teacher? I don't know.

Murders:

Abby and Andrew Borden were murdered at their home on the morning of Thursday, August 4, 1892, Abby between 9:00 AM and 10:30 AM, and Andrew between 10:30 AM and 11:10 AM.

Abby Durfee Gray Borden:

A relative had slept in the guest room the previous night, and at about 9:30 AM Abby had gone up to the room to make the bed. According to the forensic investigation, Abby was facing her killer at the time of attack. She was struck on the side of the head with a hatchet which cut her just above the ear, causing her to turn and fall face down on the floor, which created contusions on her nose and forehead. Her killer is then assumed to have sat on her back and delivered 19 direct hits to the back of her head.

Andrew Jackson Borden:

After breakfast, Andrew left for his morning walk sometime after 9 AM. When he returned at around 10:30 AM, his key failed to open the door, so he knocked for attention. Bridget (the maid) went to unlock the door. Finding it jammed, she uttered an expletive. She would later testify that she heard Lizzie laughing immediately after this. She did not see Lizzie, but she stated that the laughter was coming from the top of the stairs. This was later considered significant because Abby's body was visible through the gap between bed and floor when climbing the stairs, only becoming hidden by the bed upon reaching the top. Lizzie later denied being upstairs and stated that her father had asked her where Abby was, and she had replied that a messenger had delivered a summons to visit a sick friend. Lizzie then removed Andrew's boots and helped him into his slippers before he lay down on the sofa for a nap. Next she informed Bridget of a department-store sale and permitted her to go, but Bridget felt unwell and went to take a nap in her bedroom instead.

Lizzie gave two different accounts of what happened next. Originally, she stated that she went to the barn to look for iron or tin and remained in the loft for 20 to 30 minutes eating pears. Police were skeptical, finding it unlikely that anyone could stand the stifling heat of the loft for that long. They also reported finding no footprints in the dust.

Bridget Sullivan testified that she was in her third-floor room, resting from cleaning windows, when just before 11:10 AM she heard Lizzie call from downstairs, "Come quick! Someone has killed Father!" Andrew was slumped on a couch in the downstairs sitting room, struck 10 or 11 times with a hatchet-like weapon. One of his eyeballs had been split cleanly in two, suggesting that he had been asleep when attacked. His still-bleeding wounds suggested a quite recent attack.

At the time of the murders, Lizzie and Bridget (the maid) were known to be the only two people in the house. Lizzie's older sister, Emma (yeah, that's where it came from), was in another city visiting friends.

123 years later, and I and so many others are still obsessed with this case. It remains open to this very day.

The house where the murders took place is now a Bed and Breakfast. I have been there overnight. What an experience. The house Lizzie bought subsequent to her acquittal is now FINALLY being renovated to also become a Bed and Breakfast, slated to open in the summer of 2016. I will reserve a room in that house for a night, and one night in the murder house for my Emma and I for the weekend of March 18–19, 2017. What a great way to start my next decade.

Putting the Pee in PTSD

To show you what a crazy, bizarre life I've led, I have to tell you that the story I'm about to share with you was completely forgotten by me, until Emma reminded me of it yesterday (and this is not easily forgettable!).

Em and I were living in an apartment in Canoga Park at the time with two dogs, Joey and Yentl, and two cats, Fred and Ethel Mertz. Now Fred was an outdoor cat. Patty found him stuck up a tree and made me climb up and rescue him. So, Fred would roam in and out all day. When the sun was up, and we were home, we always left the front door open a crack for Fred to slip in and out. As the Nadler family can also attest, we had some very strange neighbors in this building. One of our female neighbors was murdered by her boyfriend, one male neighbor heard voices through his ceiling, and one guy about 40 who lived with his Mama had PTSD from Vietnam and didn't talk at all.

Well, this was during the time that I worked on "the soap", and she had asked Em and I to put together a tape of the best moments from that year to submit to some daytime award thing. So we were very proud of ourselves because we had figured out how to put two VCRs together (one to play, the other to record the tape) and were working diligently at this task.

Perhaps that was why, when the door opened all the way and the man with the PTSD who didn't talk came in, it took us a minute to notice.

He walked over to our couch, unzipped his fly, and peed all over the couch! Then without a word, he walked back out the door.

I will have to stop the story here, because all of you who feel sorry for PTSD victims, and who know my temper, will not want to know what ensued after that.

Cinco De Mayo

The other day, Em and I were having lunch in Benihana. Yeah, the same place where Tori Spelling tripped and fell onto the grill. Our table, and the cook, had a good laugh at that one, after I loudly proclaimed that I had been coming to this very restaurant since 1975 (back then, four times a week for lunch with Patty) and in the 40 years since, nobody had ever fallen onto the grill. Of course, we are talking Tori, the same person who took out the wall of a preschool I used to work at with her SUV. I don't know, between the cheating husband and the four kids so close together, maybe her brain is a bit fried.

Anyway, that is not what I want to talk about (although I certainly could sit here and fill up the show with Tori and Dean jokes). If nothing else, all those years with Patty and my beloved friend Cassandra (Mrs. Greenthumbs) left me quick-witted, at the very least.

So Em and I got into a conversation with this mother-daughter duo sitting next to him. I always have to sit with the left side empty, being a leftie in a world full of righties; 10% of us are lefties. That's the same percentage of homosexuality in the population, although I suspect it's much higher, being that being gay is so trendy now. Same percentage a woman has of developing breast cancer, although I suspect that is closer to 1 in every 7 or 8. Did I tell you I heard that Lorna (Luft) has had a reoccurrence of the breast cancer she had a few years ago? Godspeed Lorna. I wish Judy's sane little girl a quick and permanent recovery. Cassandra wasn't so lucky. She lost her life to it when she was just 55 years old.

But back to the mother and daughter we were talking to. When they found out that I could basically live anywhere in the world I wanted, the mother recoiled in horror and said, "And do you mean you picked California?"

Well, duh, lady, yeah, I chose California. It is the most logical. After spending 2013/2014 in New York, with their arctic blasts, polar freezes, and Canadian clippers, or my favorite, the nor- Easter (and believe me, that :Easter: has nothing to do with bunnies and colored eggs), what a joy to be back in the place where the warmest I've had to dress was in a sweatshirt three times this entire winter. Andy and friends are shuffling the winter clothes, and the summer clothes, and the spring coats (oh, how well I remember the spring coats of my youth) most days now. I'm throwing on a Coney Island, or my Lead Sister t-shirt and a pair of ripped jeans or shorts, and that's it. Sunshine 360 days of the year. How could anything suit me better?

But before you are all quick to defend your states, let me tell you that I have been in all 50 of them. Even Hawaii doesn't cut it. It is beautiful, and paradise, and all...But just how many days can you sit on the beach watching the waves roll in and out (since sun tanning has become taboo), or stare at the Colonel at KFC with a lei around his neck? Because I can find something wrong with every other state, (too rainy, too cold, too right-wing, too churchy, too backwards etc...).

Gayle Part Three: Who Let the Dog Out?

Now who's ready for a little—or rather, big—"Gayle in Hollywood" story or two?

I don't usually tell this one, because it's one of those unfortunate times when I was not there. But my sister Emma was, as was Craig, so any questions can be answered by either of them. Gayle had somehow found out that a cousin's, brother-in-law's, great-grandmother's, nephew's wife-by-marriage was like third cousins with comedian Buddy Hackett. So she decided that they were closely related, and she must stop off at his house while she was out here in Los Angeles for a good old fashioned family reunion—not that they had ever met before.

I think at the time Buddy lived in Bel Air. I say this because, somehow, she roped Em and

Craig into driving her, and according to her instructions from her map of the Hollywood stars' homes, they wound up right smack in the driveway of *The Beverly Hillbillys* house. People who live out here do that sometimes. We try to find the "television houses" that were real homes, not exteriors on a lot. I don't think I know a single soul who doesn't know how to get to *The Brady Bunch* house. But anyway, thank you, Gayle, because I had been looking for that one for years, and her wrong directions to Buddy Hackett's house found it for me.

Somehow, the three of them found their way to Buddy's house. Em and Craig were so embarrassed by this ploy of hers that they ducked down in the seats. Gayle boldly got out, rang the bell, got on some intercom, and spent the next hour arguing with someone, presumably Mr. Hackett, about how she was his long-lost relative from Long Beach ,New York, and she had to get in to see him.

Finally, I believe he threatened to call the police, or Bel Air Security, so they left. But not before Gayle broke off the heel of her shoe on Buddy Hackett's porch. This was a fairly common occurrence, the breaking of Gayle's heels (happened once on the Brooklyn Bridge—but that's another show.) Those shoes are only made to hold so much weight...

Now the best part about this part of the story is....that Gayle didn't seem to know her famous relative's name. Even when talking over the intercom, she kept calling him....BUDDY HACKER! Undeterred, Gayle consulted her movie star map, and decided that next, she wanted Craig and Emma to take her to Lucille Ball's house in Beverly Hills, although she had no cousin's, daughter-in-law's, nephew's, aunt's son to claim relationship to Lucy, she was—as she told them—Lucy's greatest fan.

So they pull up in front of Lucy's white house on the corner of Roxbury and Lexington, smack in the middle of Beverly Hills, and Em and Craig assume their regular positions, ducking as far down in the car seats as they possibly could. Once again, Gayle got out of the car and rang the doorbell.

Now, I know this from my goings over to Lucy's house with Patty. Although probably the biggest star at the time, Lucy had none of that fancy security stuff. When the doorbell rang, either the maid or Lucy herself answered the door (Lucy had this very nice demure Japanese couple who worked for her for many years). As luck would have it, this time the maid opened the door. Gayle said, quite abruptly, I have heard, "I wanna see Lucy." And the maid replied, "Oh no, can't. Ms. Ball very busy right now!" and was about to close the door when Gayle put her foot— the one with the broken heel—in between the door and the door jamb. "But I'm her biggest fan!" Gayle protested.

Just at that moment a little white poodle ran out of the house and started taking off up the block. That poodle was Lucille's pride and joy. The maid screamed something in Japanese, and her husband came running out, and they both ran after the dog. Then Lucy came out and started chasing the dog, too. And well, yeah, you guessed it...Gayle started chasing Lucy.

Well, they were all going crazy trying to get the dog, and Gayle was huffing and puffing behind Lucy trying to get her to autograph something. Finally one of them caught the dog, and Lucy suddenly realized that Gayle was there. Not exactly known for her tact, Lucy turned around to the maid and said, "Who is this fat woman, and why is she in my yard?" The maid explained in her broken English that Gayle was the one who let the dog out, and Gayle kept interrupting her by saying, "Oh, but Miss Ball, I'm your biggest fan." Lucy looked her up and down, and said something like, "Biggest? Yes, indeed!" before slamming the door in her face!

So off they went to see the footprints in Mann's (Grauman's) Chinese Theatre. And while Gayle didn't steal John Wayne's footprints like her idol did in an *I Love Lucy* episode, she did manage to break the heel of her other shoe when she got it stuck in Trigger's footprints.

Manson Memory

Sure enough, the most terrifying moment of my life, also had to do with the Manson Family. It was about thirty years ago, long before I knew Jo. We were living in the San Fernando Valley, not too far away from the Spahn Movie Ranch. The Spahn Ranch was an old abandoned Western studio in the North West Hills of the Valley at 12000 Santa Susanna Pass. It was there where Charles Manson had set up residency and was living at the time of the Tate - LaBianca murders horror with his "clan." The murderers were arrested from there on a hot August day in 1969. Those hills and rocks held a lot of secrets, and scary, unthinkable horrors.

But wait, more to come on that...

On this particular fall afternoon, Jill, her daughter Jeri, Emma, and I set out on an adventure. Emma and I had always been especially fascinated with infamous homicide sites such as the open field that Elizabeth Short (the Black Dahlia) had been found lying sliced in half in January of 1947, and the eerie carport alley behind the apartment building just off Sunset Boulevard where Lionel Ray Williams, in an attempted robbery, stabbed Sal Mineo to death in February 1976. We had found the Auto Upholstery shop where Angelo Buono and Kenneth Bianchi (the Hillside Stranglers) had resided in L.A., and where David Berkowitz (the Son of Sam) had lived, terrorized, and killed in New York City. In Massachusetts, we were familiar with the whereabouts of Albert DeSalvo (the Boston Strangler), and of course Lizzie Borden in St. Raymond's Cemetery in the Bronx. As a matter of fact, it's right near where my father is buried.

I could go on and on with our vast array of knowledge of famed crime scenes, but then you'd never know what was the most terrifying moment of my life.

So anyway, on the day in question, Jill, Jeri, Emma, and I set out to explore the Spahn Ranch. There were rumors that some of Manson's followers (the ones who were not involved in the murders) still lived there. But we thought it was more of a ghost story, a haunted house sort of thing to freak out one's friends from back east.

Well, I pulled into the Spahn Ranch. The Spahn Ranch, by the way, had been named for George Spahn, a very old, nearly blind man who owned the property back when. Spahn, with the help of a wannabe stuntman, Donald "Shorty" Shea, kept the ranch running at the barest minimum level. Then Charles and company moved in, and Shorty had just kind of disappeared. As a matter of fact, the last time there had been any sighting of Shorty had been in the summer of 1969, just about the time of the infamous slaughter.

The decrepit movie studio, in the late 80s, still resembled a hippie commune from the 1960s. Fluorescent-painted boulders were scattered throughout the acres of deserted land with foreboding messages, such as "Charlie is God," "Charlie is Love," "Tex Was

Here"... The most concerning of all was scrawled across a large, almost wall-like stone formation. Written in white day-glow paint was something like (but don't quote me): "Shorty was here, but now he's dead. Follow this arrow and you'll find his head." The chilling declaration was followed by an arrow poking straight down. This was beyond macabre. We were scared shitless. And just when I thought I couldn't be more frightened, a random indescribable man in a large blue pick-up trucked pulled up beside me and yelled, "Get the Hell out of here!"

Suddenly Jill, who was usually mousy, shy, and very quiet, found some courage from deep inside, rolled down the passenger side window where she was sitting, and hollered at the top of her lungs: "FUCK YOU!"

Out came the gun.

I peeled out as fast as I could. But we were high in the mountains and canyons, and the thin one- way streets were really just curvy dirt roads. Apparently, I wasn't moving fast enough for him, because the next thing we knew, the big blue pick-up was ramming the rear of my car, literally trying to push us over the cliff. Jeri and Emma were crouched on the floor of the backseat screaming and crying. I think we all were. Just by sheer luck, no matter how many times he crunched against my car, I was able to maintain control. I told Jill to look for the license plate number and write it down.

Of course, there was no license plate on the truck. You don't try to kill four people with identification on your vehicle.

He chased us as far down as the entrance to the ranch. Once we were off the property, he U- turned around and disappeared back where he came from.

Easily the most terrifying moment of my life.

Oh, and some of the Manson gang did indeed kill Shorty. They admitted that they cut him into nine sections, and scattered him throughout the movie lot.

I've heard that his head has never been found.

It Can Happen to You...

You would never believe how much strength you have until you are forced to use it...That is the true test of "Mice and Men." And I'm not ashamed to tell you that I'm sitting here on my ass, waiting for the KARMA that has already washed over me like a wave to encompass some who have never even known what it feels like to be wet. I'll wait. I'll wait forever. That's the kind of person I am.

I am a childless mother. Due to circumstances like dysfunction, codependency, illness, drugs, and a whole lot of other 12-step words I can toss around, thanks to Wally. Oh, and also a barren uterus. Mustn't forget that little problem.

But I've been raising kids in lieu of their parents going as far back as Emma (because of his mother's brain tumor when he was 13 years old). So many of you out there (of course, not Emma—I think he's my mother now) but so many of you grew up, and then what? Forgot me? Really stupid move on your part. I am a single woman, without relatives. Not buying love, anymore, so that's not the point I'm trying to make. But you, your kids, your kids' kids could have had a really good life. And I, of all people, know that that "blood is thicker than water" shit is ridiculous.

My greatest loves, my greatest joys, and I did not share one ounce of blood. All you as little kids who grew up calling me "Mama," well, you should have seen it through. It is possible to love the "Mama" who does not share your DNA, or perhaps the grandmother who does, more than genes mixing and a night of fucking can produce. And if you are reading this, and it applies.... Don't take a lifetime to realize it.

I am trying to lead up to a very difficult scenario...

In the late 1970s, Kansas City was haunted by a disgusting pervert. They dubbed him "the Babysitter Rapist." Why anyone randomly would hire an unknown person to stay alone with their children is beyond me, but he lasted there for quite a few years.

But by the early 80s, when the Kansas City police were slowly making some headway figuring out who this nut job was, the Babysitter Rapist decided to form a whole new persona. He

changed his operandi, changed his location, changed his name...
He was now "The Lost Dog Killer" of Los Angeles. No, he did not
kill lost dogs. He used the phrase, "My puppy is lost, please can
you get in the car and help me find it?" as a lure to get little girls in
his van with him. He raped the little girls, and sometimes unbelievably, he killed them. There were six in L.A. in total, I believe—
three he murdered, three he let go. My little girl was Victim #3.
She was one of the lucky ones. Sounds strange...to be lucky to be
kidnapped and raped at 9 years old.

You always think: "It could never happen to me!" *BUT IT CAN,
AND IT DOES!*

I am not going to tell you the details of that horrible night. That
only sensationalizes it. What the child endured. How I went to jail,
while the LAPD sorted things out. How my little girl went to the
hospital. How the minute they released me, I went straight to the
airport to the safety of my Grandmother's, 3,000 miles away. How
Wally and Patty had once again abandoned me in my greatest time
of need. How I had the girls' father fly out from New York, because
I was too chicken shit to wait a day to go to court and get the girls
back (my other was 11 at the time).

How it took us almost 30 years to heal the wounds. Now the
girls are doing great, married, and between them, are the mothers of four boys, and pretty fantastic mothers at that. Although I
know I had nothing to do with it, I am so proud of both of them!
I never tire of referring to them as "my beautiful girls..." (and their
beautiful boys!).

And most important, this is the closest you will ever get to
hearing me admit regret or remorse for anything that has ever
happened at any time in my life.

Bite Your Tongue

There are very few foods that sicken me to look at. Wait—I'm
lying already.

There are quite a few foods that make me nauseous just to see.
Runny eggs, melted cheese, and strings of cheese stretching (like

on pizza), spilled milk, those Filipino fish heads and eyeballs that Patty's nurses did so love to eat, tripe, anything with a lot of holes in it. But I would have to say that the very worst food that I've ever had to look at in my life, much less pretend to eat, had to be tongue! That's right, people used to eat cow's tongues. It was a delicacy in Poland called Ożór Wołowy. And as luck would have it, my father's mother was Polish.

I only met my father's mother a handful of times in my life. She was a strict, religious woman, I've heard. Had five boys (one died in infancy) and one daughter. Two things stand out in my mind about her. The first was that in 1919, she forgot to put diapers on her youngest boy, and after he peed all over the kitchen floor, and she slipped in it, she had to get her knee cap removed, so one leg always shot straight out in front of her. The second story was that when her husband, who was a bridge builder, either fell or jumped off the Brooklyn Bridge in 1933, the first thing she did was grab the youngest boy (the pee-er) and run downtown to make sure his life insurance was paid. Then when she had confirmation that it was, she identified his body.

I rarely saw her, because Bio was Jewish, and she hated that. So it was crazy when, in the early 70s, Bio was already living with her boyfriend (brother of the first husband, soon to become the third), my father was living somewhere in Brooklyn, or the Bronx, and I was living alone in what was once our apartment (at age fifteen, as you know), and my father came to Bio with this bizarre proposition—his mother was finally ready to bury the hatchet (come to think of it, if Lizzie had buried the hatchet, she might have saved herself an awful lot of trouble). Of course, he never told his mother the circumstances of our living conditions and lives. She would have been appalled, and rightly so!

Whatever he said, begged, or promised Bio, must have worked, because she agreed to have his Polish mother and one of his brothers over for Easter, and we were to pretend that we were a normal, happy family. The bribe for me must have been big, too. I don't remember right now, but it must have been money. So it wouldn't be awkward, I also had some friends come over, and Grandma (Bio's Mother) came too.

My father asked Bio to cook something traditional: Ożór Wolowy, a traditional Polish Easter dish. And once again, surprisingly she agreed willingly. I didn't know that Ożór Wolowy was cow's tongue, and there was nothing Jane liked better than boiling a tongue (never ever for me, but I guess for my father, and her boyfriend downstairs) because she was really into it!

Easter morning when I walked into the kitchen and saw what really looked like a real huge tongue, cut out of a mouth, sitting in a big pot, I almost dropped dead. Then to make it even more disgusting, Jane had sliced through a few layers of the tongue skin and had inserted peppercorns in-between the layers. Nearly 45 years later, just the memory of it makes me want to vomit.

Eventually everyone showed up. The Polish Grandmother greeted me with the usual salutation she gave whenever she saw me: "Yuck, your skin!" (Bad acne.)

Bio brought out that tongue, and I don't know if it looked better, worse, or the same, as it did before it was cooked. Just so very awful. We all sat down at the table. The Polish Grandmother said something in her native language, and the tongue was served.

Thank God for Puppy. Puppy was my slightly overweight, would eat anything, Beagle mix (she once ate a pair of my father's socks). She was right under the table, and I was shoveling that tongue right into her mouth, just as fast as she could swallow it. Unfortunately, I wasn't the only one who had that brilliant idea. Jane, seeing how quickly the tongue was disappearing kept heaping more and more on everyone's plates.

Eventually we started hearing gurgling, farting, and burping noises, too loud to ignore, coming from under the table. Apparently, all nine of us, excluding the Polish Grandmother and Bio (and I'm not 100% sure about the Polish Grandmother) had given the dog their tongue. The poor thing was nearly catatonic underneath that table.

Andy had to give her a sip of Hungarian bicarbonate beer to get her up and going again. Puppy that was, not the Polish Grandmother, who would have probably liked some, too, being that all five of her living children were alcoholics (of course, another show). But anyway, we managed to pull it off, and although my father's mother somehow outlived five of her six children (all but the daughter), she was never the wiser about us and our convoluted relationships.

And the grand finale of this story was that years later, Bio entered her tongue recipe in some recipe contest in Florida, where she then lived, and won 3rd place. She won a year's supply of apple sauce, or Rice-a-Roni, something stupid like that. But when she opened the first jar or box, she found a nice big dead roach floating right on top.

And that was the end of the tongue fiasco!

Driving Mrs. Airfart

Well, as you know, in the late 70s and early 80s, Em and I would sometimes make extended, months-long trips back to New York and stay with my Grandmother in her apartment on West 90th Street and Broadway. Now, Grandma made it quite easy for us. We never had to pay rent, or for food, or really anything. Grandma even paid the charges to get back my car when it got towed for having too many unpaid parking tickets—TWICE (another story, another day).

But there was one thing that Grandma absolutely refused to finance—my weekend antique excursions (yes, even back then). So I had to figure out some way to make money. Slacker that I am, unless I love the job, I needed to find a way to make shopping money every week with the least amount of effort I could.

So I got a job—"DRIVING MRS AIRFART." Blossom Airfart was a kindergarten teacher in the New York School System. She was in her 60s, and like most of the other characters in the play we call *My Life*, Mrs. Airfart was morbidly obese. It was obvious that the New York Board of Education was trying desperately to get her to retire. They kept sending her to schools in the worst areas of Brooklyn and The Bronx. This particular year, she was in Harlem.

The deal went like this: I got paid $100 a week to drop off and pick up Mrs. Airfart at school. And the weeks that she went to her foot doctor, Dr. Ziegfield (not kidding) in the Empire State Building. I got $150. It was not so much fun in the cold weather getting up at 5 AM to get Mrs. Airfart. She didn't have to be at school until 8, but it took her an excruciatingly long time to walk to the car, and then to get out of the car in Harlem. She was so heavy that one morning, as she was shuffling along through the snow, I got out to help her and left the car idling in neutral. Mrs. Airfart leaned on the car with all her weight and the car went rolling driverlessly down a hill before finally crashing into a snow embankment. I was damn lucky she didn't hurt anybody. This was Manhattan, after all.

Now, Mrs. Airfart had a husband. His name was RRRRRRRR-RRRRRRRRRRRRRRRRRRRichard. I only know Richard existed because I had the unfortunate luck of getting stuck on the phone with him at few times. He had a really bad stuttering problem, and it took him one half hour to get out one sentence. Mrs., Airfart must have been afraid of Richard, because every time she burst her girdle (and it happened quite often), she would not want to go to school, and she would not want to go home to Richard, so I would wind up taking her back to Grandma's apartment and poor Grandma would have to entertain (and feed) Mrs. Airfart for seven hours, until she could go home and pretend she had been at school all day. I still feel a bit guilty when I remember the look on Grandma's face when I would come in with Mrs. Airfart toddling behind me. If looks could kill, I probably would not have made it past 1983.

Skipping over when she fell face first on Broadway and it took a bunch of men to pull her up (much like Gayle, and the hole), the funniest Blossom Airfart story was when she took the kindergarten class on a field trip to the Brooklyn Botanical Gardens. Emma and I went along as "class mothers." We were three hours late getting there because they could not get Mrs. Airfart to lift her leg high enough to get on the bus. The driver got a couple of wooden milk crates, but Mrs. Airfart stepped right through those. I don't remember how they finally got her onboard, but by the time we got there, it was Mrs. Airfart's lunch hour. Mrs. Airfart sat down on one of the benches and began to eat her extremely large lunch, completely oblivious to the little girl who got hit in the head by a flying swing, or the two little boys who jumped into a fountain to see the lily pads up close. Em and I ran around like crazy trying to contain those kids. Mrs. Airfart—She ate.

When lunch was over, it was time to go back to Harlem, to the school. We saw nothing, the children saw nothing, at the Botanical Gardens. What a waste of a day, and a lot of allergy medicine. This time around, the bus driver was pissed. Not because it took so long to get Mrs. Airfart onto the bus, but because it took so long for her to get to the bus. The school bus company wound up charging Mrs. Airfart for overtime, and there were many, many hysterical parents waiting for their kids (this was before cell phones).

"Driving Mrs. Airfart" came to an abrupt end, when I went to drive her to Dr. Ziegfield, her foot doctor in the Empire State Building, with my then-best friend's four-year-old son in the car. Not only was this before cell phones, but it was also before seat belt laws. So my then-best friend's son was jumping up and down on the back seat sing-songing: "Mrs. Airfart-Fart-Fart-Fart" to the tune of "The Bunny Hop." I tried so hard to suppress it, but I couldn't. And after that, I was too embarrassed to go back to the Empire State Building to pick her up from Dr. Ziegfield. So I just left her there. My own "Ziegfield Follies."

And we never saw Blossom Airfart again.

But we'll always have our memories... Misty water-colored memories of Mrs. Airfart and Emma hand-in-hand ("David, take my hand!") going to the 1900 doll hospital on Lexington to get her babies fixed, memories of Mrs. Airfart insisting that she had to teach 30 Rhythm & Blues, Soul music-loving kids how to sing "In The Good Old Summertime..."

The 1994 Earthquake

I have to admit I am relieved that Emma is coming home from New York today. It's a bit daunting to think what I would do if we had a major earthquake, and I was all alone here with a blind dog, and Nana. And since I'm not talking to Ethel (who must be quite pissed that I've managed to recover from my back surgery without her costly help) I would probably fill up the tank and start heading East.

The last earthquake—January 17, 1994—I never felt anything like that in my life. Jill, Emma, and I lived together (no matter what anybody says, three is not a good number) and we grabbed our assorted animals and ran for my car the minute the ground stopped moving. I forgot my shoes, and Jill forgot the pills that would ultimately kill her in years to come. So I went back up, by myself, in the dark. How many people reading this know what the word "aftershock" means? I didn't...until that night.

We drove down to Patty's first. I remember it looked like the whole Valley was on fire. Buildings, strong, mighty buildings that were once hospitals and shopping malls were reduced to rubble. Patty's house survived, but all those years of Wally's food hoarding took a terrible toll on the Weschler's home. I remember walking ankle deep through broken and scattered bottles of ketchup and mustard. Everything in the music room had crashed down on top of their beautiful piano. When one of those chain stores like Target was going out of business a few years earlier, Wally and I talked them into selling us their record department—not the records, but the fixtures, the shelves that held the records, and sheet music (that I eventually came to love and collect).

Somehow that night we wound up in a motel room with the Feldmans...as in Corey and family. They were our next-door neighbors. Sheila, Corey's teaching mother (hey, he wrote a book about it, quite good and quite true), anyway Sheila had Corey and an older daughter named Mindy, who was a regular on the second *Mickey Mouse Club*. Once Sheila learned how to take little kids and turn them into child stars which brought her mega-bucks...the Coogan Law was pretty much overlooked in that family. She went on to have more kids. "More kids meant more money," she told me...only it didn't quite work out that way. The next child, a boy who had the misfortune of looking exactly like Corey. I say misfortune, because he could not get work. Nobody wanted Eden, or a Corey Feldman lookalike, when the same woman could produce the real thing. The fourth one, another boy, also fell short of Sheila's expectations. Although Devin looked nothing like Corey, he was so shy Sheila just couldn't get that "Umph" out of him...So one more try. The fifth, a girl, Brittanie. What that poor little girl endured. As you can tell by see any of Corey's movies. Sheila just loved that hair bleaching bottle. Every other week, she was touching up everyone's roots, and as she did with Mindy, kept Brittanie forever in curlers. Brittanie was going to be the Shirley Temple of the 90s. I believe she is now a stripper in Las Vegas. Oh, the fault in our stars...and their mothers!

Why am I telling you all this about the Feldmans?... Oh, I know—to point out how many of them, and the three of us were in that single motel room. With our dogs, and the Feldman dogs as well...Patty and Wally were in that motel, too. After I discovered how easy it was to sneak the dogs in, they decided to get a room of their own. I don't know why I didn't leave the super- crowded Feldman room and go stay with them. I surmise Jill was pulling some passive- aggressive shit on me, about "abandoning her and Emma" to the Feldmans. Emergencies were Jill's favorite times to do something crazy, or overdose. I didn't mention Jill on my suicide show Monday. I felt she had no place in it. "THE PAM SHOW" is about surviving, and she was no survivor. But anyway, all of us packed in that one room must have been what the tenements in old New York were like at the turn of the century. Well, without the ground shaking and rumbling every few minutes.

So I'm warning you right now....If the earth starts moving, and you live east of here, pull out the guest bed, because I'm a-coming. And I really don't eat much...if I could only have one food to eat for the rest of my life? That's easy. PEZ. Cherry flavor PEZ. No question about it (to quote Corey in *Stand by Me*). He got it pretty much right. But it's those collectible PEZ characters from the 1950s and 60s in my storage unit that make the flavor bearable. And that is the story of the 1994 earthquake, or more adequately in my case, called "Cram By Me."

The Conversation

CONVERSATION WITH MY MOTHER WHO HAS CANCER:

ME: Since you are refusing treatment, aren't you concerned that the cancer might be spreading?

JANE: I couldn't care less. I feel fine. (Translation: why think about tomorrow?)

ME: Do you want me to come down and see you?

JANE: AHHHH, they don't allow dogs down here. (Translation: You are the last person I want to see!)

ME: Glad you are so strong. (Translation: This woman was born without any emotions!)

ANDREW J. WOHL ASKS: Why can't you come to terms with Jane, and her death?

You really want me to answer that here? Okay, here goes: putting aside the fact that I was the first person in the history of the Florida Med Center who wasn't allowed to call to check on a dying family member. Putting aside that while my last words to her were "I love you" and her response was to hang up on me, even giving credence to all the Facebook people who posted that it was her body, her choice when she opted to die rather than get chemo, or a mastectomy...The fact is that it was the cap-off to a life spent doing whatever she thought would please her man of the time, at the expense of others, most especially me. Jane did not get chemo or a mastectomy simply because she did not want to have a scar, or lose her hair, which might make her less appealing to her man. The same mentality that caused her to only talk to me during 7-8 o'clock on Tuesday nights only for 21 years, when she was married to her first husband's brother. He didn't like me, so he made that Tues night only rule. Remember if I called any other time, she hung up on me? Remember how she lied to all the boyfriends about my profession, because she was ashamed of what I did? I've already gone on way too long for a Facebook page. But believe me I've got 55 years of reasons!

Soul Keepers

I don't know exactly how to begin this piece. I have always sub-scribed to the belief that there is no such thing as guilt. No "I should haves," no "If onlys" allowed to clutter up my brain. I don't want this to be interpreted to sound as if I don't have remorse for any hurt or pain which my actions may have somehow resulted in. I just believe that we (whomever "we" are) did the best we could, at the time we did it, with the knowledge, and abilities we had then.

People often hear this and ask me, "But wait—Jill killed herself, in your house, right under your nose. There must have been some signs"—and looking back, there were—"Don't you regret that you hadn't seen them, and stopped her?"

Well—of course I would have wanted it to have turned out dif-ferently. Of course it would have been wonderful, had I been able to recognize the clues that are so easy to spot in retrospect. But the reality is that I had no experience or training in suicide. How was I to know what was going on? How was I supposed to be able to dissect every word, decipher every phrase she uttered in her last days, and distinguish what or which had any alternative meaning?

My late friend Scott's funeral was on live news feed. What a world we live in, where we can sit in Cali or London, or Moscow, and watch a funeral in Ohio in real time. At one point when Scott's two sisters were speaking, his oldest sister recalled a long phone conversation she had with him, just hours before he passed. She made a reference to the fact that he complained about "This damn acid reflux hurts so much." Obviously it wasn't acid reflux. As was the case with my ex-husband, who also told himself it was indi-gestion. Both of these men suffered massive "widow maker" heart attacks. Andrew survived. Scott wasn't so lucky. I've since asked Andrew if there was any way, anything anybody could have said to make him consider that maybe it was something more serious. He told me there was not. Scott was in total denial. Apparently this is a common reaction which many people have when they suffer heart attacks, especially when they are young (my ex was 53). So if any of Scott's family or friends are reading this, please know—

there was nothing you could have done to change the outcome. Everyone did the best they could based on the knowledge they had at the time. None of you are cardiologists or, as far as I know, even remotely in the medical profession.

We can look at thousands of situations. Some are minor, some are life-changing, or even life- threatening. Do I hate that I allowed my Lorna to play video games in a 7-11, on the day she was kidnapped and raped? Well, of course. Every moment since February 25, 1982, I wish it had not happened. But I am not clairvoyant. If I had any inkling that a nine-year-old would get kidnapped off a busy street at 3:30 in the afternoon, certainly my choices as her guardian would have been different. I think all of us would agree. If we had a crystal ball to see into the future, many, many of our behaviors would have been tailored more accordingly to the final result.

I used to throw eggs at Bio. Seriously. My mother-in-law could never understand why someone who detested "chicken's periods" as much as I did (still do) bought so many cartons of eggs. I was 14/15 years old (had I not been smart and skipped a grade, I would have still been in Junior High School). I was left to live alone in an empty apartment. My words didn't penetrate. Neither did reason, or the law. So I threw eggs at her, and inside I was screaming: "Don't leave me! I'm scared to be alone! Don't make me stay all by myself. I am so frightened!"

Do I feel guilty about this, almost fifty years later?

HELL NO.

And I never ever did. I reacted as well as I could, at the time, with what I knew—then. And with a shitty role model like her, it could have been a hell of a lot worse. When words didn't work, I thought that eggs would. Normal 14-year-olds don't throw eggs at their parents. But normal parents don't abandon their 14-year-old children to go live with their former brothers-in-law. So I make no apologies.

However I do think that guilt, or "I should haves," can be unwittingly used to procrastinate growth and change. As long as one stays stuck in the mistakes (and I use the word "MISTAKES" with strong trepidation—how can it be wrong if you did not know any better?) or mismanagement of the past, there is no reason to try to do, or see, anything differently.

This is not to be used as an excuse to hurt people. We learn that is wrong as babies, the very first time we bite another child in frustration. And pretty much all children do at some point. Because word development is slower than the growth of baby teeth, we are made aware that to hurt another person is not acceptable behavior under any circumstances at a very early age.

I am speaking primarily about the instances in our lives that perhaps would have had a different outcome if we had reacted differently, If we had known there was another way. I am also referring to the things that the collective "WE" never had the chance to say, or do.

I know I've told you this story before, but indulge me. When Bio was dying, she was in hospice in a hospital in Florida. Her death was imminent. I called the hospice to see how she was doing. They told me her condition. Then they patched my call into her room. She was fully coherent, and screamed at me like I hadn't heard since my pre-Andrews Sisters days. She was furious that I dared to talk to "her" nurses. Her cancer was her business, not mine, and on and on and on. As I tried, to no avail, to explain to her that I was calling like any other relative of a patient, out of concern, she just kept yelling. Finally I said: "Okay. Die knowing that I did love you!" Her response was to keep berating me a bit more. Bio's very last words to me were, "Yeah, right!" before she slammed the phone down. I never spoke to her again.

The next night, I woke up, haunted by that conversation. So once again I called the hospice nurse's station to check on her. After the nurse gave me the update, she said: "I'll be sure to tell her you called. She'll be so pleased that you cared!" I begged this nurse NOT to tell Bio that I telephoned. I gave a brief explanation, trying my hardest to give somewhat of a look into Bio's psyche. There was a long pause after I finished. What do they call it—a pregnant pause? And finally, very quietly, she said, "I've been doing this job for forty some-odd years, and I have never before heard of a time when a patient didn't want to know that someone cared, and was concerned about them." Well... welcome to my world, lady!

Bio died the following day. I had her buried on my 58th Birthday, in a plot next to her father, which was originally bought for my grandmother. They put her in the ground at exactly 1:03 in the afternoon. I arranged it that way. This was the time, stated on my birth certificate, when I was born. 58 years before, just three miles from there.

My poor Grandmother lies alone in a Jewish cemetery in Fort Lauderdale, Florida. Her soul, though, lives on in me. Right beside Patty, and Pie Boy, and Sandra and Stewart, and all the others who went ahead. And that must bring comfort, and the fortitude to go out and live the best life you possibly can. Because, you see, you are the soul keeper for all the ones you loved, but who no longer have the physical means to live life for themselves.

It's a big responsibility. But I know you can handle it. Love you all.

Emma vs. Social Security

OK, I now officially have the funniest story of my life to share with you. I am sorry but it is not Andrews Sisters related.

I can't help but wonder how much I have to do with this chaotic mess.

You've all met my sister Emma. Long before he was my sister Emma, he was my sister LaVerne. When I do my video shows, I try to have him on twice a week, because he is hilarious. This is hilarious.

Emma has a job, spraying high-end cologne (men's cologne). He is one of those annoying people who sprays you in the department stores, and after you walk by asks: "Would you like to buy some....(whatever it is called)?

Anyway, last Friday was pay day, and Emma went to the office to pick up his check. But there was no check in the envelope, just a note that said that he needed to contact Social Security immediately. There seemed to be some pressing matter. So Em spent the whole weekend freaking out, wondering what could be wrong. It was impossible for him to get through Monday, so he called, and called, and called until he could finally get someone to help him.

Oh, they helped him alright... As soon as he gave his SSI number, the clerk said, "How may I help you, MISS Altieri?"

Miss Altieri? Okay, it's one thing to call him my sister, or pretend to be the Andrews Sisters singing for the masses in some

155

cemetery (the only place where they can't boo me out, and throw rotten fruit at me). It's even not so terrible when he calls up Streisand's brother Shelly, or Mel Torme, and impersonates Barbra... But this was Social Security. This was serious business.

Oh yes, SSI has him listed as a female!! I swear I had nothing to do with it!

So now Emma must appear at Social Security with three pieces of picture ID, his birth certificate, and—oh yes—a letter from his doctor certifying that he is male. If he indeed is. I don't know. I've never seen any proof, except he never goes to the gynecologist, and he won't get a yearly mammo. But hey, neither will some of my women friends. So there goes that theory.

I would give anything to go to Social Security with him and watch this whole thing unfold, but he's never going to take me along. I would probably fuck it up by saying, "And now...Here's my sister, Emma!"

As things go along, I'll keep you updated!

As you know tomorrow (Thursday) I am having the last of my suck out the platelets and jab them back into my spine procedures. As you also may remember, the last two times I was a bit freaked out about being alone here after the surgery, and paid Nurse Rat-Shit (Ethel) a shitload of money to stay here with me. But this morning when I woke up, as I do every morning...with one little blind girl snuggled pressed up on top of my legs, her head resting on the back of my knees, and the other little girl curled up against my chest, head on my shoulder, arms around my neck. I realized that I was the luckiest person alive.

And you don't have to pay them to love you, or take care of you. Your love is enough, and they are so grateful for it.

Now although we will discuss it tomorrow...Does anyone know if I can bring a squirrel into the house? He sits and waits for me outside my door every morning, and gets so excited when he sees me, and we've already passed the taking food out of my hand stage. Squirry would make such a nice addition to the family!

On Target

Now, I have nothing against obese people, IF they are obese because of any other means besides overindulgence. There are many reasons a person can have extra poundage—illnesses, medicines one takes, a bad thyroid, etc....When I tell a Gayle or Mrs. Airfart story, or something like that, I mention their weight because more often than not, it is a factor in the situation, and the fact that they are so overweight just adds to the hilarity of the story.

So yesterday, I was in Target buying light bulbs and things to clean the apartment. Although no sloppy presidential wives have been here for a while, I've been away for a week, and Andy arrives today from his drive down from Seattle. Yes folks, if not for my bad back, I could have been stuck in the car with him, and his stomach problems from the bad seafood and cranberry sandwich he ate, for three days! I don't even want to think about it! Bad enough he's coming here with that...but I left some things in the car from Oregon, and Washington, that were too big to take on the plane. So I need to go get them.

Anyway, I went to Target. And I'm walking around Target, minding my own business, when an announcement comes over the loudspeaker: "Will the owner of a blue Honda CRV with New York license plates please report to the security counter?" I realized that it was me they wanted, and as I rushed up to security, imaging that someone hit my car, or broke into it, and stole my precious fruit strip from earlier in the day, I actually did find something cool—a hand-painted souvenir present plate from the late 1800s from Bavaria.

I knew that whatever it was, for a change I hadn't hit anything, so it couldn't be my fault. You are not going to believe what it was that they wanted me for. Although I had parked a normal and legal distance from the car next to me, the owner of that car was (how do I say this as nicely as possible?) a very large and portly woman who could not get into her car unless I moved mine out of my parking space. I have never heard anything like this in my life. Imagine being so big that you have to go back inside the store to have the person in the parking spot next to you paged to move their car, so you can get into yours? I know a certain someone who would have been thrilled by this, but it wasn't me! It took everything I had in me, every last ounce of control. not to go off on this enormous woman.

See, when other people become my problem, then I feel I have a right to be annoyed at their lack of self-control (which by the items in her bags made me pretty sure what was the cause of her obesity). I mean, at what point is enough...enough? 200 lbs.? 500 lbs.? I'll admit to once tipping the scales at 160, but not since 1988. So my question of the day, and though this does in some way include my obsessive antique shopping, is when does enough become enough, or too much? I only partly include my compulsive antique shopping in this question because although admittedly excessive, it is contained in storage units, and the only person affected by it is me— and my wallet, when it's time to pay for those units every year.

Eat away, smoke away, drink away, etc... It's your life... But when the results of your actions inconvenience me, or any other third party, then do we have the right to say something? Of course, it was not the fat lady's fault that I lost my grocery cart, and had to start all over again picking out the stuff I needed. But the whole thing was completely avoidable. And I learned this much. I will never again move my car, nor inconvenience myself because of someone else's out- of-control eating habits (or any other behaviors done in excess.) I should have just said "NO!" And I would be lying if I didn't tell you that I am a bit pissed off at myself that I complied so readily.

You know, when I lived in New York last year, Gayle wanted me to take her to the old New York World's Fair grounds. It was the 50th anniversary of the original fair, which we had gone to together in 1964/65. I agreed that it would be amazing to walk the same grounds we did half a century ago...until I found out that Gayle doesn't walk anymore. All the years of obesity took its toll on her bones, and organs, and she is now wheelchair bound. Solely, I stress, because of a lifetime of poor eating habits, and six Big Macs at a time! Once I found out that she expected me to push her over those steep hills and dips in Flushing Meadows Park (the old fairgrounds) there was not a chance in hell.

So that's my question...When is enough enough? When is it okay to say "No Way?" It's your problem, not mine.

The Party Discount

A few months ago, my friend Kim talked me into taking a two-hour Apple (Computer) Class with her. And upon getting in the room, I was horrified to discover that I was even more computer illiterate than the oldest and dumbest person in there. But rather than admit my stupidity, I faked a Hungarian accent (courtesy of my late mother-in-law) and feigned the language barrier as my reason not to participate. "I no can speak the English. I no can under- strand vat you say?"

So, at the antique store, as predicted, the owner started with that Republican/Democrat discount business. I looked him straight in the eye, and reverted right back to my character from the Apple Class. "Vat? I no can under strand English" (yes, I know there is an extra "R" in "understand," which doesn't belong there any more than a "V" belongs in the word "what," but that's how the accent works).

So the owner left me alone, and I scrutinized that joint from top to bottom, from side to side. And when I was sure there was nothing I wanted, or would ever want from there, I walked up to the counter, and in my best Queens English (no, I don't mean The Queen's English, I mean the borough of Queens, like from Jamaica—no, not the country Jamaica, the town of Jamaica or the town of Flushing; yeah, Flushing as in what you do to the toilet. Never mind).

In my best New York English, I ripped that owner a new asshole: "How dare you push your politics on customers just coming in here to shop, and make the price of their purchase contingent on what party they are affiliated with? There must be some illegality in that!" And then I ended with a nice big "FUCK YOU!"

Which, by the way, whether spelled with letters or symbols, whether spoken by black or white people, whether used as a noun or a verb, still means the same thing!

Mini Car, Major Problems...

What I am about to tell you is 100% true. Nobody, not even the best sci-fi writer in history could come up with something as bizarre and crazy. As you know—earlier in the week my Mini Cooper blew up. Now, like pretty much everyone in America, I have AAA Roadside Service, which allows you four tows a year. My start day every year is March 8th. My end date is March 7th. My current card says "Loyal Member for 31 Years." Well, this "Loyal Member" hasn't used them in what seems like forever. However, when the Mini Cooper exploded, and after the fire was out, I had to call them to tow it somewhere. They took forever to get there, but eventually did with a flat bed, and towed it to my mechanic.

So I have been driving around in this old second car we keep for emergencies, while trying to decide my next move. Yesterday I took it to Petco to try on dresses with Nana. We came out with her summer wardrobe—only to discover that the battery in this car was dead. Once again I called AAA. They took forever to get there, but eventually did, and jumped the battery, and after several hours—we did get home.

This morning I made a decision. I knew that the dealership where I originally bought the Mini Cooper was owned by fair and decent people who would give me a good trade back, even if they lost money. This past year they went above and beyond to help me with the issues that cropped up, none of which were their fault but rather side effects of the Mini. All you have to do is Google it, or go on a forum, and they are all mentioned—134 things that can and do go wrong with that automobile. Cute car to look at. DON'T EVER BUY ONE!!

I have been a Japanese car girl since 1979 when I taught myself to drive stick shift in Manhattan, in New York City traffic in a 1976 Honda. I saw that my guys had a Nissan, only a couple of years old, with really low mileage available. Black. Not showy and reasonable with the money they would allot me back. I figured I would go down and look at it again, and if I liked it I would buy it.

And so I got back into the older car (which started up right away this time) and proceeded in the direction of the car lot. There

I was on one of the main streets of Temecula... it is at this point where I feel the overwhelming urge to sing the theme from *Arthur*, changing the lyrics ever so slightly to "When you get caught between the moon and 15 freeway"... because indeed I was, when the car died. Just stopped running in the lane leading onto the 15 Freeway North. After some very nice random guys pushed me out of the line of rush hour traffic and into the small island in the middle of this very busy street, I stared at my cell in disbelief. Was I really going to have to call AAA for the third time in almost as many days? Yes. Yes, I was. And I was told it would take forever, but eventually they would get there.

And as I sat, it occurred to me that I would not make it to the dealership, which was not very far, because AAA insisted that I stay with the car until they arrived. Then I got this outrageous idea. I called my main man at the car place and told him what had happened. I asked him if he could drive the Nissan which I liked to me, over to where I sat stranded, so I could take another look. I couldn't even hear his answer because it was crazy busy and loud. Now, in addition to the regular traffic, there was an ambulance and fire engines trying to get through the jam with sirens blasting.

To my absolute horror, it soon became apparent that the ambulance, fire trucks, the sheriff, and four motorcycle cops were there—FOR ME! I guess from the way I was sitting in the car, slumped over with my head resting on the steering wheel out of sheer disgust and disbelief, some Good Samaritan thought I was dead, and called 911.

Parli Italiano?

Today's "PAM SHOW" is dedicated to all you cynics who doubt my ability to feel sympathy, or empathy, for anything other than an animal. AND to Mr. Pintaro, my high school Italian teacher, who for two years never taught me one word of Italian (although if you saw the grades he gave me, you would think I was Carlo Ponti!).

Let me explain... Admittedly my sympathy, empathy, and compassion is very selective. And I make no apologies for it. Life tossed me around, and this is what it kicked out.

Now, I will fill you in about Mr. Pintaro. He was an old man back then, 45 years ago, so I doubt he is still alive. He was the only Italian teacher in Hillcrest High in the early 70s. My aspirations (until the day I walked through that narrow magic door in Shubert Alley) were to become a French Teacher. I was really good at languages, and took them all as credit fillers to be able to get the units I needed to graduate early. At various times during the 2-1/2 years I went to high school (I finished when I was 16, which was what enabled me to be a part of the magic in Shubert Alley), I had Mr. Pintaro for French or Spanish classes. The one Italian class he taught was the last class of the day, so when Mr. Pintaro saw me enter the room, he took me aside and said, "You are too smart for Elementary Italian. You go to the study room, and learn it on your own!" If you read my school records, I have 100% average in Italian for two straight years. But I never learned a single word. I would cut out early, and with my fake ID, go to Aqueduct, or Belmont (the horse races).

The reason I am giving you all this background info is because it filters into today's "PAM SHOW" (someday we will talk about how I never took a gym class since the 6th grade, but that's another show!).

Yesterday, I was walking into the 99 Cent Store in Reseda and saw a small crowd surrounding two very young children. There were a few store employees and a very bewildered cop on a motorcycle. From the dribs and drabs I could hear, it seemed as if the children, the boy about six, the girl about seven, were left at the 99 Cent Store and they didn't speak English, not one word. You would think that would not be a problem here in Southern California, BUT they didn't speak Spanish, either. They spoke—you guessed it—Italian.

The first thing I noticed was that all the adults who were trying unsuccessfully to talk to the children were speaking to them from high up. That is very intimidating to a small child, and to have any effective response, the adult must kneel down to the child's eye level. I discovered that I seemed to be the only one in the crowd who knew this, so I decided to give it a whirl. Plus, although Mr. Pintaro never taught me any Italian, I knew I was similar to French and Spanish, and the element that I had above the Spanish-speaking members of the mob was that I knew French, too.

So I squatted down, and somehow with this crazy made-up language consisting of French and Spanish words, I was able to find out from the kids that they were left there by their Grandmother. They didn't know where she was, or if she was coming back. By then, the real arsenal of police began coming, and they decided to take the kids out of the public area, where the crowd was growing. At this point, I've got the little girl on my lap, holding the little boy's hand (and trying to figure out how I was gonna raise two children who only spoke Italian at almost 60 years old). I asked the police if I could go with them to the room where they were going to keep the kids until Child Protective Services came for them, since I was the only one who was able to elicit any kind of response from them. They took us to this room in the back of the 99 Cent Store (I wish I could tell you that it was at Prada, or Gucci, but it wasn't...).

A little while later, another cop came in hauling an old lady who was screaming in Italian. From what I could figure out, she went to the bathroom in another store and became separated from her grandchildren. It was as simple as that.

At that point, I left. But I felt pretty damn good about myself, and that old phrase kept repeating in my mind. You know, the one that goes something like, "When am I ever going to need Algebra in my life?" Only I was remembering being 14 or 15, standing in line at the ticket window to bet on a Daily Double at the track, and thinking, "When am I ever gonna need Italian in my life? My time is much better spent playing the ponies!"

Ya never know!

Coronovirus Thoughts

I feel the need to write this because "THE PAM SHOW" does influence people. I don't know how many, or if even matters...This has to start somewhere.

As fellow human beings who must coexistent on this planet, we have a certain responsibility to each other while the Coronavirus is such a prevalent pandemic. Some of us, most of us, could probably get through it without any life-threatening effects, much like any flu that knocks the hell out of us, but we eventually recover and got on. Our core responsibility is to those who cannot—the elderly and those regardless of age with compromised immune systems and underlying medical conditions. Therefore we must take certain extra precautions. Can't be said enough—wash your hands frequently (sing the Happy Birthday song in your head two times while soaping up and rinsing). Use the anti-bacterial wipes in every store you must go into, and again when you leave. Stay out of places where people congregate. I mean, wasn't it stupid that the casinos and bars and hook-up places were open, while Disneyland and other such outdoor venues were closed?

So what I am saying is be sensible and, for now, live as risk-free as possible, if only to protect those who are too fragile to protect themselves. We owe that to the people who came before us, and the weak whose bodies are not strong enough to combat the illness.

But we are doing so much more harm dealing with this in panic mode. Look at past epidemics over the course of history. The frenzied panic and mass hysterias caused so much destruction which led to so many more deaths than perhaps there would have been. The answer lies not in the doomsday apocalyptic fear-provoking reactions but with calm, rational sensibility. I realize that this behavior is increasingly difficult when the news headlines come up with yet another fear-provoking message each time you turn on the TV or your computer.

Back in the day, it was called sensationalizing. As a matter of fact, this is how newspaper headlines were born—just taunt the people with enough information to scare them, or mesmerize them with a big blanketed fearsome foreboding message. Now I suppose it's to get one to stay on CNN or Fox or whatever you watch.

The truth is that you or I would be 100 times more likely to die of a heart attack, or cancer, or in my case, a car accident. So do what is within logic to keep yourself and those around you safe. But please, don't buy into "the world is ending, ten more years of

this catastrophic plague." We will run out of things to eat and water and starve to death. if the C-19 doesn't kill us first.

I believe that we can all get through this, if we don't buy into the
fear. There is no reason to buy out every roll of toilet paper in every
big box store or supermarket, hoard food and hand sanitizers, etc.
Those shelves are so empty, so gluttonously, selfishly empty, it makes
me ashamed to be a part of civilization in this time of crisis in 2020.

Have a great day, and thank you again.

Becoming 63

Today is my 63rd birthday.
I have lived to see the sun rise and set 23,131 times This is
the oldest I have ever been.

Until tomorrow. Then I'll be 63 years and one day. Am I old?

It depends...

According to the Corona Virus guidelines, I am right on the cusp.

According to Social Security I am a citizen of this country of
advanced age. According to the AARP and all the "Over 50" senior
discounts I've been been taking advantage of for the last 13 years:
most definitely.

To someone older to me: "Oh, I wish I was 63 again!"

To someone younger-: "Damn! You old, lady!"

To me who has the same agility and spirit I've had for the last 60
years: Shit, I am not yet even 10. Adulthood looms far ahead, way
in the vast future.

What am I going to be when I grow up?

Age is subjective.

But there is one sad concrete fact that I almost guiltily cannot
get past. As of today, I have lived one year longer than my father.

So I have decided that for him,

For the years I now am experiencing hence forward,

The ones which he never had the luxury of having,

I am going to live to be the best me I can be.

Which kinda means not to sweat the small stuff,
Just live life, find joy and good in the here and now
And not face the world with that dark catastrophic cloud loom-
ing overhead. Not be an ostrich, and hide my head in the sand.
The cloud is really there.
And every once in a while it does rear its ugly head.
But how we react in the interim is the key.
For my father, of course,
And also for my best friend Cassandra (55), for LaVerne (55)
for Scott (59), for Darryl (42), for Damien (26), for Stewart (17)
And too many others to list.
With gratitude I am going to Carpe Diem—
Actually Carpe all the Diems—
For which they never had the chance.

More Coronovirus Thoughts

I get quite a lot of PMs and desperate emails from people who are
lonely, scared, and severely depressed in the wake of the current
situation that we in the world are going through these days. Covid
19, the mass quarantine, the "New Normal"—all unprecedented
and unknown—give credence to this very real fear. "Will it really
truly ever end?" they ask me. "And if it does...then what will happen? And how can we ever come back from this?"

What surprised me the most, though, was the vast age range
of those who are teetering on the edge. It is not often (but for The
Andrews Sisters) that I am asked the same question by a 14- year-
old, as was just inquired of me by someone who is 94.

I'll do my best to give you my perspective, and maybe, just maybe, somebody will be able to see a little sliver of light at the end of
this dark, frightening tunnel.

I never imagined I would be out running around with a mask
on my face at 63. In 1963—maybe? But I hated those Ben Cooper
costumes even then, and worse yet, the suffocating plastic character masks with the one tiny air hole in the mouth. By the time I
walk out of the door these days, it pretty much feels the same sans
the Donald Duck or Woody Woodpecker painted face.

I would sooner have believed the great Nostradamus, or any soothsayer who might have predicted that in the second decade of the 21st Century we would have to shelter in place for reasons such as the threat of nuclear, or biochemical warfare—even invaders from outer space would have made more sense-—before I could fathom that more than two centuries after the smallpox inoculation was rudimentally contrived by a British Doctor named Edward Jenner, we would be hiding from a virus. A pandemic in 2020!

I mean, think about it... the year Jenner came up with his antidote to that catastrophic epidemic was 1796; George Washington was in the process of leaving office, and John Adams had

just been elected the 2nd President of the United States. This Country was just barely 20 years old. I apologize for going off again in the direction of a history lesson. My mind is a cobweb of useless trivia and historical facts, and sometimes I lose myself in it.

In the 1980s AIDS was 100% fatal. The cure rate was 0. Now with the guidance and

knowledge of modern medicine, an HIV Positive person can be completely undetectable, negating the fatality of this insidious disease. So with that kind of progress—seriously—my money would have been on the Martian invasion being the culprit of this pandemonium!

So how do we get through it?

I don't know—but we will. We are here, we are alive today. Let's live for today. I don't mean we should go out and squander everything we have to enjoy the here and now. That is reckless and irresponsible. Besides which, you'll really be screwed if you wake up tomorrow to discover that this was not the personal apocalyptical Doomsday you thought it was.

I guess what I am trying to say in my very discombobulated way is, don't let the fears of tomorrow, or next month, or next year take away the joy of being alive today. Right now. Right as you read this.

In 1960 when I was three years old, I overheard a conversation between my father and my grandmother. They were discussing a tragic accident which had happened in the subway earlier that week. Apparently an "old" lady had missed her step from the platform into the subway car and became trapped. There was not enough time to pull her out, she was lodged in there so tightly, and when the train pulled out she was killed on the spot. That one rare random event planted itself in my brain and tortured me for the next 32 years. I thought, if that could happen to one old lady, it could happen to another, and another... and one of those old ladies could be my beloved Grandma. From that day on, the fear of what could happen, the fear of losing her, became the most prevalent emotion in our relationship. Sad enough to say, it even upstaged love. I was fortunate—my grandmother lived a very long time, until I was 35 years old. But when I think about all those days, and years, that were spent worrying about losing her, when they could have been spent loving her in the time and day and the moment, overshadowed by that constant gnawing like a woodpecker in my head reminding me that someday she would be gone. If eavesdropping on one single foreboding tragedy could do that to me, I am completely devastated by the thoughts and the fears which must be so deeply burned and stained into the minds and psyches of the children today. Imagine—it is unavoidable to deafen oneself even to the slight clips of doom and death which has taken over every form of media: "60,000 people died today of Corona! No sign of lessening! The worst is yet to come!" To be a child, or even an adult, during this insane period of time... It is terrifying. "Is my mom going to catch it and die? Am I? Has my child been exposed to it?" If one doesn't find a way to stop the persistent "What if" scenarios which loom and linger like *The Blob Who Ate Manhattan* or *The Attack of The Killer Tomatoes*, some very serious PTSD can and will go on for a long, long time...

So let's look at this logically. To catch the Coronavirus is not necessarily a death sentence. Repeat that fifty times to yourself if necessary. The majority of the patients without extenuating circumstances come through it and recover. Be vigilant, Follow the rules, and as Mr. Rogers used to say, " Look for the helpers. You will always find people who are helping." If anything good has come out of this pandemic, it is the realization that true heroes are not the ones who fight windmills, or vampires, on the movie screen, or sing songs of romance and patriotism. But rather, the men and women who put themselves in danger every day, stocking the grocery shelves, filling our prescriptions, delivering the essentials which keep the rest of us alive. The nurses and medical personal for whom taking care of the ill or dying is as natural and as vital to them as breathing.

Look—everything comes with an expiration date. Somewhere probably stamped way inside our anal canals is a notation with the details. Nothing (including people) lasts forever. But if you make the useless mistake that I did with my beloved little grandmother, and spent the precious time that we were both here worrying about the day when one of us (most probably her) no longer would be, it is—in a sense—a wasted life.

So the best advice I can give is, when you wake up in the morning, look out your window at the sun and the sky and think not about what could, what possibly might happen, but rather—"It is today, and I am alive, and I am a part of this here and now." Because that is really all we have guaranteed. And don't be afraid to live and love those dearest to you if you are so fortunate as to have them sharing this day, this life, with you.

And if they have gone before you—they are still here with you in a thousand million different ways. They still gaze at the moon at night, only from a different view. And in their honor, draw a deep breath and live this day, the way Dr. Seuss so clearly and boldly advised: "Today you are You, that is truer than true. There is no one alive who is Youer than You."

Nana—can you see me?

Nana—can you see me? Nana—can you hear me? Nana—can you find me in the night? Alright—I guess that's enough of "borrowing" Barbra Streisand's lyrics. Terrific song, though.

Today is my Grandmother's 129th Birthday. She lies by herself in a cemetery in Fort Lauderdale, Florida. The rest of her family and the people she cared about are buried together at some place called Union Fields, on the Brooklyn/Queens border of New York City. It wasn't supposed to be that way. There is a place in Union Fields with her name on it, right next to her husband, the baby sister, and the parents to whom she was so devoted.

Somewhere along the way, I lost control of that decision. She lived so long she, too, lost control of that situation. My only solace is that she sleeps under the sunshine and never beneath the frozen hell of an Upper East Coast winter.

I believe that wherever we go after life here on earth is over, the love we felt on this plain is tangible, and continuing. I believe that all who want to be are reunited in death, even if their remains are housed thousands of miles apart. I believe, or hope anyway, that we have guardian angels who watch over us from that vast beyond.

So—yes—Nana, can you see me? If you can, you know that I beat all the odds. Outsmarted all the predictions, overcame the adversity of my genes (or jeans—either or both). And you can see I made it after all. I persevered despite the absurd circumstances that seemed to haunt me no matter what I did, or where I went. And I survived your daughter. Oh, you know I don't blame you for any of that. You were just as sad and perplexed as I was. Maybe that's why we were so close, bonded by her insanity. Sixty-six years separated us—Grandma—you stumbled through it as a senior, newly widowed suddenly without another soul who experienced the complexity of "our" family secrets. I as a baby. Then a child. I guess being victimized by one who is "supposed" to care about you has no boundaries, no peer group. It's not an exclusive club.

Twenty-nine years ago, I looked at my little Grandmother who, as the clock hit midnight and the date rolled to February 25th, had just turned 100, and asked her how it felt to be 100 years old? She said, "No different than 99!"

And the next day, after completing *The New York Times* Crossword Puzzle, as she did every day since its inception 64 years earlier in 1927, that woman walked unassisted into her hundredth birthday party.

And lived to enjoy two more! Happy Birthday, Nana! How does it feel to be 129?

Post-Christmas, 2019

Well, Christmas has come, and is now almost gone, forever relegated to the invisible pages of that history book entitled "2019" which we will close in just a few days.

But more important, if you are reading this, you have survived!! Another year. Whether it was Aunt Bertha's under-cooked turkey, or Uncle Fred's over-zealous political rant, or Cousin June's dismal pessimistic commentary on the state of the Stock Market and the country in general— whether you were alone with your memories, or with people in situations you absolutely detest, you got through it. Pat yourselves on the back. I am so proud of you.

I am so proud of me, too. I got through it with the help of television, YouTube, and the internet. I don't know about you, but I need background noise, especially at night, as a distraction from the ridiculously obsessive rampant thoughts one tends to have running through their mind in the deep darkness of complete quiet. And I believe (though never a proven fact) that my dogs like the TV on when I am gone. Cartoons to keep Nana occupied, and the sing-song silly sounds that at least my blind Helen K. (Mackie) can hear.

We always find a way to make the best out of anything that life throws at us. Because we are survivors. And I had a great Christmas, thanks to the miracles of You Tube. I watched all those coming-of-age programs that we so loved in the 70s. Not *The Partridge Family* or *The Brady Bunch*, but the ones which took on real issues like *James At 15* and *Family*. And *The After School Specials* that tackled the unmentionables, like anorexia and incest, topics which in hindsight they didn't always get right, but at least they had the guts to try to expose us to it, a first after the tremendous censorship of the 1950s and 60s. Right now, in 2019, I think we are more censored than we were in 1953, when Lucy was not permitted to use the word "pregnant" when she was "expecting" Little Ricky. But we will save this for a later day.

I stand by my theory that Christmas is for children, just like the Tooth Fairy. Can you imagine if the Tooth Fairy dropped some bucks every time an adult lost a tooth? Hell, I would be loaded!

I do, though, want to acknowledge that not every holiday is horrible for every person. Some of my peers got to spend their first Christmases with (gulp) grandchildren. Other friends are first-time parents, or even not-as-brand-new anything. When you have a child in your life, and are fortunate to spend Christmas with them...there really is magic in this day. Especially if you are able to see it through their eyes. I say this with no malice or jealousy, perhaps though with a bit of longing for what could have been, or what never was, and will never be—I am truly happy for those of you who have manifested into these new roles in your lives. Cherish those children and make their existence better by learning from the mistakes of our own youth and upbringing, and also interject the positive parts of the innocence of growing up when we did.

And never ever underestimate the value of being a grandmother or grandfather. For some kids whose parents just don't cut it, their grandparents can be the most significant beings in their lives. My Grandmother has been gone for almost 28 years. As most of you know, I was lucky enough to have her until I was 35 and she was 102. She was, and always will be, the MOST important, most beloved person to have ever been in my life. Maybe some of you don't realize yet the potential importance you may hold.

To some little grandchild—you may be their everything! Certainly their legacy, and way beyond.

To my friends who are now parents of young children and newborns—Well, I know most of you, when you were babies yourselves, more than likely I was your preschool teacher, when you were 2 or 3 (my favorite age to teach). Please know that although I made my mistakes, sometimes let you little devils get away with more than I should have, etc., I always tried to see the world from your vantage point. I always hung my two-year-old photo from 1959 next to all your then current two-year-old pictures, because really it was your world. I just had the good fortune to be able to share it with you for four or five hours a day. Try to remember how it felt to be 3, or 5, or 8, and you guys will be the greatest Moms and Dads ever!

So 2019 is coming to an end. We will have our last show in teens (The Best and Worst of the Years Past—on December 31st). And then Joseph Senn will Charleston us back into the ROARING 20s. And it could be roaring even louder and harder than the first time. In America, 2020 will be the Presidential Election year. Probably the most important one in the history of the United States. One hundred years ago in 1920, after a long and relentless fight, women were finally given the right to vote. On hundred years later, let's honor all those women who paved the way for us by doing the right thing and voting the right way.

You must have noticed by now how I have steered this piece away from talk of the New Year and Best and Worst of 2019. I don't want to bounce or rather drop the ball just yet. Sadly, I've learned that the very worst can happen in the last few days of the year, just when you think it is all behind you.

Please remember that in going forward, we in no way leave behind the ones we may have lost in 2019, or any year, really.

I believe that those who truly loved us would want us to be happy and enjoy life, even if they are not physically here anymore to share it with us. My long-time best friend Cassandra used to say: "Find Your Bliss!" (another very wise woman who cancer took way too soon).

See– I figure when you live the best life you can, in a way you are also living for them, and in their honor.

Random Thoughts

The beginning words to *Bohemian Rhapsody:*

Is this the real life? Is this just fantasy?
Caught in a landslide, no escape from reality
Open your eyes, Look up to the skies and see
I'm just a poor boy, I need no sympathy
Because I'm easy come, easy go
Little high, little low,
Any way the wind blows doesn't really matter to me, to me
Mama, just killed a man

Put a gun against his head, pulled my trigger, now he's dead.
Mama, life had just begun
But now I've gone and thrown it all away
Mama, ooh, didn't mean to make you cry
If I'm not back again this time tomorrow
Carry on, carry on as if nothing really matters...

Close your eyes. Start thinking random thoughts for one minute and say them out loud. Record them and play them back. It's amazing...

In 1967 Coca Cola and Tab put the pictures of baseball All Star players on the inside of their bottle caps.

Monkeys and organ grinders really did walk around the city playing and begging for money. There really were rag pickers, and rag sellers.

Mommie Dearest was on *The New York Times* Best Seller List for 42 weeks.

Mae Hirschberg was the name of the girl who got the conduct medal instead of Grandma in 1899 because her father died.

James Buchanan was the 15th president and only real known gay president.

Lizzie Borden died 93 years ago June first. "Nearer My God to Thee" was sung by her grave in the middle of the night .

When I was starting school, Robert B. sat in the second seat at the boys side of the table, and me in the second seat at the girls side. Robert B died of hepatitis when we were 5.

Peg Entwistle jumped off the "H" on the Hollywood sign in 1932. She was Brian Keith's stepmother.

Planchette was the name for the Ouija phenomenon in the 1850's and 60's.

A plinth is the base of a statue. The poem by Emma Lazarus on the plaque of the Statue of Liberty begins, "Give me your tired, your poor, your huddled masses yearning to breathe free, The wretched refuse of your teeming shore. Send these, the homeless, tempest-tost to me, I lift my lamp beside the golden door!"

Mollie Fancher got dragged through the streets of Brooklyn by a streetcar in 1865, took to her bed, had visions, never ate again, and died in 1916. She was the first known anorexic, called "the Brooklyn enigma."

Dreamland in Coney Island burned up May 26, 1911.

The Triangle Shirtwaist Factory was at about 4 PM in the afternoon of March 25, 1911 in the Village. 146 people died from smoke, burning to death, or jumping out the window.

In kindergarten in 1962 I refused to color the policeman's hat. My kindergarten Easter basket was blue, with pink crepe paper, and my cubby was pink. On the first day of school I wrote my name PAMELA on a piece of paper in orange crayon, and then suddenly got embarrassed and scribbled over it.

Rudolph Valentino died in 1926 of a ruptured stomach. He was laid out at the same place as my father and Judy Garland later were. Thousands of screaming crying women waited in line (Grandma, too) for hours to pay their respects.

Teddy Roosevelt had a big mansion called Sagamore Hill in Oyster Bay on the Island. His wife and mother both died on the same day. He was born at 28 E 20th Street in 1858. A six-year-old Roosevelt witnessed the funeral procession of Abraham Lincoln from his grandfather's mansion in Union Square. He had five children, and named the fifth one Quentin. The others were Alice, TR junior, Edith, Archie, and Kermit. Quentin was killed in the first world war.

In the 1880's window awnings became very chic and trendy.

A picture rail is a railing high on the wall near the ceiling where pictures were hung and then held to eye level by ropes or ribbons.

Queen Victoria was born May 24, 1819 and died January 22, 1901. She and Prince Albert were only married twenty-one years when he died in December 1861 at 42 years of age.

Big Edie of Gray Gardens was born in 1895, and had three children—Little Edie in 1917 and then the boys—Phelan Beale, Jr. in 1920, and Bouvier Beale in 1922. In January of 1978, after Big Edie died, Little Edie got a gig at Reno Sweeny's, a New York city nightclub. Her reviews were so bad, nobody told her. She died around January 9, 2002, in Bal Harbour, Florida—but it took a few days to find her body...

...which is nothing compared to Yvette Vickers, who was some kind of a sex symbol/actress in the 50s. She died in her house in 2010 in her home in Benedict Canyon and nobody discovered it for over a year.

Disneyland opened on July 17, 1955.

Gayle was born on July 18, 1958.

Lizzie Borden was born on July 19, 1860, and died on June 1, 1927 Emma died nine days later on June 10, 1927.

Judy Garland was born Francis Ethel Gumm on June 10, 1922 in Grand Rapids, Minnesota. Her mother, Ethel Milne Gumm, had really wanted to abort her. Ethel worked at Douglas Aircraft at a desk job, and dropped dead of a heart attack in the parking lot in 1953.

Andrew Jackson was the seventh president of the USA; his wife's name was Rachel.

We used to go Gertz department store in Jamaica, Queens each year to see the Enchanted Christmas Village. It was beautiful, but Santa was scary, so I kept my distance. Sometimes

Grandma and I took the Q-60 Bus to Alexanders in Rego Park. We always shared a soft salty pretzel from the chestnut cart outside the store. Grandma called them "Bretzels," which is the German way.

A few times a year she took me to Best and Co. Dept Store in the city to get my hair cut. But Bio always tagged along, and insisted on the Caroline Kennedy do. Every time, she said ! was not mature enough to have long hair or pony tails. I still have a multi-colored deflated balloon from the hair salon in Best and Co. from the early 60s.

The order of the coin-op rides in the Great Eastern Mills Store in Elmont, New York were the little Ferris wheel, the helicopter, the two-horse merry-go-round, Sandy the Wonder Horse, and the car. But the highlight was the Peppy the Clown push-button puppet show. They used to sell Charlotte Russes there, which was mostly pink whipped cream and sponge cake, and lady fingers.

The Ferris wheel was invented for the Chicago World's Fair in 1893. Welch's Grape Juice first came out at the 1903 St. Louis World's Fair.

Flubber was a kind of putty named after the spongy stuff in *The Absent-Minded Professor* starring Fred MacMurray. The actual Flubber came out in December 1962 and was pulled in 1963 because kids were getting rashes and sick from it. They could not find a way to get rid of it because it didn't burn, and didn't sink. Hasbro buried tons of Flubber and paved over it to make a parking lot for their new warehouse in Rhode Island.

The first time I ever went to the racetrack was in Saratoga Springs in the summer of 1964, and won $8 on a horse named "Swiss Cheese."

Richard Speck killed eight student nurses in their dorm in Chicago in July 1966.

Rosemary's Baby was named Andrew, and they lived in the Dakota, where John Lennon was killed on December 8, 1980 by Mark David Chapman.

Floating island was a dessert consisting of a meringue sort of floating on a milky custard. My friend Ramona used to call it Floating Eggs.

The main maker of the skate key was a company called Chicago Skate Company.

Fort Ticonderoga is about 100 miles north of Albany. It had battles twice during the Revolutionary War period, first in 1775 and again in 1777.

In 1973 an English pound was equal to two American dollars, and a French franc was equal to about 20 cents.

The original Bastille Day was July 14, 1789, but it didn't become a holiday until 1880.

The first American currency was minted in 1793 (I have a large cent from 1794, and one with 1799 stamped over the original 1798).

The Coney Island Cyclone roller coaster, the last wooden roller coaster, was built in 1927.

Nunley's Carousel, originally known as Murphy's carousel, was made in 1912 in Brooklyn, New York and installed in Golden City Park in Canarsie. In 1940, in anticipation of the Belt Parkway, it was moved to an indoor structure in Long Island, and became known as the Baldwin Carousel because it was in Baldwin, New York. It was there from 1940 to 1995.

There were 126 children under age 14 on the *Titanic* when it sank April 14-15, 1912. Sixty-six survived. There were also twelve dogs. Three survived. Robert Douglas Speeden (whose nanny's Titanic telegram I have) was six and survived, only to be the first automobile casualty in Maine when he was nine years old in 1915. His mother had written a book for him prior to the voyage called *Polar the Titanic Bear,* just as A.A. Milne wrote *Winnie The Pooh* for his six-year-old son Christopher Robin in 1926. I also believe that *The Wizard of Oz* was written by L. Frank Baum in 1900 in memory of his infant niece named Dorothy Gage. That Dorothy was born in June of 1898, and died at just five months old. *The Wizard of Oz* was made into a Broadway show that opened at the Majestic Theater on January 20, 1903, and ran for 293 performances, one of which Grandma saw for her 12th Birthday on February 25, 1903. L. Frank Baum died in 1919 and—in this weird coincidence—is buried in Forest Lawn in a kind of triangle from Judy Garland's father, Frank Gumm, to her mother, Ethel Milne Gilmore, in another area of the cemetery.

I read every *Dick and Jane* book in full on the first day we would get them. And then pretended to read them chapter by chapter in class.

My Grandmother made the best desserts—Bavarian Cream with chocolate or strawberry sauce. I still have the tin mold she used to make it in, which had been her mother Tillie's first. When Grandma's father died, Grandma's mother-in-law Adele moved in with Tillie. Adele had a stroke in 1944 and the doctor, wanting to go on vacation over Labor Day, signed her death certificate before she was dead.

Play-Doh was first manufactured as a toy in 1956 in Cincinnati, Ohio by Joel and Noah McVickers. Before that it had been invented to be used as wallpaper cleaner.

My father used to take me to the Rockefeller Center Christmas party and Christmas show at Radio City every Christmas. I hated those Rockettes, and so years later when I went to the Follies Bergére in Paris, I had no appreciation for the show.

Martin Van Buren, the 8th President, lived in Kinderhook, New York.

On June 10, 1692 Bridget Bishop was the first person to be hanged in the Salem witch trials of 1692. Altogether there were nineteen people hung—fourteen women, five men. There are no graves for the accused. Their bodies were left in the streets to be mocked (although some families did manage to retrieve their loved one's remains at night in the dark).

On the subject of unfair lynching as a conspirator—Mary Surratt, who was simply the owner of the boarding house where John Wilkes Booth stayed before he shot President Lincoln on April 14, 1865 at the Ford Theater while the President and his wife Mary Todd were watching the play, *Our American Cousin*. As Booth jumped from the Lincolns box seats to make his getaway, he shouted, "Sic semper tyrannis! (Ever thus to tyrants!) The South is avenged!" Poor Mary Todd Lincoln was already bat shit crazy, and this put her way over the edge. The Lincolns had four sons. Robert, Eddie, Willie and Tad. Mary had to bury the three youngest in childhood. Only Robert Lincoln lived to adulthood.

Beginning words to *The Logical Song:*

When I was young, it seemed that life was so wonderful
A miracle, oh, it was beautiful, magical
And all the birds in the trees, well, they'd be singing so happily
Oh, joyfully, oh, playfully watching me
But then they sent me away to teach me how to be sensible
Logical, oh, responsible, practical
And then they showed me a world
  where I could be so dependable

Oh, clinical, oh, intellectual, cynical
There are times when all the world's asleep
The questions run too deep
For such a simple man
Won't you please, please tell me what we've learned?
I know it sounds absurd
But please tell me who I am

My favorite line from *Le Petit Prince* by Antoine St Exupery is "Dessine moi un manton," which means "Draw me a sheep!"

Gracie Allen never said "Goodnight, Gracie."

"In the great green room, there was a telephone, and a red balloon, and a picture of a cow Jumping over the moon."

Goodnight Moon was written by Margaret Wise Brown in 1947.

My Thoughts on War

QUESTION: With The Andrews Sisters being so important to the world during the Second World War, what is your real honest thoughts/opinion on war?

PAM:
For almost 33 years now, I have been mourning the loss of a boy who was like a little brother to me. His name was Stewart Kindman (yes, Briarwood viewers, that Mrs. Kindman's son). Stewart was 17 when he died of osteosarcoma (bone cancer). It has always been the one thing in my life that I could never rationalize, or resolve in my mind on either a spiritual or intellectual level.

Then I started thinking about Memorial Day, and what the holiday really is about, and I realize there are thousands of Stewarts out there. Cancer didn't take them at 17, 18, 19 years old— WAR did. And I realize that I can't come to terms with this, either. Those boys were somebody's baby, somebody's brother, somebody's husband, and in some cases, somebody's dad. A mother carried this boy, all of these boys, inside of her, as part of her body. They were one for nine months. And then, 18 or so years later, he was ripped away and gone before his life had even really begun . And no more than I can understand losing Stew to cancer, can I understand a world that sacrifices human lives over such stupid things as land boundaries, or groups of lazy Southerns who wanted to dehumanize people of color, and make them slaves.

Or how about 16 years in Vietnam? I believe there were 58,000 plus American boys killed or MIA from that one. And what the hell for? It was a civil war in Viet-fucking-nam—why should our boys be sacrificed because the North and the South (In a country, I guarantee you, 90% of us would not even know existed had it not be for our involvement in their war) could not agree on something. Same with the Korean war. Another civil war. But back to Vietnam, I remember in 1969, every Friday morning at 10 AM, we tied a black arm band on to our left arm, and one- by-one walked out of school, without saying a word. We were 12 years old, in junior high. Some of us had older brothers fighting and dying over there. But even then, at that age, we knew it was wrong.

As I sit here just after Memorial Day thinking about those who gave the ultimate sacrifice (their lives), I can honestly tell you that I cannot find a justification for any war, except perhaps the Revolutionary one breaking us free from England's control 243 years ago...That's all.

Some power-happy nut case in Germany gets a bunch of blind, oblivious half-wits to follow him like a goddamn cult leader, spewing crazy ideas, trying to create what he perceives as the "perfect" specimens of a society. In America we call that Charles Manson and the Manson family, or Jim Jones and the Kool Aid Drinkers. In Europe in the 40s, they called it World War II, or Hitler and his Nazi followers. And I just can't understand how many boys (and they were still boys) died protecting us from these lunatics, and their disciples.

How many children never got to meet their fathers, or how many fathers never had the chance to ever hold their own child, because he died fighting the ideas and rantings of charismatic "charmers" who could dupe the masses into just about anything? I've been asking for so many years now—why did those fools drink the Kool Aid? (And don't tell me some were forced, for many did it of their own free will.) Why did any of those Manson assholes, with the swastikas carved into their foreheads, go along with a plan to kill an 8-1/2 month pregnant woman and five of her friends? For the same reason people followed Hitler, and Bin Laden—weak-minded individuals, in my opinion, are the ones who cause the wars, not the strong ones. Fucking sociopaths, with no regard for human life searching for someone to tell them what to do, what to believe in, whose child to murder.

And finally, I want to ask this question...Even at twelve with the black arm bands on, and the POW bracelets on, I knew that if I were a boy, or if they were taking girls by the time I turned 18 in 1975, I wasn't going (and the draft was on then). I didn't know how, didn't form a plan, I just knew I wasn't going to die for some country called Vietnam. So I ask, what kind of propaganda do they feed these young kids? What kind of bullshit do they promise them to make them go to foreign soil, and die for something they know nothing about?

Kids in their teens often feel like they are invincible. That is true. But how do they brainwash these young innocent minds?

For all the music and joy that the Andrews Sisters brought to the world during the Second World War, I wish it had never happened. They wished it had never happened. And yesterday, on Memorial Day, originally called Decoration Day (after the Civil War, 1861-1865) my heart was with all the parents, spouses, and children who lost someone they loved in one of these ridiculous wars.

They teach you in the playground in Kindergarten (at least Stewart's mom taught me) not to resolve your conflicts by fighting. It is so sad, such a shame, that those principles don't follow us all throughout the rest of our lives, and then maybe some mother who pushed her little boy on the swings, or held his little hand on the beach, wouldn't be putting him in a grave only a few short years later.

RIP to all the innocents. You are not forgotten.

Questions From Readers & Viewers

I 'M 60, ALMOST 61... SO MAYBE I CAN ANSWER SOME.

I still haven't found out who let the dogs out.
JOANIE SAYS: SHE ALWAYS LETS THE DOG OUT.

Where's the beef?
I HAVEN'T EATEN BEEF SINCE 1984. I ASSUME IT TURNED GREEN AND SOMEONE THREW IT OUT.

How to get to Sesame Street...
JUST FOLLOW THE YELLOW BRICK ROAD.

Why Dora doesn't just use Google Maps?
SHE IS 5 YEARS OLD AND CAN'T READ YET.

Why do all flavors of Fruit Loops taste exactly the same?
BECAUSE THEY ARE ALL THE SAME, JUST FOOD COLORED.

How many licks does it take to get to the center of a Tootsie Pop...?
I DON'T KNOW, I THROW THEM OUT AS SOON AS I GET TO THE CHOCOLATE PART...

Why eggs are packaged in a flimsy paper carton...
NOTHING MAKES SENSE ABOUT EGGS. THEY ARE CHICKENS' PERIODS, FOR GOD'S SAKE!

But batteries are secured in plastic that's tough as nails.
OLD PEOPLE ARE KNOWN TO STEAL BATTERIES!

Yet light bulbs are in a flimsy carton...
THEY COME IN PACKAGES? I GET MINE AT THE 99 CENT STORE.

Ever buy scissors? You need scissors to cut the packaging off scissors...
WELL NATURALLY! HOW ELSE ARE YOU GOING TO OPEN THEM?

I still don't understand why there is Braille on drive-up ATMs...
IN CASE SOMEONE DRIVES A BLIND PERSON UP TO ONE.

Or why "abbreviated" is such a long word...
DOES ANYTHING MAKE SENSE IN THIS LANGUAGE? THERE IS A "GH" IN THE WORD "COUGH."

Or why there is a "D" in "fridge" but not in refrigerator...
EBONICS– KINDA OF LIKE WHEN THEY SAY "BABY DADDY" INSTEAD OF BABY'S DADDY .

Why lemon juice is made with artificial flavor...
REAL LEMONS ARE TOO SOUR.

Yet dishwashing liquid is made with real lemons...
DISHES DON'T HAVE TASTE BUDS.

Why they sterilize the needle for lethal injections...
PROBABLY SO THAT THE OTHER PEOPLE WHO TOUCH THE NEEDLES DON'T CATCH ANYTHING.

And oh, why do you have "to put your two cents in" but it's only a "penny for your thoughts" — where's that extra penny going...
PROBABLY OTHER PEOPLE THINK THEIR ADVICE IS WORTH MORE THAN YOUR THOUGHTS.

Why "The Alphabet Song" and "Twinkle Twinkle Little Star" have the same tune...
SAME REASON AS THE PENN POLKA (BY THE ANDREWS SISTERS) HAS THE SAME NOTES AS WHAT THEY PLAY AT THE START OF EACH HORSE RACE.

Why did you just try to sing those two previous songs...
TO MAKE SURE YOU WERE RIGHT.

And just what is Victoria's secret??
QUEEN VICTORIA? THAT SHE DID NOT USE TOILET PAPER.

And what would you do for a Klondike bar...
NOT A DAMN THING; I PREFER ICE CREAM SAND-WICHES.

And you know as soon as you bite into it, it falls apart...
NOPE, NEVER HAD ONE!

And why do we drive on Parkways and park on Driveways? Do you really think I am this witty??
I DON'T KNOW. I DRIVE ON FREEWAYS, AND PARK IN THE STREET.

I actually got this from a friend, who stole it from her brother's girlfriend's uncle's cousin's baby momma's doctor who lived next door to an old class mate's mail man... Now it's your turn to take it from me... Peace!!
I HOPE I'VE BEEN ABLE TO CLEAR UP SOME OF LIFE'S MYSTERIES FOR YOU!!!!

Pam-Tication: Fads

Fads and trends have been around since the beginning of time. It's almost as if the logical little kid who tells Mommy and Daddy to "put down that cigarette because it's yucky!" hits those teen years, and as the breasts, and penis's grow, the mind seems to shrink. I'm not trying to be funny (although it is). This is really the truth.

Now because I have a few things I have to do while I am still 61, we will only go back to 100 or so years. In the 20s the fad was to sit on flag poles. Looks it up. They climbed up and sat on flag poles as kind of an endurance thing. And teen boys of the 20s were really, really cool, if they could muster up the coin to buy an authentic racoon coat. What trendy kids of the 20s did could have put all three of the Gabor Sisters to shame.

In the 30s, teenagers, especially in the universities (where parents are in trouble these days for bribing and cheating on their child's admission qualifications to get them accepted), the big fad was swallowing live goldfish. Oh, yes. One kid set their record by swallowing 89 live goldfish in one sitting. And there were dance marathons—another contest of endurance to see who could stay on their feet dancing for the most amount of hours. People passed out from exhaustion, or dehydration, and the marathoners just kept dancing around them. The girl who lasted the longest that we know of danced (in 1932) for 27 straight hours, with six different partners before collapsing.

In the 40s it was stuffing a phone booth, seeing how many teenagers could be crammed inside a telephone booth. If you are too young to know what a telephone booth is, look it up. Once I bought an old wooden phone booth and put it in the middle of the living room. I thought Patty would kill me. She owned the townhouse I was living in at the time. But that's a whole other show. Phone booth stuffing came to an abrupt end when the kids on the bottom of the booth began suffocating and lives were lost.

By the 50s, phone booth jamming had morphed into automobile stuffing. Pretty self-explanatory. Only this time, they filled the car to capacity, kind of like those clown cars in the circus. There were sock hops (shoes scratched the school gymnasium floors) and around this time, drive-in movies attained popularity, and so did hiding in the trunk, or under blankets, to see how many teens could be snuck in to watch the film without paying the admission.

Now—oh, yes, we have reached the decade where I not only remember the fads, but participated in them. We were peace advocate, love-beads-wearing, tie-dyed hippies. We wore micro miniskirts which left nothing to the imagination, white go-go boots, and bell-bottomed pants. We twisted, and jerked, and frugged, and shimmied, and shook as if we were having epileptic seizures.

And we stood up to authority. We had "sit ins" and moratoriums. We put black bands on our arms to protest the war in Vietnam.

In Southern California the surfing craze was in full swing. If you couldn't get to the beach to "hang ten," you did it on land—skateboarding.

In the 70's the the trend was "streaking"—removing all one's clothing, and running totally naked through a large sports event or venue (somebody actually streaked their way through the Academy Awards in 1974). We put on our fancy roller skates and that became serious business. We wore mood rings and had Pet Rocks (look it up). Both of mine (mood ring and Pet Rock) came from Maxene in the mid-70s. I still have them.

And then towards the end of the decade—DISCO came and went very quickly. Side story which I think you will find kinda cool: disco was a rhythmic beat. In the haste of the trend, performers tried to "disco-tize" everything, even already-written songs. One day, I was driving along on the 405 freeway in my originally red, then painted yellow, Dodge Duster, blasting the FM radio, when the theme to *I Love Lucy* came on, jazzed up and with a whole new Disco beat. When I got home and told Patty, her first thought was, "Well, I hope Lucille is getting royalties from this!" And she immediately picked up the phone and called Lucille Ball. As I tuned out, Lucille knew nothing about "Disco Lucy" and since I was the one who who had actually heard it, Patty put me on the phone and I told her all about it. Now, these were the days before the infamous backgammon game, and Lucy still liked me. I had met her a year or so earlier when Patty took me with her to Lucie Arnaz's 25th Birthday party.

I loved the fads and styles of the 80s. Big hair, neon clothes, spandex, thick socks, and Reeboks. And where I lived in the San Fernando Valley was right smack in the middle of the hugely popular, trending "Valley Girl" phase. Although I would never have been caught dead telling anyone to "Gag me with a spoon," the 80s would have been a lot more fun for me had I not quit smoking in 1981 and spent the majority of that decade—until 1988—being overweight and unable to fit in a lot of the clothes, and mindset, of the time.

It is at this point in my writing that I must look up the origin of the word, "FAD."

Fad (noun) 1834, "hobby, pet project" (adjective—faddy is from 1824), of uncertain origin. Perhaps shortened from fiddle-faddle. Or perhaps from French *fadaise*, "trifle, nonsense," which is ultimately from Latin *fatuous*, "stupid." From 1881 as "fashion, craze," or "trivial fancy adopted and pursued for a time with irrational zeal."

In the 90's, Grunge came into being. Saggy baggy pants, multiple piercings. Beanie babies and Pokemon trading cards were the "thing" And for most of us, our world changed forever. Cell phones and computers became a part of our regular lives. For me, eBay became an integral part of my life, prompting me to buy a Web-TV.

The first 10 years of the 21st century, the fads which stand out the most for me are Flash Mobs, and MySpace. I had the best MySpace page. The profile started out as a joke, which my friend wrote, but soon I changed it, line by line, until even though still funny, it was the truth. I thought there would never be anything better than MySpace. Remember the top 8? Then came Facebook.

And to round out the past 100 years, let's look finally at the 2000s teens. Well, we all knew the day would come when everyone would be walking around, with green, pink, blue, and rainbow hair, *à la The Simpsons*, or *The Jetsons*. The ripped, frayed pants we wear today look ridiculous. As do the many, many selfies we take and post of everything from our infected fingernail to what we ate for lunch. Social media has become our main form of communication and interaction. However, I am just as guilty as anyone of being a very willing, and active participant in all of these trends and fads.

The hours of my 61st year are ticking away and I still have not gotten to my topic of choice yet. So okay, here it is. Some of you, I know, have asked me to discuss the disgusting trend that originated in Indonesia of boiling up bloody tampons, or pads, and then drinking the "tea" made from it to get high. This has been going on for a while, and the reason I didn't touch it before is because they also eat dogs in Indonesia. And you certainly are aware of my feelings on that taboo subject. I figured if they didn't ingest a piece of poodle infected with rabies, maybe at least toxic shock from the used feminine products would do them in. The less of them, the less dogs would be sacrificed. And meals like "Leg of Lab" would cease to be.

But now teens in the US and the UK are doing it. Apparently, it is not the blood that gets them high. It is a hygiene product which contains dioxins, gel, bleach, chlorine, synthetic fibers, and unknown petrochemicals which, when heated and drank, makes one sort of drunk.

The blood is just for color, to give the mixture a grenadine-like tinge (this one beats eating the Tide Pods!).

My Left Hand

Once Upon a Time...being left-handed was a sign of evil.
In ancient times, people believed that left-handed people were truly evil individuals. There is evidence of a large number of very ancient tools that have been used by left-handed people and human remains which showed dominance in the left hand in carrying out daily activities.

So why did ancient people consider the left-handed to be evil?

A woman, supporting a child with her left hand, reaches for a fig, from the 25th Dynasty Palaces Inlay found in a Monument on the West Bank at Luxor, Egypt.

All of the early great civilizations of the world, from the ancient Mesopotamians to the Egyptians, Greeks, and Romans, have been strongly biased towards the right hand. The right hand of the gods was considered to be healing and beneficent, while their left hand was used for curses or inflicting injury. In almost all of these cultures, the right hand was used for ceremonies and for eating, and the right-hand side was always the favored position.

In drawings, the Ancient Egyptians depict all the good armies as being right-handed, while their enemies are left-handed.

Plato and Aristotle almost always associated the right with good and the left with evil and criminality. The great philosopher Plato was convinced that the limbs are naturally of equal strength and ability, and that any handedness is culturally imparted. In fact, he went so far as to blame left-handedness on inept mothers and nurses who failed to adequately school their children in the correct way of doing things. Aristotle, on the other hand, believed that a person's handedness was natural but an indicator of good versus evil.

Ancient Romans shared similar beliefs about the left-handed. According to some, wearing a wedding ring on the third finger of the left hand originated with the Romans, the idea being to fend off evil associated with left-handedness.

The modern practice of shaking right hands in greeting dates back to the Roman custom of touching right hands to demonstrate the absence of hidden weapons.

Little is known of the practices and attitudes towards left-handedness during the Middle Ages.

Despite the limited reforms of the Age of Reason and the Age of Enlightenment, the 18th and 19th centuries were particularly hard on left-handers, and discrimination against them became ingrained and institutionalized.

Austrian physician and psychologist Wilhelm Stekel wrote in 1911 that "the right-hand path always signifies the way to righteousness, the left-hand path the path to crime. Thus the left may signify homosexuality, incest, and perversion, while the right signifies marriage, relations with a prostitute, etc."

Even in the relatively free societies of North America and Western Europe, deliberate and sometimes brutal attempts to suppress left-handedness and impose conformity in the education system were endemic during this time, including such practices as tying a child's left hand behind his chair or corporal punishment for anyone caught writing with the left hand.

Until only recently, left-handed children were forced to learn to use their right hands in school.

There are a lot of things you can try to take away from me. Oh, I'll fight you alright. Maybe you'll win. Maybe I will. Maybe it will be negotiable. Go for it. Take my car. Take my house. Take my antiques. Take my Andrews Sisters possessions (oh, of course if you try that one, you'll have to deal with Lynda, as well.) Take my pills. Take my friends. Take my food. Take my beliefs.

But you are not allowed to take away, or tinker with, my inner core. You know—that part inside of me which makes me—ME. Please never ever try to change me. For I am who I am, and very very few people can say that they like themselves as they are. I will always be loud. I will always be opinionated. I will always speak as a straight shooter. There are no filters here.

Wally died eight years ago today, and I vowed that was the last time I would ever pretend to be someone I was not. If anything good came out of all the years of dealing with him, it was that I could now be true to myself, and never let anyone have the power over me to say and do what is not in my heart, or my soul. He dangled Patty in front of me as one would do with a carrot to a rabbit, a one-trick pony, or a race horse. Just far enough, or rather close enough, to make me chase that inevitable reward, if he/she performed on point. I spent forty years of my life running around that track like a greyhound in Florida (Hialeah? By the way, I think it's a horrible sport on all levels!).

I will try to be polite, but I can't promise to always be politically correct. Some of that stuff, some of the things people get offended over, are just nonsense. I've said this before–I never in a billion years imagined that the 21st Century would be so conservative, so overly insulted by, whomever makes the P/C rules, "words." Like tattle-taleing in the schoolyard. "So and so called me skinny, fat, ugly, a baby, etc...." As eight-year-olds, we were taught to shrug it off. In 2018, we are taught that those same stupid childish taunts can destroy a human being. WOW.

I will never conform to who or what I am not. Hate me. Like me. Stop watching my show. Criticize me all you want. Most probably you will never get the reaction or the results from me that you want.

You see, I am a cultivated machine. I had to learn to conform, to survive in this world one way or another to suit the wants, needs, and comforts of those who dangled that fish hook. The ones that had the control of feed me, or leave me, or sign me into "a place for troubled kids." And then later the ones who had the power to throw me out literally into the streets, on a whim, and out of the lives of those I most needed and loved.

This person you watch spewing my stories, and opinions, and reflections daily on "THE PAM SHOW" began as a role I created many years ago as a means of survival. This fearless person afraid of nobody in the world (except maybe Judge Judy, a little bit!) was a mask that a shy, inept little girl kid hid behind. It took many years for me to grow into that character I created. Many years until it was no longer a pretend game, or costume. I grew over time to become the woman you see before you. I cannot tell you what was the single moment when I integrated the survivalist me comfortably and naturally with the world. I would have, should have, always been allowed to be.

So if you are to take something away from you from this rambling jumble of thoughts, know that you can be whoever, and whatever (personality-wise) you want to be, even if it's not in your initial make-up. Play the part even if you are just pretending. Become the role, and one day– the role has become you.

Did I Offend You?

I seem to have lost a few viewers over my post regarding the 2,800 Orthodox Jews in Brooklyn who illegally and immorally disregarded the current social isolation orders and gathered together to celebrate the life of one of their own—a Rabbi...ironically, who had died from the Coronavirus.

I also seem to have lost some viewers, a couple of weeks ago, on Easter Sunday, when I posted about those selfish Mega-Church Pastors who went against everyone, right on up past the Pope—and opened their doors to the throngs of "Kool-Aid Drinkers" assuring them that "GOD would spare the true believers." Several of them and their sheep (followers) passed into the Holy Kingdom within a few hours or days, suffering and terrified, because they knew what was happening as they gasped for their last breaths.

And am I in the wrong because the "Religious Extremists" take it upon themselves to deem whether to follow ancient rules or customs of their faith recklessly—while endangering the lives of innocent living people? I am accused of demeaning their ancestors.

Well, FUCK YOU!! I am their cultural ancestry, born to a woman whose entire heritage goes back hundreds of years—total German Jewish descent. By blood, I come from a long line of Levys, Zimmers, and Goldbergs.

The other 23 and me combo consists of a long line of Polish and Austrian Catholics. My father's family were deeply devout "Hail Mary," "Praise Jesus," "Pray 50 times a day" folks since way, way back.

So cut the bullshit. I'm not disparaging anyone's heritage, including my own. What I am vehemently opposing is EXTREMISM, and THE BLATANT DISREGARD OF SCIENCE AND COMMON SENSE.

Let's say it again: EXTREMISM! And not just those of matters of the cloth. Think for a minute. There is a reason why a program like *My 600 lb. Life* ("FATTIES") is among the most-watched shows on television. EXTREMISM. That is what I am protesting. Not religion, or anyone's right to worship anything, as long as it does not harm another living being in any way.

Let me try this another way.

In a little over a week it is going to be Mother's Day. There are sons and daughters out there that will not be seeing their mothers, because SHE IS DEAD—something so remote that two or three months ago, it was the last thing on their minds, but she now is gone—she died of Covid-19. They will never again see her in this world, because of some random encounter perpetrated under the guise of tradition.

You want to see it in an even more horrifying light? Probably not, but I'm going to tell you anyway. Much as we hate to think about it, it's sort of a given that children will outlive their parents. But next Sunday, on May 10th, there are going to be an awful lot of childless mothers, devastated by their horrendous losses, which they also gave no credence to the idea of just a short time ago.

And in a month or so, it will be Father's Day. Please do me a favor—on June 21st, read this again, only every time I used the word "Mother" replace it with "Father."

AND FOR ALL THE MOTHERS WHO LOVE THEIR CHIL-DREN- DUMP THE GUILT, AND TELL THEM TO NOT VIS-IT. THIS YEAR. THEIR WELL-BEING IS YOUR PRIORITY, NOT THE STUPID GIFT AND OBLIGATORY MOTHER'S DAY BRUNCH.

Now this would have probably been a poignant and appropriate place to end this piece. And ordinarily- I would have. But my friend Kurt brought to my attention the plight of the most vulnerable victims of all. At least, to me. When thousands of people die during a pandemic, thousands of dogs and cats are left homeless. Most of them will be killed. It's hard enough to get animals adopted under normal circumstances.

So the pets die because the older people die, and husbands, and wives, and brothers, and sisters, and children, and loved ones die... because some damn group of assholes feel the need to say goodbye to Rabbi Mertz (I kid you not—MERTZ, as in FRED and ETHEL) or commemorate the rise of Christ from his grave. They've been waiting for the second coming for over two thousand years—could they take a year off for the sake of all humanity?

It's Not All Black and White

OK, so I want to weigh in on this horror that has gone down in Dallas. Of course those innocent policemen did not deserve to lose their lives because of some perceived prejudice. I use the word "perceived" because black lives do matter, ALL lives matter. But how much of this is really black and white?

There is a motorcycle cop whose area is the little village of Tarzana here in the San Fernando Valley. Tarzana was originally the estate of Tarzan creator Edgar Rice Burroughs. When Burroughs died, his vast estate was turned into a small town. Now for me to tell you that I have been stopped, detained, ticketed, etc. by this same police officer no less than five times would be an understatement. He is black, by the way. I am white. In all the stops, it never crossed my mind that race was the issue. I thought of all kinds of crazy reasons...My car is purple, and stands out? The New York license plates that I finally got around to changing? The crazy Coney Island bumper stickers plastered all over the car? And then I remembered something from a long time ago...

When Kim and I were friends, many years ago, this same officer pulled her over while I was a passenger in her car. He detained us, but had absolutely nothing to cite her for. So after about half an hour, he decided that her license plate was loose, and forced her to bend over in a short skirt to tighten it, while he watched. He even provided her with the screwdriver.

Do I believe that this macho, power-happy man sitting out in the heat all day targeted us because we are white? Because we are women? Of course not.

One has to look at the element of what causes someone to choose this profession. To become a police officer. A small penis perhaps? Someone who was targeted by a bully? A person who craves the power that one obtains while hiding behind a badge?

What I am getting at is, how much of this is really a black/white thing? A man/woman thing? And how much is an over-eager, power-crazy person looking to get back at a world that somehow (real or imagined) made him feel powerless and inadequate?

As for me, I don't think I'll be getting stopped in Tarzana anymore by the motorcycle cop. The last time, I went to court and smeared his ass from one side of this Valley to the other.

OK – NOW I DEMAND APOLOGIES UP THE ASS, AND REPARATIONS GALORE BECAUSE I WAS PERSECUTED BY ANCIENT HISTORY RIGHT THROUGH THE EARLY 20TH CENTURY.

I. AM. OFFENDED.

I AM OFFENDED AND INSULTED BY RIGHT-HANDED SCISSORS, AND SCHOOL DESKS, BY NOTEBOOKS THAT OPEN ON THE RIGHT SIDE MAKING IT IMPOSSIBLE TO WRITE WITHOUT SMUDGING THE PAPER. AS A MAT-TER OF FACT: I AM OFFENDED AND INSULTED BY EVERY PUBLISHING COMPANY OUTSIDE OF ISRAEL WHO BIND THEIR BOOKS ON THE LEFT SIDE, THUS MAKING ONE UNABLE TO TURN THE PAGE WITH THEIR LEFT HAND. I AM OFFENDED BY THE U (UNSATISFACTORY) GRADE I RECEIVED FOR MY HANDWRITING IN MRS. ROLNICK'S 4TH GRADE CLASS (1966–1967) BECAUSE I COULD NOT WRITE THE SAME AS THE RIGHT–HANDED CHILDREN.

FOR 62 YEARS, I HAVE BEEN PERSECUTED IN EVERY WHICH WAY POSSIBLE FOR BEING BORN WITH THE EVIL LEFT–HANDEDNESS. AND JUST LIKE THE CHINESE

ARE OFFENDED BY THE IMPROPER REPRESENTATION OF CHOPSTICKS AND EYE SHAPES, THE HANDICAPPED ARE OFFENDED BY ANY WORD THAT DOESN'T MAKE THEIR DISABILITY SOUND LIKE A WONDROUS GIFT, AND THE ENTITLED ARE OFFENDED BY JUST ABOUT EVERYTHING, I AM INSULTED, OFFENDED, AND PERSECUTED. AND I WILL NOT BE A VICTIM OF HATE NO MATTER HOW MANY HUN-DREDS OR THOUSANDS OF YEARS AGO THIS HAPPENED.

LEFT LIVES DO MATTER!

If I Were a Candidate...

Just like my idol Gracie Allen did 75 years ago, I too am thinking of tossing my hat in the ring, (yes, that would be Johnny Fedora) and running for president on the Surprise Party ticket which has not been revived since 1940...Gracie always said: "Everybody has a platform, except Kate Smith...She broke hers!"And now that I am addicted to *My 600 lb Life* on TLC, I can concur.

I looked up the questions that would be most likely asked of a person interested in running (well, with me back-walking). And here is what I came up with, along with my answers...

1. What's the biggest crisis you've faced in your professional life and how did you handle it?

PAM: The biggest crisis I ever faced in my professional life was trying to return all the white babies back to their mothers, after an intellectually disabled Black teen in my care snatched about five of them at the local park.

2. What's the biggest personal crisis you've faced and how did you handle it?

PAM: The biggest personal crisis I've ever faced in my personal life had to be Gayle. That's a big one. I handled it by not paying for more than the equivalent of six meals at a time for her. I also had a priest sit in my car and talk to her at Denny's at 2AM when she pitched a fit because she wanted a seventh. The Priest told her that even God rested after six! (but I think he was talking about days, not pork chops).

3. What's your greatest political triumph?

PAM: Vice President of the 5th grade Class 5-4, Mrs. Serbin's class 1967–1968, PS 117 Queens, NY. I'm ready to be the president now. But Mrs. Serbin died, so this is the next best thing.

4. What's your greatest governing triumph?

PAM: Governing Triumph... Easy. My former classmate from Hillcrest High, Franny, had a super hit TV show called *The Nanny.* Another word for Nanny is "Governess." And if you have ever wondered where that Nanny AKA Governess got that voice from... well, look no further. Definitely my biggest governing triumph!

5. What experience have you had that will serve you well as president?

PAM: I personally stood between, behind, and beside The Andrews Sisters for many years. Next to that, negotiating any Peace Treaty would be a piece of cake!

6. What historical presidential moment tells us the most about your vision of the office?

PAM: That stupid LBJ picking his beagle up by the ears. Under my term, he would be in jail for animal abuse.

Pam Courageous

QUESTION: You are so outspoken mostly in a good way. Are you ever afraid to speak your mind? Where do you get your courage?

PAM:
It seems that after the last few "PAM SHOWS" I've gotten so many posts and PMs telling me about how brave I am, and asking me how to have more backbone, more courage, in this world of ours. I have to tell you, that—

1. It hasn't always been this way, and

2. I found my true courage after "The Great Plague of 2013" wiped out most of my loved ones.

I was a very shy kid, far from the attention whore I am today. I hated any interest focused on me, to the point that if I were at a birthday party and it looked like I might be winning a party game, I deliberately lost, so all that praise, and congratulations would not be put on me. Same thing at school. I could easily ace any history test (I read encyclopedias in the bathroom from the time I was seven) but would answer some of the questions wrong on purpose, so as not to be singled out for getting the highest grade. That's what bad parenting can do to you—make you afraid to be good, to be better than good.

So I don't know if I'm brave or if I'm lucky. At 12 years old, I found my voice. I found it because I realized finally that nobody was going to stand up for me, but me. However, first I found it in order to defend my teacher, of all things. A brand new, just-out-of-college foreign language teacher who had absolutely no clue how to control a rowdy group of 7th graders. And especially my class. We were the ones who had been chosen to skip from the 7th to the 9th grade. We were the best, the brightest, and we knew it. Our young teacher did not have a chance, unless one of us spoke up and told the others to cut out their crap. I was the one voice. And do you know, fifty years later, we (me and my junior high school teacher) still talk to each other at least once a month.

Bravery, to me, is not giving a shit what other people think about how bad or good you are at something. If you like to do it, just go on and do it full on. Do it with gusto. And enjoy every minute of it! I can't tell you how many people I've now met, who have told me about an encounter they had with one of the Andrews Sisters, and that they were too frightened to speak to her. I want to scream at them, "Do you know what you missed out on?"

You've heard how awfully tone deaf I am, how horrible my singing voice is (I've been known to sing in three keys—all off key, and all at the same time). But that never stopped me from belting out "You're a Lucky Fellow, Mr. Smith" or "Any Bonds Today?" standing in-between Emma and our late friend, Darryl. Did I mention this was always at the top of our lungs in a crowded shopping mall? When you are enthusiastic about something, very little is met with discord— even my chords!

And never be afraid to go against the grain for fear of people disliking you if you don't agree with them (I can say this freely, now that Wally is gone, and I don't have to nod my head up and down like one of those bobble baseball characters in order to be able to see Patty.) If you are the only one in the world who believes something to be the way you see it, don't ever be too intimidated to say what you feel. A lot of times in groups, or on forums, I am apt to take the side of the person who is in the less sympathetic position. Such as that case in Cleveland where the three girls had been "held captive" by Ariel Castro for 11 years. Or, perfect example, I got into it on an online "discussion" over Jim Jones and the 900 Kool Aid drinkers. I will always have my set opinions on the death penalty, gay marriage, right to choose, animal rights, etc., and never waver from them. What other people think is really of no consequence to me. I hope whoever is reading this can find that strength, too. It makes life so much better when you don't have to sell out for someone else's approval

When I die, people are going to have plenty to say, not flattering, I'm sure. I've been Facebook jail and blocked more times on Facebook this year than ever, by those who did not like my "drama." But the one thing no one will ever be able to say about me is that I didn't laugh, and love, and live life on my own terms. And so far it's been a blast. Fear is sometimes the best motivator. Or the worst, depending on how you look at it. But from someone who has acted out every scene from *The Wizard of Oz* and half of *Meet Me in St. Louis, Yentl* and *The Way We Were* before thousands in cemeteries all over the country (I always said that with my voice, the dead were the best audience, since they couldn't just get up and walk away), I'm gonna leave you with this one thought to ponder. Words of wisdom from Miss Minnelli:

"Life is a cabaret, old chum (not a dinner theatre) and I love a cabaret."

Which in essence means don't settle for less than you want, ever. Go forward and seize the whole dream! I've danced with original Munchkins, I've sang "Have Yourself A Merry Little Christmas" to Margaret O'Brien. I've done everything from pass myself off as a man in the gay bath houses to ride wild horses on beaches in remote little towns in Spain. And why? Because in the end, it's the things you didn't do that you regret, rarely the things you did.

An Easter (Passover) Message

Before you sit down to take that first bite of your Easter ham—which always reminded me of a giant hemorrhoid, but was in fact, somebody's beloved baby piglet—"THE PAM SHOW" would like to wish you a Happy Easter holiday, and to my Jewish readers, a happy Passover Seder. Please be conservative, and use the same baby lamb which you've already slaughtered to smear the blood on your front door to fool the Angel of Death in your heart attack-inducing lamb stew dinner. And remember, as anxious you are to dig into that widow-maker meal, you must pray in all four languages (English, Hebrew, Yiddish, and Ancient Arabic) for at least four to five hours to make sure it sticks. I assure you that the lamb will still be soaking up the juices in the pot until you are ready to stuff your already clogged arteries.

But this year...

Please allow me to put a different spin on the Easter egg (roll, or rolls) with my kind of roll!

With all the strife and turmoil going on in the world...it just didn't seem inspirational enough to use my usual annual clip of Judy and Fred Astaire gliding down 5th Avenue in New York singing "Easter Parade," so I went to the place that brings me the most enlightenment, the most introspection, the most perspective—TLC—to the raw honesty of "Fatties!"

Yes, *My 600-lb.Life* does begin every episode with a shot of nature and a memorable life-affirming quote, delivered by the person about to embark on their weight loss journey. Because I care deeply about every one of my viewers, I watched about 50 hours, and have listed the most motivational quotes below (no need to thank me, your continued viewership is enough!).

HERE GOES:

Sometimes the only apology for how you lived your life is to change it.

Life has a way of taking you to a low place you never thought you would be. But you have to find the motivation not to stay there.

Sometimes the safest paths in life can take you to the most dangerous places. I can't clean my own vagina.

It's hard to make a change in your life when you've given up on yourself for so long. It's even harder when everyone else has as well.

The only thing that's harder than fighting for your own life is fighting for the life of someone you love.

You think about things you miss, life passing you by, because you're so big. Moooooooom—can you wipe my butt?

Sometimes you can't control the choices you make in life, and the places you end up, and the hard choices in life determine where you end up above all else.

Some people can hide their pain on the outside; it's much harder to hide it on the inside.

A journey starts with putting one foot in front of the other, but sometimes the journey starts just getting on your feet.

My boyfriend has to hose me down in the front yard in a trough like an animal; I'm too big to fit into the bathtub.

When you missed out on so much in life it will make you so desperate you will do anything to change.

It's hard when you see how you're hurting the people you love, and you can't stop making the choices that hurt them.

Pain can make you stop completely or pain can make you start again. It's up to you.

Son, boy, bring the bucket. I have to pee. Too late. You'll have to change the bed now. Ya gots to move faster, boy!

You never can predict how things will go, but the more you run from the past, the harder it is to face the present.

Life will always be full of a lot of twists and turns, and when it's a big turn, your biggest struggle will be to stay on the road.

Life can be completely unpredictable and the more you try to control it, the worse it can get.

I am knowledge'd. I know if I don't stop this behavior, I'm gonna die. I'll have a number 3 combo, supersize the fries. A number 6, no, make that two number 6's, extra cheese. And four tacos, three burrito supremes, and don't be stingy with the sauce, an extra-large plate of nachos, and a Diet Coke!

Enjoy your day!

The Meaning of Life? Orgasms.

QUESTION: What do you think most people feel is the meaning of life?

PAM:
The Ultimate Orgasm.
See—I got your attention.
So among other things, let's talk about the ultimate orgasm. We've all had one. That epic orgasm that—well, in my case—shattered glass doors. And then we spend years trying again to reach or surpass the height of that feeling once again.

It's like that with so many things in life, some good, some very bad. There are medicinal orgasms. Anyone who's ever experimented with substances knows what I'm talking about. That time, that one time, when you felt freer and lighter than ever before. When you actually did fly. I think drug addiction stems from a quest, a continuous never-ending search to feel that way, one more time, and an inability to recognize when the need has turned from recreational to dangerous.

In my life, I am on the ultimate quest—the hunt to find the perfect antique, the one that might get away. Many years ago, I found a print by James Rizzi (look him up) in a thrift store in Los Angeles. I think I paid five dollars for it; certainly no more. The next time you stumble upon a rerun of *Seinfeld* on one of those old cable channels, look at the baseball picture on the wall in Jerry's apartment. That's my Rizzi. It appraised in the double digit thousands. The rush, the adrenalin, that consumed me on that day, in the thrift store, is the same one which sends me out every single day trying to replicate that find. I'm good at what I do, antique wise, and knowledge is power, so I do come close often (as I've shown you on "THE PAM SHOW").

Gambling is another start out problem-less activity that enhances that "Chasing the High" behavior. I've never been very lucky in the betting department (except for a few horse races when I was much younger, and had not yet understood the brutality of that sport). The only real "take a chance on luck" that I can remember is the night I won a huge psychedelic giraffe at a Church Street Fair, when the spinning wheel stopped on the number 19, where I had placed my dime, and on the red bar, which meant I also won one of the big prizes on the bottom shelf. I was 12 then, it was 1969, and that multi-colored giraffe was larger than me.

Now Emma, on the other hand, is the luckiest person I have ever known. The first time in his life that he bought a scratch-off lottery ticket, he scratched his way to $1000. I was there. Eyewitness. First freaking time ever. But certainly not the last. He won on the Powerball, and the Mega-millions. Not the huge money, but a couple of thousand here and there, matching like three numbers and the special one, or four numbers out of the six. He was pretty good on the slots, as well. I defy any 90-year-old woman wearing a diaper, sitting in front of the same machine for ten hours, to beat out Emma. He's the person who walks through a casino with his last quarter, drops it in a random slot machine, and the bells and whistles and alarms go off. Another type of euphoria one can lose themselves in chasing after it time and again.

Maybe we are all wrong. Maybe we should just cherish that incredible moment, embrace it, enjoy it while it's happening, and the memory of it after it's over. Maybe we cause ourselves too much trouble—seeking, seeking, seeking.

Maybe there is only one ultimate orgasm in a lifetime.

I make no secret of the fact that while I grew up in a wonderful tree-lined neighborhood, with many little friends, and great memories of living through the 1960s, I hate Queens New York. And I have a hard time understanding why some people live and die spending their whole life in that place. Surprisingly, I really only know of a couple of people who haven't made the precarious journey out at least to Long Island, or into Manhattan, and have remained in Queens for what now equates to 50 or 60 years.

Recently I heard about the untimely death of one of those such people from my hood. A Mets loving, fuhgeddaboudit, *Daily News* rolled up and stuffed in his back pocket, every Friday night Gino's pizza, and beer with da boys for the last half century kind of guy. A job— and a life—that absolutely paralleled the character Kevin James in *The King of Queens.*

Now even on the show the players openly acknowledge that "Queens" is just a stepping stone to something so much better. A starting-out place to strive to get out of that blue collar Archie Bunker-type of existence.

So anyway, when I heard that this guy, a bit younger than me, most likely shoveled the driveway and path after one too many snowstorms, keeled over, and dropped dead. My first thought after learning this was, "Oh my god! I babysat him, when he was a little kid!" Wow! Such a sweet, bright little boy. Why didn't he ever get out?

Maybe because it was good enough for him. Some, I suppose, are correct to remain "the cricket on the hearth," never traveling far from the world they were born into. Maybe not everyone has the need to strive for the ultimate orgasm, or the perfect antique discovery. Maybe for him, he did it just right.

RIP—my friend.

Gayle, Part Four: The Adventures Continue

I'm always being asked to tell about more Gayle and her adventures, and there are so many stories, like the time Emma and Craig took her to Mexico and she waited in line to have her picture taken on a donkey, as all the previous people had. After a loud argument, half in Spanish, half in English, the donkey's owner went and got a milk crate for Gayle to sit on in front of the donkey.

Or the time she and my ex-husband went on a spinning whip ride at a carnival, and all the while she was squealing and laughing, completely oblivious to the fact that one by one, the rivets were flying off the car they were riding in.

Or the time I pushed her into a wheelbarrow full of cement in the summer of '61 (she still brings up that one).

Or how about the time when Gayle couldn't find any toilet paper in the Chinese restaurant, and grabbed a fancy linen napkin off a table and wound up having a tug-of-war fight over the napkin with the owner?

Or maybe how she would kneel on the couch backwards looking out the window, and her ass looked like a billboard for Jordache Jeans?

Alright, finally, I'll tell you another story from her month-long stay with Emma and I, after she got thrown out of the hospital for smuggling in candy bars.

At that time, I worked as a personal assistant, but not for any of the Andrews Sisters. For the prior three years I had been working for the woman who was the "It Girl" of soap operas in the day—Kristian Alfonso, a former figure skater who played "Hope" on *Days of Our Lives*. This happened to be Gayle's all-time favorite show, and Kristian was her all-time favorite actress.

I was determined that there was no way I was going to let Gayle meet Kristian.

I compensated by taking her to one of the charity baseball games my friend and I produced at that time, where the cast of *Days* played against the casts of other West Coast-based soaps, and introduced her to the rest of the actors. I knew that Kristian couldn't play that weekend, so it was safe to bring Gayle. I have a photo of the cast and fans on the field from that game, and there is Gayle, right in the middle, taking up most of center field.

I did whatever I had to in order to keep Gayle away from Kristian. I would sneak out of the house at 4:30 AM to sit in front of the Sunset Gower Studios until it opened at 6. I told Gayle it was

Patty on the phone, asking me to pick something up for her, when it was really Kristian. How I got away with buying birth control in front of Gayle, and telling Gayle that it was for Patty—who was nearly 70 at the time—is anyone's guess!

Finally, the longest month of our lives passed, and at last it was the night Gayle was scheduled to go back to New York. I had successfully kept Gayle away from both Patty and Kristian for an entire month. On the way to the airport, Gayle asked if we could stop at Kentucky Fried Chicken, so she could get a little snack for the plane (in those days, you could bring your own food on airplanes). Out she toddled with her "little snack"—a 16-piece bucket of fried chicken, with—oh, yes—mayonnaise poured over it (Gayle ate everything with mayo). We got to LAX, got her checked in, and went to the gate (yes, these were still the times when you could actually go to the gate and watch the plane take off).

Then it happened...

Actually, it was a series of events that happened.

First Gayle dropped the bucket of mayonnaise-laden fried chicken, and pieces went flying all over the terminal. Undeterred, Gayle was still going to eat it. So we both got down on the ground, and started picking up this greasy, slimy chicken. What a sight we must have made.

And then I heard it...that unmistakable voice I become used to hearing at every hour of the day or night for the last three years: "Pammy, what are you doing here?"

I looked up, and there stood my boss. And thirty days of keeping Gayle away from her went down the toilet.

I said, "Wait, what are you doing here?" hoping Gayle would not notice her...but she was a well- known woman, and Gayle and half the terminal did indeed recognize her.

Kristian reminded me (I had totally forgotten) that over three months ago, I had booked her on an American Airlines flight to go home to Massachusetts to see her family. That flight made a quick stopover in New York. OH MY GOD! Gayle and Kristian were on the same flight!

My last memory of that nightmare was of Kristian going through the gate with Gayle trying to catch up to her, huffing and puffing, the chicken flying out of the KFC bucket once again, and Gayle yelling, "Kristian Alfonso! Wait! I'm Pammy's oldest and dearest friend! I wanna tawk to you."

I never knew exactly what transpired on that five-hour flight back East, but I can only imagine, because Kristian's first words to me when she returned were: "I need my house keys back." And within three weeks, I was no longer welcome on the Sunset Gower Studios lot, or at Kristian's home. To this very day, I cannot tell you why. God only knows what Gayle was spewing into that poor woman's ears that entire flight. But whatever it was, it sure traumatized her enough to get rid of me in a hurry!

Five foot two, eyes of blue,
But oh, what those five foot could do,
Has anyone seen my gal?
Turned up nose, turned down hose,
Never had another beau,
Has anyone seen my gal?
Now if you run into five foot two covered with fur,
Diamond ring and all those things
Bet your life it isn't hers.
Could she love? Could she woo?
Could she love? Could she coo?
Has anyone seen my gal?

Now imagine these lyrics turning into a quick Charleston, at an Amateur Night in a Long Island Night Club...and being sung and danced to by a 550-pound woman dressed as a Flapper? I think it was a satin blanket with tears in it to look like fringes. I wasn't there. My ex-husband was. When I asked him to describe it, he said, "It looked like what they cover the horses with was about 200 Ibs ago."

Now I am not going to brag, but one of my many talents is guessing the tonnage on morbidly obese people. (I've been watching a lot of *My 600 lb. Life* on TLC), and have gotten pretty good at figuring it out. I could have been one of those carnival barkers who yell, "Step right up, lady, and I'll guess your weight within ten pounds!" (Oh, if not for those Andrews Sisters.)

So naturally, when the phone rang last week and I recognized that 516 area code, I figured Gayle wanted something, I just didn't know what. I've made it clear for everyone...NO MORE MONEY (hmmm, I just realized that I have not heard from Ethel in a while). It turns out Gayle wanted to make another television appearance, and wanted my help. Now when someone of that weight calls and asks for one's help to get on TV, you figure that she didn't want to be on *Say Yes To The Dress*, right?

I presumed she wanted the operation, and wanted me to get her on *My 600 lb Life*. Boy, was I wrong. "No, PAMMY, I want you to call Ellen. I want to go on *Ellen*, and tell her my troubles and despairs."

So stupid me, who didn't want to get involved anyway, said, "Gayle, what about Dr. Phil? As nuts as I was, they all really liked me over there, maybe I could call someone over there."

And then the arguing starts...."No, no, no, it has to be Ellen."

And I'm going back and forth with her, about how I don't know anybody at *Ellen*...But *Dr. Phil?* You never know. I would not know who to talk to or what to say to Ellen's people.

"Darling, I anticipated that, so I wrote you a script." And sure enough, a few emails later, I did indeed receive a script from Gayle. Sweet as Pie. Everything from how we have known each other for over 55 years, to how much I love Gayle, etc., etc. Not that I had any intention of making that phone call, but I thought it would make for good conversation and laughs over a meal with Emma. So we go out to eat, and I start to tell him about Gayle's latest...but he is not laughing. In fact he is getting paler and paler. It seems Gayle had him make the very same phone call to Ellen's people last week, but they turned him down because they said, "Ellen only likes to do happy, upbeat shows!"

So Gayle (as told to me later) was going to have me get us on the show as lifelong bosom buddies, and once she had Ellen's attention, she was going to turn the whole show around about her poor pathetic life, and her liver which is the size of a small aircraft, in hopes that Ellen would buy her a new Hoveround mobility scooter.

Now why did I start this story out with Gayle dancing and singing the Charleston at Amateur Night in a Long Island Night club? Of course—I know!!! They were using those Ted Mack hooks (canes) to pull the bad talent off the stage, but they broke all three hooks on Gayle before they had to get security to escort her off the stage...

Five foot two, eyes of blue,
Could she, could she, could she coo? Has anybody seen my Gayle?

What I've Learned

(AUGUST 19th, 2014)

Tomorrow, it will be the one year anniversary of Jill's death, and since I came back from that failed disaster of trying to live in New York again, a friend of mine asked me to share what I learned in this transitional year. So here goes:

I learned that I am a strong, smart, independent woman, who can pretty much get anything done on my own, and get myself in or out of any situation I may find myself involved with. I learned that I am not afraid to be alone, and that I really do not want to be dependent, or co-dependent, on or with anyone (been there, done that). I may complain, but at the end of the day, I am damn proud of all I've accomplished on my own. I've also learned never ever to trust another human being—100%, no matter how long you've known them, or how well you think you do. Never put all your eggs in one basket, and also that if something sounds too good to be true, it probably is. I've learned that having money does not change anything, except perhaps, it is one thing less to worry about. I've learned that there are some people who like me only because of the Andrews Sisters, which for the most part, I don't mind—if I like the other person. I've learned never to put stock in the words of naïve, gullible people, or people with a history of malice. It destroys otherwise solid relationships. I've learned that I am a lot less P/C pertaining to certain health issues and illnesses than I pretend to be. I've learned that Karma does exist, and what goes around does indeed come around. I've learned to have a home with a lease or title in your name, not to live in someone else's home, no matter how easy it might make life seem. Do your own banking, pay your own bills, live within your means, whatever that may be. I've learned that we must take care of ourselves first, and then the innocents—the animals and children who cannot do for themselves. Above anything else. I've learned to find my bliss, and live it, as everyone should do, as long as it doesn't hurt oneself or others. I've learned that as long as I live, I'll never stop antique shopping. I've learned to keep promises, or agreements, even if the other person has reneged on theirs long, long ago. And finally I've learned that you cannot go home again since people rarely change, even if it kills them. Case and point right here.

(AUGUST 19th 2019) – THE WHALES OF AUGUST:

Here I am, five years later. and I still agree with every word I wrote on this day in 2014. I just might add that since I first wrote this, I have also learned to never stop my quest for knowledge, and laughter, and whatever it is that makes one's little heart do cartwheels. Speak your best truths, and Carpe Diem, My Friends (Seize The Day), because there are a lot of our loved ones who no longer have that luxury. This earth, this life, is a gift—such as it is. And just when it looks the darkest and feels the scariest, somehow, some way, from out of the shadows, a "Mata Bond" of your own will show up, and all will be right with the world once more.
If you do believe in fairies—clap your hands!

Time and Again

The best book I've ever read in my life was called *Time and Again* by Jack Finney. When Cassandra gave it to me about 35 years ago, she said, "I envy you being able to read this for the first time." So I am passing the info on to you... if you ever get the opportunity, read it, and you too will wish Cassandra was still alive to thank her. Phenomenal...Jack Finney is perhaps best remembered for his genius work *The Invasion of the Body Snatchers*— but today, I want to talk to you about yet another of Mr. Finney's publications: a short story turned into a novel in the late '60s called the Woodrow Wilson Dime..

Now before I lose your attention completely, indulge me for a moment. Go into your purse or pocket and take out a dime, and look at it. Is Woodrow Wilson depicted on that dime? Of course not. It's FDR. His image replaced the Mercury head in 1946, a year after his sudden death in April 1945, while serving his fourth term as U.S. president. But what if, as Jack Finney imagined, it was different? What if there were slight little changes that often occur and are enjoyed by many another sort of parallel existence? What is the serendipitous nanosecond which shapes our "destiny"? Would our lives be altered in some way if it was indeed Woodrow Wilson on this piece of American ten cent coinage? Or if Dewey did indeed defeat Truman?

I mean think about it. The millions of slight differences of events that could have, and maybe did change the course of your day? If you are married—where did you meet your spouse? What if you had not gone to that bar, or that bank, or that party on that day? Your entire life as you know it would not be. Your children would be different children. Your partners would be other people. I'm not saying this is a good or a bad thing. It happens both ways.

What if I had not left my then nine-year-old kid at that particular 7-11 in Los Feliz, California, on that particular day, 36 years ago— Feb 25th—at 3:30 in the afternoon? She would not have been kidnapped and raped by the infamous Babysitter/Lost Dog Rapist.

By the same token, what if I had not seen that show (either *Here's Lucy* or *Over Here*)? What if I had not been backstage on the day Patty decided she needed an assistant? If things had worked out as planned, a wardrobe woman would have introduced me to Patty and Maxene. I would have shook their hands, probably told then how much I enjoyed their music, and never seen them again. But a change, ever so small, occurred. The wardrobe woman never showed up, and so I talked to Wally, clueless to who he was, but simply because he was there. And though I didn't yet know how he held all the power over Patty, I was at least able to impress him with my knowledge of early 1970's current events and Watergate, which of course altered the course of my life.

I was ready to become a high school French teacher in the New York Public School System, and most probably take over my

Grandmother's apartment on the Upper West Side. My only interaction with the state of California would have been, at most, a short trip to Anaheim to check out what this Disneyland deal was all about. Would I—could I—have thrived, or even survived that?

Why was it that Dave Kapp, president of Decca Records, happened to be in one of the few taxicabs in New York with a radio tuned into the Andrews Sisters broadcast from the Edison Hotel in 1937? Their time was over. They had failed to prove themselves in the three months allotted and were on their way back to Minnesota. This had been their last chance. And they had been fired just after that broadcast aired. What fate, what mysteries of the universe, intervened at that moment? And why?

I realize that this might be sounding a bit *Night Gallery*-ish or *Twilight Zone*-ish, but maybe because it really truly is. How is one to ever predict which moment, which decision, which event might have steered us in one direction to another that might be the one to change our very existence?

I have a friend who was at the Harvest County Music Concert in Las Vegas with her husband last year. You know the one, where that lunatic Stephen Paddock went nuts, and fired off high powered weapons from the window of his room at the Mandalay Bay Hotel, killing about 60 people, and injuring nearly 1000? My friend and her hubs were okay, and recently had their first baby. If you do the math, that little girl was conceived roughly two weeks, maybe within days, of that horrific event. Were the Gods of Fortune smiling on them that day? Or on the baby yet to be? If so... where were they for Connor Peterson, or Paul Polanski?

Why wasn't Joanna killed that August night at her best friend Sharon Tate's house when the Mansons turned it into a place of murder and carnage? She had been there only hours earlier, sitting on the same furniture, walking on the same rugs that were soon to be covered with her beloved friends' blood and gore. By all accounts, and by all previous actions and plans, she was supposed to be there. Why was Joanna "The Girl That Got Away" (a term that curiously was applied to her once before in the wake of another high profile mass murder case)?

Cassandra and I used to play this wonderful game. We would stare into a photograph taken in the 19th Century, usually in New York, and Cassandra, who was very, very smart, would start talking about the scene—the sights, the sounds, the smells, the feelings, the perspectives at that exact moment. New York City was a very dirty place in the 1800s. Horses pulling carriages and wagons in all different directions. The clip-clop sound as the horses plodded along the crowded brick-paved roads. The air was stale, and stank with the odor of horse manure that the city street cleaners found to be an impossible task to keep up with. There were no garbage receptacles on every corner—trash was strewn wherever it had been dropped. The El (elevated train) screeched from above, and vendors and peddlers yelled, and screamed, and sweated, and froze as they tried to sell their wares. Those long dresses that the women wore were filthy from the trim. They trailed along the dirty ground. Nobody ever tells you that. But they were all permanently encrusted and stained. As long as Sandra spoke, it was as if we were transported into that picture, into that time. And that was the closest I ever felt to being in a parallel world that really did exist.

Did I mention that I still have my Grandmother's wedding dress? She wore it only once, on Christmas Eve 1912, mostly inside the Banquet Room of Dominic's Restaurant in lower Manhattan. The bottom is indeed dirty, if only from the short walk from the snow-piled sidewalk into her wedding. That dress did not age well. Even when I was young, and it was still in Grandma's closet in its original box, it crinkled and ripped at the slightest touch. I'd like to think that I am aging better than that poor dress did.

SERENDIPITY: An unforeseen piece of good luck that results in unplanned good fortune. That is my second favorite word in the English language, surpassed only by the word ECLECTIC (read it again—I did not say "electric"). ECLECTIC—a mismatched hodgepodge of items or things that have absolutely no semblance to each other mixed together... It's pretty obvious why I would love that word.

Now these happenstances are very different than the "If onlys..." or the "I should haves...", although I tend to stay away from those ideas, choosing more to believe that "I did the best I could, with what I knew, at that time." When Jill killed herself, I was angry (I'm still angry), and I felt betrayed. Out of respect for her children and grandchildren, I won't go into the really crazy stuff. But the best way to explain it is I felt betrayed that she could just off herself after all the worrying I did. Now in Jill's defense, she never did ask me to worry, nor did she ever really know the extent of my worrying. The two-week wait every three months for the blood test results from the oncologist for years...the rooms where they pumped stomachs, and administered charcoal to absorb the drug overdoses...the big metal doors that were locked round the clock, where I would sit with others, on the side where the sane stayed, waiting for them to be unlocked by some uniformed guard for the daily half-hour visits... I bring this up now to tell you that after Jill died, I resigned myself to keep the few close friends I had left. To be friendly, and helpful, and kind, but to not allow myself to ever again get close to another human being who could elicit that kind of emotion from me. And for the most part I have done that. Made lovely new friends—mostly online—but not giving anyone the power to provide a circumstance, or circumstances, that would rain such terror and shame on me.

And I see now that maybe, just maybe, all that horror was meant to be in this constantly twisting and turning and challenging thing called life. That is why we are ambiguous, open-minded, and unique. That is why we hold on, and don't take any one thing or person too seriously. It can and often does change in an instant. It's the ride, folks, not the results that count. Enjoy your roller coaster or yellow brick road—no matter where it takes you. Maybe that's why "THE PAM SHOW" aired in Temecula. Maybe that's why it still does. Journey on, my friends. I hope you have the time of your lives!

Good Times, Good Advice

QUESTION: What was the single best moment of your life? And what was the best advice anyone ever gave you?

PAM:

This was the very first question I received, and therefore the one I have put off the longest answering. But I don't want the viewer who asked it to think I've forgotten about him. So here is the obvious—the day, the moment I met Patty backstage at the Shubert Theater, when I was 16 years old. Standing there right in front of me in the wings of the Broadway stage, dressed in that spangled, glittery red-white-and-blue costume, looking than life to me. I'm glad I had this moment, for within a half hour, she was a normal run-of-the-mill middle-aged lady, sitting across from me in a robe, asking questions about my life. Not even looking like the same person. My moment with the big legend had come and gone. The very next time she put on that sparkly, patriotic costume, and every day thereafter, I would be on the other side, stuffing her and zipping her into it. There were to be forty more years, but never one more momentous as that first one.

The second part of this question is...What was the best advice you have ever gotten? And that, too, refers to that magic first day backstage. And it came from—believe it or not—Gayle's father, Seymour (the man who could only eat hot dogs, fried salami, and French fries). It was the night before I was supposed to meet Patty and Maxene, and I was hanging out at Gayle's house. Gayle's father Seymour was an uber-Andrews Sisters fan, so he got it (as a matter of fact, it was on Seymour's two Andrew Sisters 78s that I ever first heard The Andrews Sisters sing—but more on that later).

On this, the evening before, Gayle's father asked me how I felt about the upcoming events of the next day. I told him that I was excited, but also a little sad, because after tomorrow, all it would be was a memory (little did I know!).

Seymour said, "Listen, what you are about to do is something many people dream of, but never remotely get the chance to do. So just be happy and savor every moment. You are luckier than most!"

I never forgot those words. And in time— I was able to make his dream (the same one) a reality, and introduce him to The Andrews Sisters.

NOW...HERE'S THE KICKER...

Nobody can sustain life eating just French fries, and fried sala-mi. And most of the time, the hot dogs, too, were fried. And after 60 years of doing just that— his liver exploded, and he died. He was 61 years old. Seymour was a hoarder, and had a second small apartment attached to his house. That other apartment was full, piled from floor to ceiling with junk! Everything he could get off the streets before the garbage trucks beat him to it (it was a daily contest between him and the Long Island Department of Sanitation).

Anyway...a few months after the liver blew out, the house was condemned. In order for Gayle's mother to get out of there, and maybe make a few bucks on the land (it was beach property) after the house was demolished, she had to rent one of those gigantic in-dustrial trash dumpster things that sit outside on the curb, while the house slowly is uncluttered and trashed by the men in Hazmat suits.

It was around 6 or 7 months after Seymour's death when I called up his wife—Gayle's Mommy—and asked her if I could please have the two 78s he owned of The Andrews Sisters (By the way, they were kept in a clean, non-toxic part of the home). Of course, by then I had them in all kinds of different formats. But those two tangible records held such a special meaning to me. It was on those records at Seymour's house in the 1960s that my future, without even me knowing it, had started to sprout fragile roots. Gayle's mother, who had known me since I was two years old, and whom I really believed liked me, let loose a barrage of nasty, awful words at the top of her lungs, most of which were so garbled that I couldn't make them out. But the gist and conclusion was that because I dared to ask, she would never give them to me. And SLAM went the phone. No, wait—DOUBLE SLAM; she picked it up again and slammed it down with more gusto.

Shocked? Stunned? I don't know what words to use to describe it. Let's see—Seymour died in December 1991, so this had to be in the summer of 1992. I called my Grandmother, who at the time was 101 years old. Grandmom had known Gayle's parents for as long as I had, and they really seemed to like her. They certainly acted like they did. Grandma—I repeat, 101-year-old Grandma—offered to call Gayle's mommy and straighten this out. These records had absolutely no value (except emotionally to me). They could be bought for under one dollar a piece at any used record store, eBay, or flea market (probably still can).

Well, Grandma got a repeat performance of the blast Gayle's mother gave me the day before. With one extra bonus—she made Grandma listen as she cracked and snapped the records into tiny pieces, yelling at the centenarian that she would rather see it broken and smashed beneath the waste in the big trash bin out front, than give it to me.

The 5 Most Beautiful Things

Having led the life you've led, and seen the things you've seen—what do you think are the five most beautiful things in the world?

PAM:
I am pretty sure that when the writer of this question asked this, he/she thought I'd come back with things like the Louvre, or Versailles in France, Niagara Falls at night, the Aurora Borealis soaring across the Anchorage sky, Stonehenge, the Coliseum in Rome, Yosemite National Park, Sunset over the Mediterranean Sea in Spain, or—for Gayle—the KFC in Hawaii where the statue of Colonel Sanders has a water spout coming out of his mouth. These are *all* beautiful sights, granted. But the question asked me was—what I thought were *the 5 most beautiful things in the world.*

1. The look in a dog's eyes of complete adoration and devotion is, to me, the most beautiful thing.
The moment when an abandoned puppy or re-homed dog in a strange situation takes that deep breath, and they allow all their fear and apprehension to turn into acceptance and trust. It is almost like a complete submission. In a way, given the choice between love and hate, this powerful animal who has the means (and teeth) to harm someone very badly, and who has probably been hurt at some time in their short little life, will always undoubtedly choose

good over evil once the slightest bit of kindness is perceived. They are the only unconditional living beings that want nothing besides your affection and attention, and are so very grateful when it is received. A dog will stay by your side for hours, for days, if you are sick, or sad, or just in need of some company. They may not be able to give you the answers to your problems, but they will listen to your words more intently than any person possibly could, and sometimes that's the best solution of all. Yes—a dog's eyes. When they greet you at the door, whether you've been gone 3 minutes or 3 months, it doesn't matter. There is sincere gratitude and relief in their eyes, because once they see you, all is right.

2. A Baby's First. I

nitially, I was going to say a Baby's First Laugh. But then I realized that a baby's first everything fits into this category. First smile, first words, first steps...think about it. A baby who has not yet had the life experiences which make one fearful, and ashamed. They are completely un-jaded, and so do things for the sake of doing them. They haven't learned about Political Correctness, Social Etiquette, or "Social Ineptness." Or reasoning. For example: why bother trying to stand up and take a step on two feet, when you're obviously better balanced crawling on all fours? Why do babies laugh? They certainly don't understand what's so funny. Why do they smile? Because they have not learned to worry about events yet to be. They smile because they are happy and content with what is happening at that moment, in the here and now. They aren't aware of delayed gratification, or the potential dangers that await them in this cynical Me-Me-Me, "I'm being offended by..." world. Their innocence, there lack of "BEWARES" and warnings is truly magical. And should be cherished because this is the purist kind of beauty you will ever see.

3. Altruistic Kindness to one who could never ever repay the deed.

The act of physically helping one in a weaker, more vulnerable position (not just not writing a check to some charity, or shopping at the Salvation Army). The homeless, especially the children, and the animals whose only crime was being born into an impoverished situation, through no choice of their own. Or the elderly, those living hand-to-mouth on a fixed income, rationing out their meager allotment to get them to the next Social Security payday, with too-old eyes or crippled in some way that makes it virtually impossible for them to supplement their monthly money. These are the ladies in the market who don't have cats yet buy cat food, or the old men who must choose between their heart medicine or a sandwich. I remember once, I was in a 99 Cent Store. The very ancient woman in front of me had to packages of ham (there was a sale going on at the time—four packs for a dollar). The elderly lady was struggling to count out pennies and nickels, trying desperately to get up to 50 cents to buy that ham. It was truly heartbreaking. You know what I did? What we should all do if we are not struggling financially in our own lives. These people, the ones who lived, and fought in wars to protect us, who once had husbands and wives and children but now sit all alone at tables in empty apartments, the helpless ones who are the victims of circumstance and, on occasion, bad genes—there is nothing better than making their scary, mundane lives a little easier. These people are hungry. They are cold. Pay for their groceries. Buy them a warm coat. Because there by the grace of God goes...any of us. And the act in itself will be so much more beautiful than any pearl or diamond trinket you could have used that money for.

4) The rebirth of life.

We have a grape arbor in our yard. The trees from when the leaves grow are completely dead. As dry and brittle as Betty White's bones must be. What hadn't died we chopped up with an axe (a fun day on my part, to be sure!). Now, it is Spring again. And from the dead, brittle, hatchet-slaughtered, disintegrating pieces of wood, the grape vines have sprung and are growing with abundance. For someone like me who was never be able to procreate life, this is indeed a miracle. I have never much of a gardener. That chance passed by me when Cassandra died seventeen years ago. Although to be fair, I never had much interest when she was alive. But to witness life being reborn from a dormant tree, or bush, to see a tiny cutting no bigger than an inch, cut off from some random plant, or a little sprinkle-sized seed now growing into a field of flowers, or untamed ivy, just totally blows my mind. I don't know if it's just me and people like me who do not reproduce, or if it's everyone, but nature's ability to wait patiently under the months of snow, or in our case, torrential rain, and then BOOM—be back just as beautiful and healthy as it was last year at this time, amazes the hell out of me.

5. Joanna

Letter to My 12-Year-Old Self

Hey Pammy,

It's almost 50 years later in your life, and I'd like to tell you some things that I wish you had known in 1969. I won't lie to you. You've got a life full of great, and many, losses in front of you. That little baby boy that you are probably carrying around with you right now won't live past his teens. The grandmother whom you've always worried about losing will live until you are 35 years old. I wish you could have known that, so you would not have wasted all that time worrying about her dying, and just enjoyed having and loving her for all the years to come. Your father will be gone very soon, and your mother...well, you've always known that this she wasn't there. It wasn't your fault. She was mentally ill.

In another year or so, you will lose all semblance of trust of anyone in your life you thought would protect you. I won't tell you why, or what Janie is going to do to you, but know this action will have an impact on you for the rest of your life. Just know that it is scary, and unnecessary, and will take away the part of you that believed that anyone ever would truly have your back, unconditionally (even Grandma). But you got out. You went back to school, skipped 8th grade, and finished high school when you were 16. Those pimples your Dad said would be gone when you turned 18 weren't. More like when you were 38.

That love of antiques and old things that he is instilling in you will last a lifetime. It will be your passion always.

The funniest thing is (get this) that the woman you saw a few weeks ago on *Here's Lucy* (the one with the two sisters that intrigued you so), will one day be your adopted mother. Not kidding. And next to Grandma, she will be the most important person ever in your life. You will love her so much, that you will actually move to California for her. That's right...you'll live in California. Well, even now, you want to go there, even if it's just to see Disneyland. And when you do finally get to Los Angeles, it will feel like a place you always belonged. And in the end, the place, the people, your life will turn out better than you could have ever imagined.

No babies. Sorry... It's not that you will not have tried, it's just that sometimes things don't work out the way you hope they will. But you will grow into that fake strength which you are just now learning how to perfect, and someday it will be real. It will see you through some of the worst tragedies, images, and moments of your life.

So 1969 Pammy, the best advice I can give to you, since I am sure you have figured out by now that you will basically be on your own, is to count on yourself as much as possible, because really only you can take care of yourself. As the *Here's Lucy* show lady, whose songs you don't even know yet, will teach you: anything and everything is possible. And there is always someone (human or animal) that is weaker than you. You will discover that you prefer animals, and the greatest joy in your life is making theirs that much better.

And just when you think it's all over... and there is nobody left to care about you...

Along will come Jo. The pretty lady from that *Casino Royale* movie, which you saw recently at the Valencia Theater and didn't understand. And everything will be right again! Except that you still won't understand the movie!

Enjoy the ride. It's a roller coaster for sure, but for the most part, it's up, and fun, and exciting.

And you know that button you bought last week in Central Park commemorating the moon landing? You are still going to have it when you are 2018 Pam (and those damn newspapers are going to be worth a fortune!).

Loving Your Life

Dear 2048 Pam,

I am hoping that you are alive in 30 years to see this.

Since your mother lived to be over 90, and your grandmother lived to be over 100...here's hoping! If you are still here, you will have finally experienced the 40s. OK, so not exactly the 1940s, as you would have liked, but the 40s anyway.

I hope that you never ever get old. "OLD" is an innate state of being, not a physical one. Just like you could not stave off the blemishes of teen-hood, most probably, you will deal with the inevitable progression of age (wrinkles, brittle bones, failing eye-sight and hearing, etc., etc.). What's the alternative? I would like to believe that it is in your genes (and that at still in your jeans) to stay free thinking, free speaking, and free willed. I know that you, 91-year-old Pam, will have a dog, at least one, probably some sort of Chihuahua. You will pamper and love a dog 'til your last breath. And then you will make sure that he/she/they have an easy and safe transition to their new life.

Probably by now, there are five storage units. I want you to be one of those old ladies, whom I now see in the antique stores, and wonder why bother? Save history. Yours, and theirs, for genera-tions to come. Somebody must. And I hope that even after all this time, you have never let the Andrews Sisters be forgotten. They were there for you in your darkest time. You need to be acute-ly aware that they're remembered and revered forever. I'm pretty sure you have figured out by now how to keep the legacy alive and flowing. That you have found someone much younger to pass your memories, and their stories, on to. The music, I am quite sure, will persevere itself.

You already know that your situation is different than most. It would be amazing if you still have a family of choice like I had when I wrote this to you in 2018. But for many years now, you have not had any blood relatives (children, grandchildren, siblings...) I assume you've learned to live with this over the years. It is a part of your destiny. Don't feel badly that the photographs and tangible memories of your life will seem to be meaningless to any other human being. There are plenty of people, like you, who preserve the lives of people they've never known. 2048 Pam must believe that someone will pay it forward. And someday, somebody will look at those long ago photos, and although not quite sure where or when, marvel at your childhood in the 1950s and 60s, and wonder what it felt like to be a child at that turbulent time in history. Your father was right, you know, back in 1963, when he sat you in front of that television for hours, as the Kennedy assassination and aftermath unfolded before your eyes, and he kept repeating "This is history, you are watching history." Now here you are, 80-some-odd years later, one of the few people left who can actually say they saw it in real time.

I wish for you that 2048 still holds the same tenacity as the years always have. And that you will ride out the storms and tidal waves that way you learned to so many years ago. With an eye to the horizon, the sunrise, may the glass always, ALWAYS, continue to be half full. Remember when your grandmother was 91, she still had over a decade left to live. She walked into her 100th birthday party without a cane, and completely sane. Since you were always a little crazy, that's not likely. But the lesson is that it's not over until it's over.

And when it is, may it be without regret. A life well lived. Remember the only regrets are really the things you've never done. Stay fearless. Stay independent. Love someone or something, but stay autonomous. Of course, never be afraid to ask for help if you need it. Needing is not a sign of weakness. Strength is in the perseverance, no matter what it takes to achieve the outcome you want.

I owe it to you, my future self, to take care of this body we share. To feed it better. To stay on top of "what could happen" and take the necessary tests and precautions. Just as the 24-year-old Pam of 1981gave 2048 Pam the consideration to stop smoking before the lungs collapsed on themselves, I must give you the "armor" you will need to survive the best you can, to be the happiest and healthiest, and strongest, 91-year-old you can be.

And finally, should this letter find you plagued with the dementia that sometimes comes with age, I hope that, like Patty did, you are reliving only the best times of your life, over, and over, every day for as long as you live.

About the Author
Pam DuBois

Pam Dubois with Patty Andrews

I was born in Queens, New York in March of 1957 to a man who already had two grown children with children of their own, making him a grandfather, and a very cold, non-affectionate woman who really did not like or want kids. However, the 'normalcy' of the 1950s was to have a pretty little child to dress up and parade around the neighborhood in a fancy English pram. It was enticing enough for Jane to go for it. However, she soon discovered that she was ill-equipped for the other 90% of the necessities for taking care of a baby or toddler. So, she dumped me on her mother—my recently-widowed 70-year-old grandmother.

My grandmother and my aunt had a lucrative business supplying Broadway shows, the circus, the Icecapades, etc. with stockings, gloves, and other specially-requested accessories. And that is how I first encountered the Andrews Sisters. If you want to know how I became Patty's adopted daughter....well, read the book.

Thank you for reading

My Adventures with the Andrews Sisters and Beyond

by Pam Dubois

Please leave a review on the website of your favorite online bookseller

MORE GREAT READS FROM HENRY GRAY

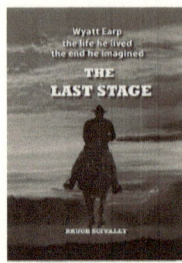

THE LAST STAGE by Bruce Scivally
In his final days, lawman Wyatt Earp dreams of one last showdown—gold, gunmen and love with his devoted wife, Sadie.

VEIL OF SEDUCTION by Emily Dinova
In 1922, journalist Lorelei Alba infiltrates a gothic asylum for "troublesome" women—and falls into the orbit of a dark, mysterious doctor.

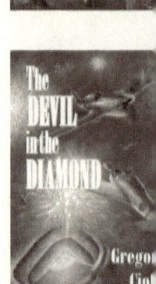

THE UNDERSTUDY by Charlie Peters
A kidnapping plot during a high-stakes merger quickly unravels, exposing every flaw in a "perfect crime."

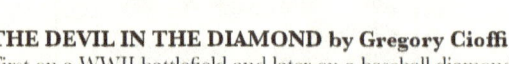

THE DEVIL IN THE DIAMOND by Gregory Cioffi
First on a WWII battlefield and later on a baseball diamond, two soldiers, once enemies, find themselves bound by history, family, and the game they love.

A PRAYER FOR THE DAMNED by Joe Cornet
Bounty hunter Cole faces a deranged preacher and seeks a lost Confederate treasure in a town on the brink of violence.

THE MAN FROM BELIZE by Steven Kobrin
Dr. Kent Sterling's perfect life in paradise shatters when his past as a government hitman catches up—and the Viper comes calling.

SINS OF THE RAVEN by Steven Kobrin
Dr. Kent Stirling returns to face adversaries from his past, forcing him to confront buried secrets and fight for his life before the sins he thought forgotten consume him completely.

SHELBY'S VACATION by Nancy Beverly
Shelby runs from heartbreak into the arms of Carol, a woman carrying her own relationship scars. Together, they discover love worth risking.

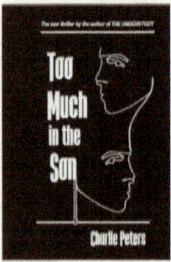

TOO MUCH IN THE SON by Charlie Peters
Mistaken identity plunges Leo Malone into a twisted web of lies, gangsters, and family deception.

I CONFESS: DIARY OF AN AUSTRALIAN POPE by Melvyn Morrow
An Australian pope battles corruption, blackmail, and betrayal as he tries to reform the Vatican from within.

visit www.HenryGrayPublishing.com

THE ANTAGONIST by Emily Dinova
A mysterious note shatters Dave Collins' quiet life, unraveling his world piece by piece. Who is behind it—and why?

WHILE WE'RE HERE by T.A. Manchester
A heartfelt coming-of-age story of football, family, first love, and tragic loss. This YA debut captures the fragile beauty of youth and the heartbreak of growing up too soon.

WASTED by Sam F. Park
When a drunk with amnesia—known only as 'Wasted'—is forced into brutal labor on a powerful rancher's land, he becomes tangles in a web of violence, redemption, and truth.

POETIC ANARCHY by Gregory Cioffi
Raw, fearless, and unfiltered—Gregory Cioffi's poetry explodes with passion, humor, and rebellion. From love and loss to art and anger, every page is rallying cry for authenticity.

BILLION DOLLAR BATMAN by Bruce Scivally
From dime comics to billion-dollar blockbusters, discover the amazing story of Batman's rise from Bright Knight to Dark Knight.

REJECTED: ESSAYS ON BELONGING by Michelle Fiordaliso
Through humor and honesty, Fiordaliso explores heartbreak, rejection, and the quest for acceptance and belonging.

MIRROR OF MY WORLD: REFLECTIONS ON AN UNDIAGNOSED AUTISTIC CHILDHOOD by Christian Karen Berman
A moving memoir of growing up neurodivergent in the 80s and 90s.

HIGH: FROM CANNABIS TO CLARITY by Leonard Lee Buschel
From addiction to transformation, Buschel shares his raw, funny, and inspiring journey through decades of drugs, Hollywood, and recovery.

ABNER THE CLOWN by Jeffrey Breslauer
Young clown Abner hates his name until an expected adventure teaches him the magic of self-acceptance.

BENNETT WILL ONLY EAT BLUEBERRIS by Nicole Dillenberg (available in English & Spanish)
In this whimsical picture book, anique toy bears bring Bennett's picky-eating tale to life.

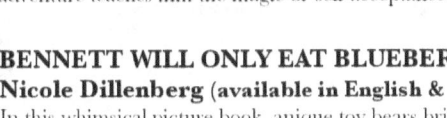

SEARCH FOR FUN WITH PAPA ROCK!

PAPA ROCK'S HORROR MOVIES WORD SEARCH
by Rock Scivally & Jeffrey Breslauer
150 puzzles based on horror films from *Frankenstein* to *Godzilla* equals 150 reasons to keep the lights on all night!

PAPA ROCK'S SON OF HORROR MOVIES WORD SEARCH by Rock Scivally & Jeffrey Breslauer
Looking for more Word Search chills? In this edition, monsters from the 1960s and 70s haunt every page!

PAPA ROCK'S REVENGE OF HORROR MOVIES WORD SEARCH by Rock Scivally & Jeffrey Breslauer
Looking for more monter Word Searches? Here you'll find the classic movie monsters from the 1980s and 90s!

PAPA ROCK'S ROMANCE MOVIES WORD SEARCH
by Rock Scivally & Jeffrey Breslauer
From *Casablanca* to *Titanic*, here's 150 Word Searches based on romance movies, so pick up a pen and turn on the love light!

PAPA ROCK'S WESTERN MOVIES WORD SEARCH
by Rock Scivally & Jeffrey Breslauer
Hop into these 150 Word Searches and ride with John Wayne, Randolph Scott, Clint Eastwood, and cowboy favorites!

PAPA ROCK'S ANIMATED MUSICALS WORD SEARCH by Rock Scivally & Jeffrey Breslauer
You'll be humming along as you do 150 Word Searches on favorite animated musicals from *Snow White* to *Strawberry Shortcake!*

PAPA ROCK'S WAR MOVIES WORD SEARCH by Rock Scivally & Jeffrey Breslauer
Climb into your foxhole and challenge yourself with Word Searches based on classic war films from *Sergeant York* to *Saving Private Ryan*.

PAPA ROCK'S SCI-FI MOVIES WORD SEARCH by Rock Scivally & Jeffrey Breslauer
Relive science fiction's greatest hits with these Word Search puzzles covering classics from *Metropolis* to *Star Wars!*

PAPA ROCK'S DETECTIVE MOVIES WORD SEARCH by Rock Scivally & Jeffrey Beslauer
Solve 150 puzzles inspired by classic detective films, from Sherlock Holmes and Sam Spade to noir favorites.

PAPA ROCK'S MOVIE COMEDY TEAMS WORD SEARCH by Rock Scivally & Jeffrey Breslauer
From the Marx Brothers to Abbott & Costello to Martin & Lewis to Cheech & Chong, celebrate the greatest comedy teams with this laugh-out-loud puzzle collection!

Stay in touch with Henry Gray Publishing!

Follow us on Facebook

Subscribe to our YouTube channel

Sign up to our mailing list at

www.HenryGrayPublishing.com

Granada Hills, CA
"Select books for selective readers"

www.ingramcontent.com/pod-product-compliance
Lightning Source LLC
Chambersburg PA
CBHW020444130626
46549CB00001B/291